REAL ESTATE SALES HANDBOOK

10th Edition

GAIL G. LYONS

Consulting Editor

Dearborn™
Real Estate Education

RS RESIDENTIAL SALES COUNCIL

While a great deal of care has been taken to provide accurate and current information, the ideas, suggestions, general principles and conclusions presented in this text are subject to local, state and federal laws and regulations, court cases and any revisions of same. The reader is thus urged to consult legal counsel regarding any points of law—this publication should not be used as a substitute for competent legal advice.

Publisher: Kathleen A. Welton
Acquisitions Editor: Patrick J. Hogan
RS Council Product Director: Christine M. Drover
Associate Editor: Karen A. Christensen
Senior Project Editor: Jack L. Kiburz

Published by Real Estate Education Company, a division of Dearborn Financial Publishing, Inc., and the Residential Sales Council℠ of the REALTORS NATIONAL MARKETING INSTITUTE®

Printed in the United States of America

09   10   20   19   18

Library of Congress Cataloging-in-Publication Data

Real estate sales handbook / Gail G. Lyons, consulting editor.—
    [10th ed.]
      p. cm.
    Includes index.
    ISBN 0-7931-0947-7
    1. Real estate business—Handbooks, manuals, ect. I. Lyons, Gail G.
HD1375.R3933   1994
333.33′068′8—dc20   94-7176
                                                              CIP

Contents

Chapter 4.   Time Management   56

Chapter 5.   Selling and Listing with
Psychology   68

Chapter 6.   Obtaining the Listing   77

Chapter 7.   Servicing the Seller   114

Chapter 8.   Advertising and Public Relations   128

Chapter 9.   Finding and Working with the Buyer   137

Chapter 10.   Negotiating and Closing   165

Chapter 11.   Financing   179

Chapter 12.   Expanding Your Services   193

Chapter 13. Technology and Real Estate   209

Glossary   217

Appendix: Exterior Structural Walls and Framing   258

Index   261

About the Residential Sales Council   274

Foreword

The *Real Estate Sales Handbook* has been part of the educational publishing program of the Residential Sales Council for more than half a century. With distribution of more than *one million copies* in nine previous editions, the Handbook has become an essential tool for real estate salespeople.

This reference book will not solve salespeople's problems but can help them when they have problems to solve. Any mention of local and state laws and methods of operation mentioned in this Handbook refers only to specific instances and/or sources cited and does not apply generally. Readers are advised to check policy and procedures, forms and contracts against whatever regulations apply in their company, municipality and state and to keep informed of changes in the laws at all levels.

Among the changes in society in the United States in the last quarter of the 20th century, two notable ones are the professionalism in the real estate industry and the sophistication of the consumer and business public. Both demand of real estate salespeople the fullest knowledge obtainable and a real dedication to serving the public. Continuing education in their chosen profession is available through print and audiovisual materials and attendance at courses offered by local, state and national real estate organizations. Real estate salespeople who avail themselves of these educational opportunities will be better equipped to render the kinds and quality of service both buyers and sellers have come to expect.

The Institute wishes to acknowledge with gratitude the contribution made to this tenth edition by real estate writer William H. Pivar and RS Council members James Abell, Germantown, Tennessee; John Cotton, Osterville, Massachusetts; Taylor N. French, Memphis, Tennessee; Scott Frohm, Omaha, Nebraska; Gail Hendley, Brentwood, Tennessee; Susan Kingsley, Ocean City, Maryland; Richard Lentfer, Orland Park, Illinois; Jeanne Logosz, Boise, Idaho; Michael McGaughan, Champaign, Illinois; David Siweck, Tucson, Arizona; James Warren, Tucson, Arizona.

Chapter 1

Getting Started

The real estate profession is really a people profession as much as it is one that deals with property. By understanding people and their needs and then fulfilling those needs, you will be successful. Your rewards will be commensurate with how well you are able to help others.

In addition to financial rewards, the real estate profession can provide you with the psychological reward of knowing you have helped people in their life's goals and have guided them through decisions.

Meeting the needs of others requires enthusiasm, both people and property knowledge, creativity, self-discipline, a determination to succeed and an understanding of basic motivating factors. Every day presents new challenges that a real estate professional views not as a problem but as an opportunity for success.

A successful real estate professional must be self-motivated. There is no one to tell him or her what to do and when to do it. The commodity that a real estate professional really offers is his or her time. It is a precious commodity that must be jealously guarded and used wisely.

The arrangement of working hours in real estate usually differs from selling in other fields. Although unusual hours and weekend work may be necessary, well-managed schedules can provide freedom at other times. And as a real estate salesperson learns how to make maximum use of each working hour, the same time use habits will spill over to help him or her enjoy every free hour to its fullest.

Successful real estate salespeople must sincerely like to work with people and find them interesting. They will be working with a wide range of people, from young families striving to obtain a home of their own to sophisticated investors and affluent retirees. In real estate, the people "mix" changes with every transaction.

SUBJECT KNOWLEDGE NEEDED

Real estate salespeople need to be skills-oriented. They should understand the following areas:

- Market analysis: understand market conditions in order to advise both buyers and sellers of the proper time to act.
- Appraising: be aware of the approaches to value of property, which include being versed on neighborhood trends, the climate of opinion and municipal ordinances that might affect values.
- Finance: be able to guide buyers and sellers on how purchases can be financed and help to arrange the financing.
- Law: advise potential parties to a contract of the need for expert legal counsel.
- Duties: understand his or her legal as well as ethical duties, including any agency relationship. The salesperson must make certain that both buyer and seller understand the salesperson's roles and duties.
- Interior decorating: be able to present a word picture of how a different color scheme could change the appearance of a room or how rearrangement of furnishings could alter the illusion of space.
- Landscape architecture: know what changes in planting can do to improve the appearance of a property.
- Construction and architectural details: be capable of advising buyers and sellers on the value of home improvements or point out to buyers how major or minor changes could enhance the value of a property they are considering. The agent should be able to recognize visible signs of structural and/or systems problems so as to advise both buyers and sellers.
- Community information: introduce new buyers to neighbors; show them nearby schools, churches and recreational facilities.
- Psychology: know how to lead a person in the fulfillment of his or her needs.

SOME PROBLEMS IN SELLING

Like every other business, real estate has problems. Sometimes they approach crisis proportions, either for the salesperson or his or her family. The most common ones are listed here, with a reminder of the ancient Chinese calligraphy for *crisis,* which combines the forms for both danger and opportunity.

Real estate salespeople learn to deal with "down" periods common to every selling field. They are almost predictable in both character and timing. After a period of perceived failures, there is a great risk of becoming negatively motivated. If a salesperson believes that he or she is a failure, this belief can become a self-fulfilling prophecy. A successful real estate salesperson must view the glass as "nearly half full" rather than "more than half empty." Real estate is very similar to baseball in that you can't get a hit unless you get to the plate. In real estate, being at the plate means making a listing or sales presentation, and a hit is a successful transaction. The more times you can get to the plate, the more chances you have of getting a hit. A successful ballplayer rejoices in a 300 average rather than laments the seven times out of ten he has struck or flied out. You must rejoice in your hits and try to learn from the times you strike out.

The first critical period is likely to come after you get your first contracts and have conquered a natural fear of failing. You may be discouraged by more experienced salespeople who tell you the good habits you've just begun to establish aren't necessary.

That is the time to forget how other people work. Do things the way you've been taught: use a daily work plan; follow up every lead and every sale; maintain a prospect list and work it regularly for development and follow-up; and work a full day, free of excess socializing and paper shuffling.

The next critical period usually comes during the second year. The second-year slump might be due to feeling that you know more than you do. Making decisions hastily, such as "They aren't buyers," or "No one will come to an open house on a rainy day," will decrease your efforts and your earnings. Maybe you've become a little cocky or a little sloppy and thus less efficient and effective. You may have begun to think you don't really need your broker and you can make it on your own. You may have become lazy and let good habits slide; you may have turned away from working to get listings, taking the easier route of walk-in buyers and ad calls. Or you may have gotten so enthusiastic about your own real estate investment program that you are looking at every property for your own potential use and not that of your clients. Now is the time for some retraining and self-analysis.

The third critical period is largely ego-centered. You may become bored with residential sales, or you may begin to think about opening your own office or going into some other phase of real estate. It's great to grow. New fields bring new challenges. But remember, you can grow right where you are.

Before making any major change, analyze carefully just what it is you think you can do and analyze that market just as carefully. Find out what special real estate knowledge and administrative know-how you will need in the new field. How much lead time will you need before a new venture is profitable? The industry is littered with case histories of people who plunged into new ventures without enough preparation and capital and ended in failure.

Smart salespeople recognize any of these periods for what they are—temporary slumps. The smartest ones take effective action to work out of their slump.

WHAT THE BUSINESS IS LIKE FOR FAMILIES

Real estate has been likened to the medical profession in that family matters always seem to take second place. The spouse has to know what to expect and what's involved in being successful in real estate. A supportive family can go a long way toward ensuring success.

One answer to this is to make whatever time is available quality time. Good time-management practices can be carried over to personal time with the family. Rearrangement of children's schedules can give more time with parents.

Vacations can be difficult to schedule. Even when the real estate salesperson is an independent contractor whose vacation schedule is not controlled by a broker, the timing of a transaction can cause delayed departures or cancelled trips. This is just as common in many other businesses.

In addition to personal slumps, there are market slumps when activity and earnings decrease. However, there are also periods of great sales activity when buyers will seem to be coming at you from all directions. Two old cliches are important for success in real estate: "Make hay while the sun shines" and "Put something aside for a rainy day." Some families can budget; some can't. Some find it best to pay bills in advance when big commission checks come in. Others are able to save enough from big checks to carry them over lean months. Some take out a short-term loan at the bank.

Your family members should be active members of your team. They can serve as extra sets of eyes and ears that are constantly alert for opportunities to list and sell real estate.

CAREERS IN REAL ESTATE

Real estate offers a wide range of sales careers. Residential selling is a challenging, rewarding career. Success demands the discipline of good work habits and mastery of selling skills. Other fields such as commercial, industrial and investment require special knowledge and training; each offers unique opportunities.

A specialty may be defined by a type of real property—residential, commercial, office, industrial, shopping centers, etc. A specialty can also be a price range or even a defined geographical area, or it can relate to serving users or investors, buyers or sellers. In any specialty field, services your firm may offer include exchanging, trade-ins, leasing, appraisals, syndication, renovation and redevelopment, counseling, selling for builders, referral services, property management, insurance and financing. The purpose of specialization is to provide the best possible service to your client.

Whatever the specialty and its required body of technical knowledge, selling skills remain at the heart of success. Specialties will be covered in greater detail in Chapter 12.

YOUR LICENSE

Licensing laws give both the public and real estate brokers protection against unethical and irresponsible operators. Fifty states, the District of Columbia and several provinces of Canada regulate real estate brokerage through a system of licensing brokers and salespeople.

Although licensing requirements may differ from one state to another, all states and the District of Columbia require prospective salespeople and brokers to pass written exams that cover the fundamentals of real estate and laws affecting the sale of real estate. Some states require prospective licensees to complete educational courses accredited by the state licensing agency before they can qualify for the exam, while other states will allow these courses to be taken within a specified time after licensing. Overall, more than half of the states specify special education and/or experience or their equivalents to obtain a broker's license.

Most licensing laws have been drafted and sponsored with the assistance and cooperation of REALTORS® to strengthen the professional standing of people legitimately engaged in the real estate business. Your license is your "right to work." Your obligation as a licensee is to work professionally, legitimately and ethically.

For detailed, up-to-date information, contact the Real Estate Licensing Commission in the state(s) where you'd like to practice.

PROFESSIONAL ASSOCIATIONS

Firms that encourage professional attitudes among their salespeople usually belong to the local board of REALTORS®, where people associated in the same field work to maintain both the spirit and letter of professionalism. When you become an active member of your local board, you will benefit from the exchange of ideas and experiences of fellow professionals. Make every effort to carry out the special assignments given you and to participate in all the programs and discussions at board meetings.

There are also many real estate–related associations in existence today. Most are as concerned with professional conduct and ethics as with educating and informing their members. The following list provides the names, addresses, telephone numbers and membership category of these associations. The NATIONAL ASSOCIATION OF REALTORS® and its institutes, societies and councils are covered in Chapter 2 and are not included here.

American Industrial Real Estate Association (AIR)
Sheraton Grande Office Center
345 S. Figueroa, Suite M-1
Los Angeles, CA 90071
213-687-8777
Real estate men and women specializing in industrial properties; affiliate members are title companies, banks and other lending institutions, mortgage loan companies, railroads and public utilities. Membership concentrated in southern California. Has developed industrial listing system and lease forms. Sponsors annual seminar.

American Land Development Association (ALDA)
1220 L St. #510
Washington, DC 20005
202-371-6700
Developers of residential, resort and recreational communities; large corporate land owners; suppliers to the land development industry. Offers seminars and conferences; maintains database.

Apartment Owners and Managers Association of America (AOMA)
Box 238
65 Cherry Ave.
Watertown, CT 06795-0238
203-274-2589
Builders who also manage the multifamily housing they construct. Sponsors regional seminars.

Building Owners and Managers Association International (BOMA)
1201 New York Ave. NW, Suite 300
Washington, DC 20005
202-408-2662
Owners, managers, investors and developers of commercial office buildings. Provides courses; awards designation.

Appraisal Institute
875 N. Michigan Avenue
Chicago, IL 60611-1980
312-335-4100
Commerical and residential real estate appraisers. Full range of professional development programs.

American Association of Certified Appraisers (AACA)
800 Compton Rd., Suite 10

Cincinnati, OH 45231
513-729-1400
Building and loan appraisers, bank appraisers, real estate brokers, and city, county and state tax assessors. Offers continuing education through seminars.

American Society of Appraisers (ASA)
P.O. Box 17265
Washington, DC 20041
703-478-2228
Professional appraisal testing/certifying society.

National Association of Independent Fee Appraisers (NAIFA)
7501 Murdoch St.
St. Louis, MO 63119
314-781-6688
Appraisers for real estate groups, savings and loan associations, title companies and related industries. Conducts career training and professional development programs.

International Association of Corporate Real Estate Executives (IACREE)
440 Columbia Dr., Suite 100
West Palm Beach, FL 33409
407-683-8111
Executives, attorneys, real estate department heads, architects, engineers, analysts, researchers and anyone employed by an industrial, commercial or retail corporation to manage a real estate–related function. Conducts seminars and workshops; offers computerized corporate real estate data network.

International College of Real Estate Consulting Professionals (RECP)
297 Dakota St.
Le Sueur, MN 56058
612-665-6280
Individuals proficient in fields related to the real estate profession, including sales, accounting, law, consultation, education, finance and government. Conducts seminars; awards designation.

Motel Brokers Association of America (MBAA)
10220 N. Executive Hills, Suite 610
Kansas City, MO 64153
816-891-7070
Real estate brokers specializing in sales of and investment in motel properties.

National Association of Real Estate Brokers (REALTIST)
1629 K St. NW, Suite 306
Washington, DC 20006
202-785-4477
Members of the real estate industry. Conducts research, educational
and certification programs.

National Association of Real Estate Buyer Brokers (NAREBB)
490 El Camino Real, Suite 209
Belmont, CA 94002
415-591-5446
Real estate licensees. Conducts educational seminars.

National Association of Real Estate Investment Trusts (NAREIT)
1129 20th St. NW, Suite 705
Washington, DC 20036
202-785-8717
Real estate investment trusts and others who manage or have an
interest in real estate trusts, associations, corporations and funds.

National Association of Review Appraisers and Mortgage
Underwriters (NARA/MU)
8383 E. Evans Rd.
Scottsdale, AZ 85260
602-998-3000
Real estate professionals who aid in determining value of property.
Conducts educational seminars; maintains speakers bureau.

National Motel Brokers (NMB)
P.O. Box 5446
Three 37th Ave.
San Mateo, CA 94402
415-349-1234
Brokers who arrange sales, leases, exchanges, financing and other real
estate transactions related to motels, motor hotels and hotels.

National Multi Housing Council (NMHC)
1850 M St. NW
Washington, DC 20036
202-659-3381
Builders, developers, owners, managers of multifamily housing.

National Realty Club (NRC)
60 E. 42nd St., 2303
New York, NY 10165-2303
212-532-3100

Real estate and leasing brokers, investors, builders, architects, attorneys and bankers from throughout the United States and Canada. Founded as a social and luncheon club for New York men identified with all phases of real estate.

National Realty Committee (NRC)
1250 Connecticut Ave. NW, Suite 630
Washington, DC 20036
202-785-0808
Business league of real estate owners, developers and investors.

Property Management Association
8811 Colesville Road
Silver Spring, MD 20910
301-587-6543
Property managers who manage real property.

COMMISSIONS

In real estate brokerage today, money is made from commissions earned. Most salespeople work on a commission basis, operating as independent contractors. In some states real estate salespeople are regarded as employees of the broker even though they are paid on a commission basis. But some firms now employ salespeople and offer them a salary in lieu of commissions. Because compensation arrangements vary from company to company and even from salesperson to salesperson within a company, the arrangements are whatever the broker and the salesperson mutually agree on, within the acceptable legal limits for independent contractors and employed salespeople.

WORKING WITH OTHER SALESPEOPLE

Cooperation with other salespeople and coordination of effort is important to the success of a sales staff. It is not unusual, for example, for two salespeople to team up on certain transactions, dividing the commission on a predetermined equitable basis. Joint efforts of this kind often lead to a sale that might otherwise be lost.

Some salespeople actually work as a team, dividing the commissions earned. Generally, these salespeople enter into short-term, renewable written agreements. The advantages of this sort of sales team is that team members tend to help motivate other team members. By planning together, members can maximize the use of their time, and having others to help or take over a transaction will often mean success instead of failure.

Occasional efforts of this sort should not be confused with the need for a continuing willingness of salespeople to help one another without expecting to be paid for it. A true spirit of cooperation exists in an office where everyone both gives and accepts help, knowing that such coordinated efforts result in greater volume for all. Conflicts of interest will occur from time to time but can be worked out in an office where a spirit of fairness prevails and judgments are made on *what* is right rather than *who* is right.

Listings are the property of the company. Your broker will tell you what the firm's procedure is for obtaining and filing listings. The sooner a new listing is filed and every salesperson is informed of it, the more active a sales staff can be. A salesperson who holds a "hot" listing is unfair to his or her associates and can give the broker cause to terminate their relationship. A good stock of listings helps build the firm's reputation with customers and clients, because they know their needs can be met.

THE COMPANY YOU WORK WITH

It pays to work for a reputable firm. Whether you work as an independent contractor or an employee, it is important to spend your working hours among people you respect and who respect you. You need your company's prestige, and you have an obligation to maintain its good reputation, being careful to do nothing that will lessen the public's regard for it.

Large Firm, Small Firm

Whether a small, owner-operated business or a massive, multioffice operation, each size has advantages and attracts good salespeople. Small offices give salespeople an opportunity to work closely with the broker, learning and being guided on a one-to-one basis. This same advantage can be found in some large companies with a strong training program. Many large firms offer salespeople a chance to train for and move into a specialty without changing companies.

Most good real estate firms share the following attributes:

- principals with sufficient experience to understand the fundamentals of real estate practice
- a staff of efficient, effective people
- enough capital to conduct the business without limitations
- principals who are service-minded and civic-spirited
- sensitivity to changing conditions
- strictly professional attitude toward the public
- memberships in good standing in local, state and national real estate organizations and specialized institutes as well as active participation in their programs

- considerate treatment of salespeople and employees
- training and educational programs for personal and professional development

Services Supplied by the Company

In addition to office facilities, REALTORS® provide their salespeople with the name and image they have built in the community. This is complemented by an advertising and public relations program.

One important service the company may provide is a referral program or network of offices with which it is affiliated—a service valuable to salespeople, because such a high percentage of real estate listings and sales originate in referrals. As you become well known and fully productive, you will build your own referral business. Until then, you will depend heavily on business that comes to you through the firm.

Successful real estate firms understand the value of computers and computer training. The computer in real estate does not replace people; it makes them more effective. What was formerly scattered forms and unrelated data can now be readily accessed from computer files.

Training Programs

Your broker may have a system for training new salespeople. Many brokers also have a continuing training program that keeps the whole staff up-to-date on real estate practices in general and the company's response to changing conditions in the market, whether local, regional or national. In addition to the firm's training program, an occasional training session may be organized by a cooperating group of brokers.

Training at some firms may be less formal and structured than at others, but all training is important. Sales personnel should avail themselves of every learning opportunity presented even though attendance may be optional. Employee-salespeople can be required to attend whatever training the firm offers.

On-the-job training is often utilized along with formal training programs. A veteran salesperson may take a newcomer under his or her wing, going along on the first calls or perhaps working with him or her until several sales have been made. This is often called a mentor program.

Before choosing an office, you should consider talking to recent licensees working there about their perception of the training provided.

The REALTORS NATIONAL MARKETING INSTITUTE® offers training courses for members to help them develop professionally and learn to serve buyers and sellers more effectively. These courses cover professional sales techniques, human behavior, self-awareness, awareness of others, setting personal and professional goals, and the concepts and techniques that build professional stature. They challenge the individual to increased personal development and growth and provide guidelines to successful client counseling.

Real estate salespeople should also consider training programs put on by other professional organizations as well as private seminars. While many of these programs are costly, many are also well worth the cost. It is suggested that you talk to successful agents who have attended courses and programs you are interested in to obtain their opinions as to the value and relevance of the material presented. You should discover that the more successful an agent is, the more that agent values continuing training.

Sales Meetings

Sales meetings can be an excellent training ground. Here, with fellow salespeople, sales managers and management, you will discuss company policy and procedures, hear sales ideas being developed and exchange information. Sales meetings are often planned around role playing or audiovisual training materials or lectures by experts in real estate–related topics.

POLICIES AND PROCEDURES

A policy and procedures manual helps an organization run smoothly and effectively. When important guidelines are put in writing, they save time and help prevent misunderstandings. Knowing exactly what the company policy is on listings procedures, commissions and the differences between what is mandatory for employees and optional for independent contractors can prevent abrasive situations from developing.

Checklists of the steps followed in taking and servicing listings, qualifying and servicing buyers, and handling closings go beyond being guidelines and become salespeople's tools.

The nature and content of a policy and procedures manual varies widely from company to company. However, most manuals include sections on advertising, commissions, disputes, ethics, financing, interdepartmental cooperation, job descriptions, securing and servicing listings, office procedures, sales techniques and time management.

THE COMPANY DOLLAR

Although many brokers manage their firm's finances by monitoring the gross commission coming into the firm and treat all payments (commissions, rents, ads, etc.) as gross expenses, some brokers find that monitoring the company dollar is a useful management technique.

After a broker pays sales commissions, fees, and splits to the staff and cooperating brokers, the remaining money is known as the "company dollar." From these funds must be paid the bills that provide a place to work and the services and supplies needed to do business. This may include such expenses as office furnishings, a pro rata share of office space and related maintenance costs, telephone, stationery and printed forms, clerical and secretarial services, advertising, promotion and publicity programs, salaries of supervisory and management personnel, and any other items necessary to the operation of the business.

Many brokers also monitor desk cost. "Desk cost" is the term used to describe that portion of the company's expense allocated to each salesperson. It is determined by dividing the number of salespeople into the total operating expense. Therefore, desk cost becomes the yardstick for measuring your goals against what it costs the company to have you associated with or employed by it. Because most brokers expect each salesperson to generate enough income to at least cover his or her desk cost, it is important to plan your time so you achieve your goals and cover this cost to the company as well.

Salesperson's Commission

Commission splits vary between brokers. However, it would not be wise for a new licensee to choose a broker based on the commission split offered. Generally, offices offering higher commission splits do so because they do not or cannot provide the same level of services, support and name recognition as firms offering a lower percentage. For new licensees, training and support are far more important than share of commission. After all, 100 percent of nothing is still nothing.

BROKER-SALESPERSON RELATIONSHIP

The relationship between a broker and the affiliated salesperson is that of either employer/employee or broker/independent contractor. It is of critical importance that every salesperson clearly understands the respective rights and responsibilities of each.

To ensure this understanding, it is highly desirable that a written agreement exist between the broker and at least those salespeople who function as independent contractors. The terms of such an agreement should be carefully reviewed and strictly adhered to. The agreement has effect only to the extent the parties to it observe its requirements.

Employees

A salesperson employed by a broker is under his or her direct supervision and control. The broker may determine not only the objectives to be attained by the salesperson-employee but also the manner and means of accomplishing them.

The broker may pay expenses, license fees and board dues; compel attendance at training sessions; require floor time; and assign administrative duties and organization titles. The salesperson-employee is subject to federal withholding tax on the compensation received from the broker-employer, who is required to pay FICA taxes and any other applicable workers' compensation, unemployment compensation or other federal, state or local employment taxes. Moreover, the salesperson-employee is entitled to participate in the broker's pension and profit-sharing plans, if any, on a nondiscriminating basis with all other employees. The broker must cover employees with workers' compensation coverage. However, if the employee is paid solely by commission for successful transactions, the broker is not generally required to pay for unemployment compensation.

Independent Contractors

If a salesperson is affiliated in an independent-contractor status, the broker may still determine the objectives to be attained by the salesperson but may not control the manner and means whereby those objectives are attained. He or she may not reimburse or pay selling expenses, license fees and board dues; compel attendance at meetings or adherence to a specific schedule; require attainment of sales quotas; or control vacation times. The broker may not include the salesperson in employee benefit programs. Salesperson-independent contractors are obliged to pay their own income and FICA taxes and may, if they desire, establish their own Keogh plan or, if they are incorporated, have a qualified corporate pension plan set up.

The Internal Revenue Service will view a real estate salesperson as an independent contractor if three criteria are met:

1. The salesperson is properly licensed to sell real estate.
2. All compensation is based on success (not hours worked).
3. There is a written contract that states that for tax purposes the salesperson shall be treated as an independent contractor.

By meeting the above criteria, the broker is not responsible for withholding federal income taxes from the salesperson's commission, nor does the broker contribute to FICA (Social Security) contributions.

Comparison of Relationships

The relationship that exists between a broker and salesperson must be mutually satisfactory. There is no one ideal relationship; indeed, the relationship may change from time to time.

A newly licensed salesperson may find the employee relationship most satisfactory, as it furnishes a higher degree of security. The broker may find the employee relationship desirable because it permits closer supervision and training of inexperienced salespeople.

On the other hand, an experienced salesperson may find the freedom and independence offered by the independent-contractor relationship most desirable and profitable. At the same time, the broker may find this relationship entirely consistent with his or her operational and administrative objectives and capacities.

The important point to be observed is that the broker and the salesperson select the relationship they want and adhere to its requirements. Any attempt to create an "independent-contractor/employee" status could defeat the objectives of broker and salesperson alike and result in confusion and misunderstanding, which could lead to disputes and possible litigation.

Some state courts have determined that the real estate salesperson is an employee regardless of the contractual agreement between broker and salesperson. The employee status is important in these states primarily in regard to broker liability for wrongful acts of the salesperson, because by meeting the IRS requirements, the IRS will still regard the salesperson as an independent contractor.

Regardless of the relationship established, the REALTOR® provides an office for the salesperson and pays the overhead expenses of maintaining it. He or she contributes a stock of goods to sell (listings) and is available as a counselor and negotiator, especially in complex transactions.

Chapter 2

Profession-
alism

Brokers and salespeople have certain legal performance responsibilities as well as ethical standards to maintain if they are to enjoy professional standing. Fifty states, the District of Columbia and several provinces of Canada regulate real estate brokerage through licensing. Most real estate licensing laws have been drafted and sponsored with the assistance of REALTORS® to strengthen the professional standing of people legitimately engaged in the real estate business. Licensing laws protect both the public and real estate brokers against unethical and irresponsible operators.

Professionalism is strengthened by continuing education. Information covered in state licensing exams should remain part of the salesperson's store of knowledge and be enhanced by reading and keeping abreast of trends in the real estate business. In this context, professionalism requires that although you will not always have the answer, you must know where to look for it and be willing to find answers that satisfy the needs of buyer and seller.

One of the basics of professionalism is a clear understanding of the roles people play in real estate and the organizations through which they operate, whether as a principal, a sales associate or an employee.

A principal, in the law of agency, is the one giving authority to another to act for him or her. This person is one who employs a real estate broker, is the broker's client and is responsible for paying his or her commission. An agency is an agreement between an agent and the principal wherein the agent represents the principal in dealing with a third party.

A REALTOR® is a professional in real estate who subscribes to a strict Code of Ethics as a member of the local board and state association and of the NATIONAL ASSOCIATION OF REALTORS®. The term REALTOR® is a trademark owned by the national association. It was adopted officially in 1916 and since then has been used continuously. Similarly, the term REALTOR-ASSOCIATE® is a registered trademark. The designation refers to a membership classification that permits a salesperson employed by or affiliated with a REALTOR® to join the local board, state association or national association.

A board of REALTORS® is the REALTOR® organization at the local level that exemplifies the REALTOR® concept and organizational intent. It is the organization that is most visible and best known to the general public.

Local boards consist of REALTORS® and REALTOR-ASSOCIATE®s who are members of the national association through the local board or state association. Local boards provide many services to members, including but not limited to a library on real estate; training films for REALTORS® and REALTOR-ASSOCIATE®s; training cassettes; standard business forms; decals, engravings, mats, pins, emblems, maps and other supplies related to the business; advertising, publicity and public relations on behalf of the board and its membership; and opportunities for civic participation and educational meetings and seminars. The possibilities of service to its members are limited only by the imagination and determination of the board's leaders.

THE NATIONAL ASSOCIATION

Professionalism has been the concern of real estate leaders since the beginning of the movement for a national organization in the 1890s. The National Real Estate Association, formed at meetings in Birmingham, Alabama, in 1891 and Nashville in 1893, was the forerunner of the present NATIONAL ASSOCIATION OF REALTORS®.

The panic of 1893 and ensuing depression killed the infant organization; but its aims of making real estate rules and regulations uniform from state to state, making title to real estate more secure and having real estate recognized as a profession remained uppermost in the minds of early leaders. Several meetings were held between 1894 and 1908, when the National Real Estate Association was officially founded. The name was later changed to the National Association of Real Estate Boards. In 1973 the NATIONAL ASSOCIATION OF REALTORS® came into being.

The NATIONAL ASSOCIATION OF REALTORS® is the nation's largest trade association. It presently serves more than 750,000 members in 50 states, Guam, Puerto Rico, the District of Columbia and the Virgin Islands. Members belong to one or more of some 1,864 local boards, 54 state associations and the NATIONAL ASSOCIATION OF REALTORS®. A REALTOR® or REALTOR-ASSOCIATE®, by virtue of his/her membership in the local board, is automatically granted membership in the state association and the National Association.

Working for America's property owners, the National Association provides a facility for education, research and exchange of information among its members, the public and government. The Association assists in preserving the free enterprise system and the right of free people to own real property in the interest of public welfare.

DIVISIONS OF NAR

Finance Management

The Finance Management division provides the Association and its institutes, societies and councils with necessary financial and budgetary controls and reports; provides financial expertise to staff and helps implement fiscally responsible programs; prepares monthly financial and managerial reports to the membership about the Association; and prepares all NAR tax returns and a year-end audited report attesting to the Association's financial condition.

Research

The Research division consists of three programs:

1. The *Existing Home Sales* program collects data on home sales and prices from local and state associations and outside multiple listing systems. Statistics are released to the news media the 25th of each month for the preceding month.
2. The *Investment Real Estate* program collects and analyzes information on commercial/investment real estate markets and produces *National Real Estate Review,* an acclaimed report that provides background and forecast information on all property types.
3. The *Operation of the Firm* program provides research-based tools to help members become more productive and profitable, often utilizing local boards/associations to assist in dissemination of the findings. Typical projects include an analysis of income/expense/ profits of real estate firms; how to establish a value for a real estate company; or understanding changes to the characteristics of customers and clients.

Education

Education is provided through five programs:

1. The *Association Executives Institute* (formerly EO Institute) is a five-day educational program for executive officers and staff

specialists focusing on aspects of association administration and management such as MLS policy, professional standards, political strategy, fair housing, association law, membership development and other areas.

2. The *Certified International Property Specialist* program is NAR's newest designation. REALTORS® earn the CIPS by submitting data on international transactions they have participated in and by taking five CIPS courses. Courses focus on International Business, Europe, Asia/Pacific, the Americas and financial analysis.

3. The *Certified Professional Standards Administrators* program trains executive officers and staff specialists in proper administration of ethics complaints and requests for arbitration.

4. The *Convention Education* program offers a selection of timely education sessions during NAR's three national meetings.

5. The *REALTOR® Institute* establishes national curriculum standards and certifies state programs relative to the Graduate, REALTOR® Institute (GRI) designation.

Convention

The mission of the Convention division is to coordinate logistics and negotiate solid contractual arrangements for the three annual national meetings of NAR—the Mid-Winter Meetings, Mid-Year Conferences and the Annual Conventions.

Member Services

Publications include the *Roster of REALTORS®* and the *State and Board Leadership Directory.* This division of NAR has negotiated group buying discounts with AT&T, Budget Rent-a-Car, Oldsmobile and Xerox for NAR members. It also offers risk reduction programs and recruiting programs for state and local boards.

Member Policy

The Member Policy division serves members through four programs:

1. The *Member and Board Policy/Support* program provides policy and guidance to local and state associations to assist them in maintaining compliance with NAR policy, thereby minimizing potential legal exposure and insurance costs.

2. The *Multiple Listing Policy Compliance* program disseminates MLS policy information to local and state associations and members through NAR publications, and provides policy guid-

ance to local and state associations and members on multiple listing policy.

3. The *Professional Standards Policy Compliance* program supports the ongoing review and revision of the Code of Ethics to provide a viable guide for ethical business practices and provides locally deliverable training programs on the meaning of the Code and how its principles are to be applied in everyday practice.

4. The *Multi-Board Management Services* program is designed so state associations will be able, at their option, to provide a menu of needed and wanted management services to small to medium-sized boards.

Computer Services

The RCS/MLS is a computerized multiple listing system of state-of-the-art computer hardware and the latest in computerized MLS software, developed by the National Association. The system is currently being maintained in 63 sites around the country and in Australia.

Political and State Affairs

The Political and State Affairs division provides services through six programs:

1. The *Housing Needs* program is an outreach program to local associations and demonstration cities that provides information and educational and technical assistance for a variety of afforda-ble housing programs. This information is made available to members interested in solving their local housing needs problems.

2. The *Independent Expenditures* program seeks to help achieve the political and legislative objectives of NAR by using RPAC funds, separate from RPAC direct campaign contributions, to make campaign expenditures on behalf of a select number of federal candidates.

3. *Issues Mobilization* provides financial support to local and state associations for issues confronting the real estate industry and the ownership of real property.

4. The *Political Communications Network* is the grassroots lobbying arm of NAR. It currently consists of over 50,000 REALTORS® who have stated their willingness to write, call or visit with members of the U.S. Congress or their staffs on issues of impor-tance to the real estate industry.

5. *REALTORS® Active in Politics (RAP)* activates REALTORS® in the political process on the federal, state and local levels.

6. *REALTORS® Political Action Committee (RPAC)* raises $2 million a year from REALTORS® for RPAC and contributes those funds to federal candidates who support NAR's legislative agenda in Washington, D.C.

Legal Affairs

The Legal Affairs division is made up of five programs:

1. The *Arbitration Award Enforcement Fund* can provide up to $1,500 to the prevailing member in a board arbitration to defray the legal costs incurred if the losing party refuses to pay the award.
2. *Board/Association Professional Liability Insurance* provides insurance coverage for local and state associations in the area of errors and omissions and directors and officers liability.
3. The *Legal Action* program provides financial assistance in cases of national industrywide legal significance.
4. *Legal Counseling* responds to the fundamental legal needs of the Association, affiliates, and local and state associations.
5. *Trademark Protection* preserves and strengthens the proprietary rights of the Association in its registered trademarks.

Publications

NAR offers the following publications:

- *EO Update Newsletter* is distributed free to local and state associations to provide brief updates on NAR programs, policies, products and services that affect local and state associations.
- *The Executive Officer Magazine* is a 32-page magazine distributed four times a year free to local and state associations. Offers in-depth review of management and policy subjects.
- *Manuals for REALTOR® Association Operations* on all aspects of REALTOR® association management.

REALTORS® Library Service

This division maintains a comprehensive library of real estate information for dissemination through individual responses and by the Real Estate Index and responds to the information needs of members, staff and executive officers by acquiring and organizing materials relevant to the real estate industry and by maintaining the National Association's archives.

Public Affairs

The National Association provides a variety of programs to members and the general public. These services include board publication support, community service programs, media relations consulting, officer talking points and spokesperson training. Public Affairs also organizes American Home Week, which celebrates the right to own private property, and distributes awards for excellence in association service.

SPECIALIZED DIVISIONS

In 1923 the national association began to develop specialized divisions to aid members in perfecting their skills. These divisions grew into the present institutes, societies and councils of the national association. REALTORS® and REALTOR-ASSOCIATE®s who avail themselves of these organizations of specialists are offered professional publications, technical journals, educational programs and research facilities as well as the business contacts essential to progress.

Education and certification in each of these specialties enable association members to receive professional designations that mark them as qualified specialists to their business associates and the public.

Residential Sales Council

The Residential Sales Council (RS Council) is a professional organization dedicated to providing superior member benefits to enable residential sales specialists to maximize their professional performance. Their objectives are to enhance members' continuing competency through providing superior educational opportunities in a cost-effective manner; to provide and promote benefits that enhance the economic value of membership in the Council; and to create and maintain organizational systems to ensure the integrity of the Council.

The Council offers the Certified Residential Specialist designation (CRS), which is the highest designation awarded in the residential sales field. Members earn the designation through advanced course work, experience and elective credits.

Publications   *Real Estate Business,* a quarterly magazine, focuses on current business practices in finance, marketing, computers, management, sales and investment. The *RS Insider* is a quarterly newsletter highlighting programs and services of the Council, with articles covering the most innovative sales techniques.

Advanced Professional Training RS Courses are advanced courses leading to the CRS (Certified Residential Specialist) designation. They include the following:

- RS 200—Business development for the Residential Specialist
- RS 201—Listing Strategies for the Residential Specialist
- RS 202—Sales Strategies for the Residential Specialist
- RS 203—Personal and Career Management for the Residential Specialist
- RS 204—Building Wealth through Residential Real Estate
- RS 205—Financial Skills for the Residential Specialist
- RS 206—Computer Applications for the Residential Specialist
- RS 207—Sales and Marketing Strategies for the New Homes Specialist

Books and Products The RS Council publishes books and products to improve the knowledge and ability of residential sales agents. The Council also provides access to a variety of products produced by leading educators in the residential sales industry.

Recommended Software The RS Council has established a rigorous, three-part review process for real estate software programs. They are tested by a software testing laboratory and by members of the Council's Computer Services Committee. To earn RS Council recommendation, the programs must demonstrate the highest levels of accuracy and user-friendliness, use the most current technology, display a superior quality of output, completeness and documentation, and provide exemplary technical support.

Other Programs The RS Council has chapters nationwide where members can meet locally. They also hold three national business meetings per year in conjunction with the National Association's meetings. In addition, the Council sponsors a national sales rally for members only.

OTHER INSTITUTES, SOCIETIES AND COUNCILS

American Society of Real Estate Counselors (ASREC)

ASREC was formed in 1953 to enhance the quality of advice available to the public on property matters. The Counselor of Real Estate is the ultimate source of knowledge available to meet the needs of property owners, investors and developers. The CRE designation recognizes the individual's demonstrated judgment, integrity and experience in real estate matters and client service. Compensation is by a prearranged fee or salary for services, rather than by commission or contingent fee. Membership is by invitation only, on either a self-initiated or sponsored basis.

CRE® (Counselor of Real Estate)   All members hold the CRE designation and provide objective advice on real estate–related areas to investors, builders and various financial institutions.

Commercial-Investment Real Estate Institute (CIREI)

The Commercial Investment Real Estate Institute, through an extensive educational curriculum, enhances the competence of those engaged in commercial investment real estate. Membership includes specialists in commercial property development, brokerage and investment analysis, as well as allied professionals in banking, taxation and law.

CCIM (Certified Commercial Investment Member)   This designation is conferred upon members after successful completion of 240 hours of graduate-level study in property analysis, valuation, cash flow projections and analysis, taxation, syndication, investment, development and marketing; submission of resume of qualified consummated commercial-investment transaction and/or consultations; and successful completion of an eight-hour comprehensive examination.

Institute of Real Estate Management (IREM)

IREM was established in 1933 to develop and ensure high standards of professional practice in the field of property management. IREM creates and sponsors a wide variety of courses, seminars and continuing education programs at both the national and local levels. IREM's membership is composed of property managers and real estate asset managers who have achieved designation requirements in the areas of experience, education and ethics.

CPM® (Certified Property Manager)   Members earn this designation by meeting required standards in property management experience and education while subscribing to a code of ethics.

AMO® (Accredited Management Organization)   Property management companies that meet established standards of experience, integrity and fiscal stability can receive this designation.

ARM® (Accredited Residential Manager) This is an educational accreditation awarded to on-site managers specializing in residential property who meet specific requirements in education, experience and ethical behavior.

REALTORS® Land Institute (RLI)

RLI, established in 1944, helps members improve their professional competence and marketing expertise in all phases of land brokerage, including agricultural and urban land, and transitional and recreational properties. The Institute offers the RLI Land University, the ALC designation, a monthly publication and national marketing sessions.

ALC (Accredited Land Consultant) This designation is earned by members who meet educational standards, have professional experience and complete service requirements.

RNMI (REALTORS® National Marketing Institute)

RNMI, founded in 1923, promotes professional competence in residential sales and brokerage management through its two independent Councils:

1. The *Real Estate Brokerage Managers Council* provides broker managers of residential, commercial, industrial, relocation appraising and property management companies the working knowledge and skills necessary to profitably manage their companies.
2. The *Residential Sales Council* and the Certified Residential Specialist designation (CRS) are explained earlier in this chapter.

CRB (Certified Real Estate Brokerage Manager) The CRB is awarded to those who successfully complete the CRB management series, fulfill experience requirements and apply learned management concepts to daily practice.

Society of Industrial and Office REALTORS® (SIOR)

SIOR was established in 1941 for individuals specializing in all phases of industrial and office real estate activity. SIOR offers a full range of educational courses in marketing industrial and office properties and is dedicated to maintaining high professional standards while meeting the needs of its corporate clients.

SIOR®   This designation is earned by industrial and office REAL-TORS® who complete required course work and fulfill professional experience criteria.

PRE (Professional Real Estate Executive)   Corporate real estate executives earn this designation by completing required course work and fulfilling professional experience criteria.

Women's Council of REALTORS® (WCR)

WCR, founded in 1938, provides a referral network, programs and systems for personal and career growth, and opportunities for the development of leadership skills through its local and state chapters and the WCR Leadership Training Graduate program. In 1990, WCR introduced a Referral and Relocation Certification program. RRC is the only relocation certification offered through NAR or any of its affiliated Institutes, Societies and Councils.

LTG (Leadership Training Graduate)   Awarded after completing four leadership training courses and meeting leadership experience requirements.

CODE OF ETHICS AND STANDARDS OF PRACTICE OF THE NATIONAL ASSOCIATION OF REALTORS®

The word *ethics* comes from the Greek word *ethickos,* meaning moral, and *ethos,* meaning character. Ethics is regarded as "doing what is right."

The NATIONAL ASSOCIATION OF REALTORS® has taken the position since its inception that REALTORS® are bound to a code of conduct greater than that set forth in statutes. (Laws set a minimum standard of acceptable behavior.) The Code of Ethics and Standards of Practice that has evolved is based on what is right and the belief of REALTORS® that the best measurement of what is right is the Golden Rule.

Code of Ethics and Standards of Practice of the National Association of REALTORS® Effective January 1, 1993

Where the word REALTORS® is used in this Code and Preamble, it shall be deemed to include REALTOR-ASSOCIATE®s.

While the Code of Ethics establishes obligations that may be higher than those mandated by law, in any instance where the Code of Ethics and the law conflict, the obligations of the law must take precedence.

Preamble: Under all is the land. Upon its wise utilization and widely allocated ownership depend the survival and growth of free institutions and of our civilization. REALTORS® should recognize that the interests of the nation and its citizens require the highest and best use of the land and the widest distribution of land ownership. They require the creation of adequate housing, the building of functioning cities, the development of productive industries and farms, and the preservation of a healthful environment.

Such interests impose obligations beyond those of ordinary commerce. They impose grave social responsibility and a patriotic duty to which REALTORS® should dedicate themselves, and for which they should be diligent in preparing themselves. REALTORS®, therefore, are zealous to maintain and improve the standards of their calling and share with their fellow REALTORS® a common responsibility for its integrity and honor. The term REALTOR® has come to connote competency, fairness, and high integrity resulting from adherence to a lofty ideal of moral conduct in business relations. No inducement of profit and no instruction from clients ever can justify departure from this ideal.

In the interpretation of this obligation, REALTORS® can take no safer guide than that which has been handed down through the centuries, embodied in the Golden Rule, "Whatsoever ye would that others should do to you, do ye even so to them."

Accepting this standard as their own, REALTORS® pledge to observe its spirit in all of their activities and to conduct their business in accordance with the tenets set forth below.

Articles 1 through 5 are aspirational and establish ideals REALTORS® should strive to attain.

Article 1: In justice to those who place their interests in a real estate professional's care, REALTORS® should endeavor to become and remain informed on matters affecting real estate in their community, the state, and nation. (Amended 11/92)

Article 2: In the interest of promoting cooperation and enhancing their professional image, REALTORS® are encouraged to refrain from unsolicited criticism of other real estate practitioners and, if an opinion is sought about another real estate practitioner, their business or their business practices, any opinion should be offered in an objective, professional manner. (Amended 11/92)

Article 3: REALTORS® should endeavor to eliminate in their communities any practices which could be damaging to the public or bring discredit to the real estate profession. REALTORS® should assist the governmental agency charged with regulating the practices of brokers and sales licensees in their states. (Amended 11/87)

Article 4: To prevent dissension and misunderstanding and to assure better service to the owner, REALTORS® should urge the exclusive listing of property unless contrary to the best interest of the owner. (Amended 11/87)

Article 5: In the best interests of society, of their associates, and their own businesses, REALTORS® should willingly share with other REALTORS® the lessons of their experience and study for the benefit of the public, and should be loyal to the Board of REALTORS® of their community and active in its work.

Articles 6 through 23 establish specific obligations. Failure to observe these requirements subject REALTORS® to disciplinary action.

Article 6: REALTORS® shall seek no unfair advantage over other REALTORS® and shall conduct their business so as to avoid controversies with other REALTORS®. (Amended 11/87)

- **Standard of Practice 6-1:** REALTORS® shall not misrepresent the availability of access to show or inspect a listed property. (Cross-reference Article 22.) (Amended 11/87)
- **Standard of Practice 6-2:** Article 6 is not intended to prohibit otherwise ethical, aggressive or innovative business practices. "Controversies", as used in Article 6, does not relate to disputes over commissions or divisions of commissions. (Adopted 4/92)

Article 7: When representing a buyer, seller, landlord, tenant, or other client as an agent, REALTORS® pledge themselves to protect and promote the interests of their client. This obligation of absolute fidelity to the client's interests is primary, but it does not relieve REALTORS® of their obligation to treat all parties honestly. When serving a buyer, seller, landlord, tenant or other party in a nonagency capacity, REALTORS® remain obligated to treat all parties honestly. (Amended 11/92)

- **Standard of Practice 7-1(a):** REALTORS® shall submit offers and counter-offers as quickly as possible. (Adopted 11/92)
- **Standard of Practice 7-1(b):** When acting as listing brokers, REALTORS® shall continue to submit to the seller/landlord all offers and counter-offers until closing or execution of a lease unless the seller/landlord has waived this obligation in writing. REALTORS®

shall not be obligated to continue to market the property after an offer has been accepted by the seller/landlord. REALTORS® shall recommend that sellers/landlords obtain the advice of legal counsel prior to acceptance of a subsequent offer except where the acceptance is contingent on the termination of the pre-existing purchase contract or lease. (Cross-reference Article 17.) (Amended 11/92)

- **Standard of Practice 7-1(c):** REALTORS® acting as agents of buyers/tenants shall submit to buyers/tenants all offers and counter-offers until acceptance but have no obligation to continue to show properties to their clients after an offer has been accepted unless otherwise agreed in writing. REALTORS® acting as agents of buyers/tenants shall recommend that buyers/tenants obtain the advice of legal counsel if there is a question as to whether a pre-existing contract has been terminated. (Adopted 11/92)

- **Standard of Practice 7-2:** REALTORS®, when seeking to become a buyer/tenant representative, shall not mislead buyers or tenants as to savings or other benefits that might be realized through use of the REALTOR®'s services. (Amended 11/92)

- **Standard of Practice 7-3:** REALTORS®, in attempting to secure a listing, shall not deliberately mislead the owner as to market value.

- **Standard of Practice 7-4:** (Refer to Standard of Practice 22-1, which also relates to Article 7, Code of Ethics.)

- **Standard of Practice 7-5:** (Refer to Standard of Practice 22-2, which also relates to Article 7, Code of Ethics.)

- **Standard of Practice 7-6:** REALTORS®, when acting as principals in a real estate transaction, remain obligated by the duties imposed by the Code of Ethics. (Amended 11/92)

- **Standard of Practice 7-7:** REALTORS® may represent the seller/landlord and buyer/tenant in the same transaction only after full disclosure to and with informed consent of both parties. (Cross-reference Article 9) (Adopted 11/92)

- **Standard of Practice 7-8:** The obligation of REALTORS® to preserve confidential information provided by their clients continues after the termination of the agency relationship. REALTORS® shall not knowingly, during or following the termination of a professional relationship with their client:

1) reveal confidential information of the client; or
2) use confidential information of the client to the disadvantage of the client; or
3) use confidential information of the client for the REALTOR®'s advantage or the advantage of a third party unless the client consents after full disclosure unless:
   a) required by court order; or

b) it is the intention of the client to commit a crime and the information is necessary to prevent the crime; or

c) necessary to defend the REALTOR® or the REALTOR®'s employees or associates against an accusation of wrongful conduct. (Cross-reference Article 9) (Adopted 11/92)

Article 8: In a transaction, REALTORS® shall not accept compensation from more than one party, even if permitted by law, without disclosure to all parties and the informed consent of the REALTOR®'s client or clients. (Amended 11/92)

Article 9: REALTORS® shall avoid exaggeration, misrepresentation, or concealment of pertinent facts relating to the property or the transaction. REALTORS® shall not, however, be obligated to discover latent defects in the property, to advise on matters outside the scope of their real estate license, or to disclose facts which are confidential under the scope of agency duties owed to their clients. (Amended 11/92)

- **Standard of Practice 9-1:** REALTORS® shall not be parties to the naming of a false consideration in any document, unless it be the naming of an obviously nominal consideration.
- **Standard of Practice 9-2:** (Refer to Standard of Practice 21-3, which also relates to Article 9, Code of Ethics.)
- **Standard of Practice 9-3:** (Refer to Standard of Practice 7-3, which also relates to Article 9, Code of Ethics.)
- **Standard of Practice 9-4:** REALTORS® shall not offer a service described as "free of charge" when the rendering of a service is contingent on the obtaining of a benefit such as a listing or commission.
- **Standard of Practice 9-5:** REALTORS® shall, with respect to the subagency of another REALTOR®, timely communicate any change of compensation for subagency services to the other REALTOR® prior to the time such REALTOR® produces a prospective buyer who has signed an offer to purchase the property for which the subagency has been offered through MLS or otherwise by the listing agency.
- **Standard of Practice 9-6:** REALTORS® shall disclose their REALTOR® status and contemplated personal interest, if any, when seeking information from another REALTOR® concerning real property. (Cross-reference to Article 12) (Amended 11/92)
- **Standard of Practice 9-7:** The offering of premiums, prizes, merchandise discounts or other inducements to list, sell, purchase, or lease is not, in itself, unethical even if receipt of the benefit is contingent on listing, purchasing, or leasing through the

REALTOR® making the offer. However, REALTORS® must exercise care and candor in any such advertising or other public or private representations so that any party interested in receiving or otherwise benefiting from the REALTOR®'s offer will have clear, thorough, advance understanding of all the terms and conditions of the offer. The offering of any inducements to do business is subject to the limitations and restrictions of state law and the ethical obligations established by Article 9, as interpreted by any applicable Standard of Practice. (Amended 11/92)

- **Standard of Practice 9-8:** REALTORS® shall be obligated to discover and disclose adverse factors reasonably apparent to someone with expertise in only those areas required by their real estate licensing authority. Article 9 does not impose upon the REALTOR® the obligation of expertise in other professional or technical disciplines. (Cross-reference Article 11.) (Amended 11/86)

- **Standard of Practice 9-9:** REALTORS®, acting as listing brokers, have an affirmative obligation to disclose the existence of dual or variable rate commission arrangements (i.e., listings where one amount of commission is payable if the listing broker's firm is the procuring cause of sale and a different amount of commission is payable if the sale results through the efforts of the seller or a cooperating broker). The listing broker shall, as soon as practical, disclose the existence of such arrangements to potential cooperating brokers and shall, in response to inquiries from cooperating brokers, disclose the differential that would result in a cooperative transaction or in a sale that results through the efforts of the seller. (Amended 11/91)

- **Standard of Practice 9-10(a):** When entering into listing contracts, REALTORS® must advise sellers/landlords of:

  1) the REALTOR®'s general company policies regarding cooperation with subagents, buyer/tenant agents, or both;
  2) the fact that buyer/tenant agents, even if compensated by the listing broker, or by the seller/landlord will represent the interests of buyers/tenants; and
  3) any potential for the listing broker to act as a disclosed dual agent, e.g. buyer/tenant agent. (Adopted 11/92)

- **Standard of Practice 9-10(b):** When entering into contracts to represent buyers/tenants, REALTORS® must advise potential clients of:

  1) the REALTOR®'s general company policies regarding cooperation with other firms; and

2) any potential for the buyer/tenant representative to act as a disclosed dual agent, e.g. listing broker, subagent, landlord's agent, etc. (Adopted 11/92)

- **Standard of Practice 9-11:** Factors defined as "non-material" by law or regulation or which are expressly referenced in law or regulation as not being subject to disclosure are considered not "pertinent" for purposes of Article 9. (Adopted 11/92)

Article 10: REALTORS® shall not deny equal professional services to any person for reasons of race, color, religion, sex, handicap, familial status, or national origin. REALTORS® shall not be parties to any plan or agreement to discriminate against a person or persons on the basis of race, color, religion, sex, handicap, familial status, or national origin. (Amended 11/89)

Article 11: REALTORS® are expected to provide a level of competent service in keeping with the standards of practice in those fields in which the REALTOR® customarily engages.

REALTORS® shall not undertake to provide specialized professional services concerning a type of property or service that is outside their field of competence unless they engage the assistance of one who is competent on such types of property or service, or unless the facts are fully disclosed to the client. Any persons engaged to provide such assistance shall be so identified to the client and their contribution to the assignment should be set forth.

REALTORS® shall refer to the Standards of Practice of the National Association as to the degree of competence that a client has a right to expect the REALTOR® to possess, taking into consideration the complexity of the problem, the availability of expert assistance, and the opportunities for experience available to the REALTOR®.

- **Standard of Practice 11-1:** Whenever REALTORS® submit an oral or written opinion of the value of real property for a fee, their opinion shall be supported by a memorandum in the file or an appraisal report, either of which shall include as a minimum the following:

1. Limiting conditions
2. Any existing or contemplated interest
3. Defined value
4. Date applicable
5. The estate appraised
6. A description of the property
7. The basis of the reasoning including applicable market data and/or capitalization computation

This report or memorandum shall be available to the Professional Standards Committee for a period of at least two years (beginning subsequent to final determination of the court if the appraisal is involved in litigation) to ensure compliance with Article 11 of the Code of Ethics of the NATIONAL ASSOCIATION OF REALTORS®.

- **Standard of Practice 11-2:** REALTORS® shall not undertake to make an appraisal when their employment or fee is contingent upon the amount of appraisal.
- **Standard of Practice 11-3:** REALTORS® engaged in real estate securities and syndications transactions are engaged in an activity subject to regulations beyond those governing real estate transactions generally, and therefore have the affirmative obligation to be informed of applicable federal and state laws, and rules and regulations regarding these types of transactions.

Article 12: REALTORS® shall not undertake to provide professional services concerning a property or its value where they have a present or contemplated interest unless such interest is specifically disclosed to all affected parties.

- **Standard of Practice 12-1:** (Refer to Standards of Practice 9-4 and 16-1, which also relate to Article 12, Code of Ethics.) (Amended 5/84)

Article 13: REALTORS® shall not acquire an interest in or buy or present offers from themselves, any member of their immediate families, their firms or any member thereof, or any entities in which they have any ownership interest, any real property without making their true position known to the owner or the owner's agent. In selling property they own, or in which they have any interest, REALTORS® shall reveal their ownership or interest in writing to the purchaser or the purchaser's representative. (Amended 11/90)

- **Standard of Practice 13-1:** For the protection of all parties, the disclosures required by Article 13 shall be in writing and provided by REALTORS® prior to the signing of any contract. (Adopted 2/86)

Article 14: In the event of a controversy between REALTORS® associated with different firms, arising out of their relationship as REALTORS®, the REALTORS® shall submit the dispute to arbitration in accordance with the regulations of their Board or Boards rather than litigate the matter.

In the event clients of REALTORS® wish to arbitrate contractual disputes arising out of real estate transactions, REALTORS® shall arbitrate those disputes in accordance with the regulations of their Board, provided the clients agree to be bound by the decision. (Amended 11/92)

- **Standard of Practice 14-1:** The filing of litigation and refusal to withdraw from it by REALTORS® in an arbitrable matter constitutes a refusal to arbitrate. (Adopted 2/86)
- **Standard of Practice 14-2:** Article 14 does not require REALTORS® to arbitrate in those circumstances when all parties to the dispute advise the Board in writing that they choose not to arbitrate before the Board. (Amended 11/92)

Article 15: If charged with unethical practice or asked to present evidence or to cooperate in any other way, in any disciplinary proceeding or investigation, REALTORS® shall place all pertinent facts before the proper tribunals of the Member Board or affiliated institute, society, or council in which membership is held and shall take no action to disrupt or obstruct such processes. (Amended 11/89)

- **Standard of Practice 15-1:** REALTORS® shall not be subject to disciplinary proceedings in more than one Board of REALTORS® with respect to alleged violations of the Code of Ethics relating to the same transaction.
- **Standard of Practice 15-2:** REALTORS® shall not make any unauthorized disclosure or dissemination of the allegations, findings, or decision developed in connection with an ethics hearing or appeal or in connection with an arbitration hearing or procedural review. (Amended 11/91)
- **Standard of Practice 15-3:** REALTORS® shall not obstruct the Board's investigative or disciplinary proceedings by instituting or threatening to institute actions for libel, slander or defamation against any party to a professional standards proceeding or their witnesses. (Adopted 11/87)
- **Standard of Practice 15-4:** REALTORS® shall not intentionally impede the Board's investigative or disciplinary proceedings by filing multiple ethics complaints based on the same event or transaction. (Adopted 11/88)

Article 16: When acting as agents, REALTORS® shall not accept any commission, rebate, or profit on expenditures made for their principal, without the principal's knowledge and consent. (Amended 11/91)

- **Standard of Practice 16-1:** REALTORS® shall not recommend or suggest to a client or a customer the use of services of another organization or business entity in which they have a direct interest without disclosing such interest at the time of the recommendation or suggestion. (Amended 5/88)

- **Standard of Practice 16-2:** When acting as agents or subagents, REALTORS® shall disclose to a client or customer if there is any financial benefit or fee the REALTOR® or the REALTOR®'s firm may receive as a direct result of having recommended real estate products or services (e.g., homeowner's insurance, warranty programs, mortgage financing, title insurance, etc.) other than real estate referral fees. (Adopted 5/88)

Article 17: REALTORS® shall not engage in activities that constitute the unauthorized practice of law and shall recommend that legal counsel be obtained when the interest of any party to the transaction requires it.

Article 18: REALTORS® shall keep in a special account in an appropriate financial institution, separated from their own funds, monies coming into their possession in trust for other persons, such as escrows, trust funds, clients' monies, and other like items.

Article 19: REALTORS® shall be careful at all times to present a true picture in their advertising and representations to the public. REALTORS® shall also ensure that their professional status (e.g., broker, appraiser, property manager, etc.) or status as REALTORS® is clearly identifiable in any such advertising. (Amended 11/92)

- **Standard of Practice 19-1:** REALTORS® shall not offer for sale/ lease or advertise property without authority. When acting as listing brokers or as subagents, REALTORS® shall not quote a price different from that agreed upon with the seller/landlord. (Amended 11/92)
- **Standard of Practice 19-2:** (Refer to Standard of Practice 9-4, which also relates to Article 19, Code of Ethics.)
- **Standard of Practice 19-3:** REALTORS®, when advertising unlisted real property for sale/lease in which they have an ownership interest, shall disclose their status as both owners/landlords and as REALTORS® or real estate licensees. (Amended 11/92)
- **Standard of Practice 19-4:** REALTORS® shall not advertise nor permit any person employed by or affiliated with them to advertise listed property without disclosing the name of the firm. (Adopted 11/86)
- **Standard of Practice 19-5:** Only REALTORS® as listing brokers, may claim to have "sold" the property, even when the sale resulted through the cooperative efforts of another broker. However, after

transactions have closed, listing brokers may not prohibit successful cooperating brokers from advertising their "cooperation," "participation," or "assistance" in the transaction, or from making similar representations.

Only listing brokers are entitled to use the term "sold" on signs, in advertisements, and in other public representations. (Amended 11/89)

Article 20: REALTORS®, for the protection of all parties, shall see that financial obligations and commitments regarding real estate transactions are in writing, expressing the exact agreement of the parties. A copy of each agreement shall be furnished to each party upon their signing such agreement.

- **Standard of Practice 20-1:** At the time of signing or initialing, REALTORS® shall furnish to each party a copy of any document signed or initialed. (Adopted 5/86)
- **Standard of Practice 20-2:** For the protection of all parties, REALTORS® shall use reasonable care to ensure that documents pertaining to the purchase, sale, or lease of real estate are kept current through the use of written extensions or amendments. (Amended 11/92)

Article 21: REALTORS® shall not engage in any practice or take any action inconsistent with the agency of other REALTORS®.

- **Standard of Practice 21-1:** Signs giving notice of property for sale, rent, lease, or exchange shall not be placed on property without consent of the seller/landlord. (Amended 11/92)
- **Standard of Practice 21-2:** REALTORS® acting as subagents or as buyer/tenant agents, shall not attempt to extend a listing broker's offer of cooperation and/or compensation to other brokers without the consent of the listing broker. (Amended 11/92)
- **Standard of Practice 21-3:** REALTORS® shall not solicit a listing which is currently listed exclusively with another broker. However, if the listing broker, when asked by the REALTOR®, refuses to disclose the expiration date and nature of such listing; i.e., an exclusive right to sell, an exclusive agency, open listing, or other form of contractual agreement between the listing broker and the client, the REALTOR® may contact the owner to secure such information and may discuss the terms upon which the REALTOR® might take a future listing or, alternatively, may take a listing to become effective upon expiration of any existing exclusive listing. (Amended 11/86)
- **Standard of Practice 21-4:** REALTORS® shall not use information obtained by them from the listing broker, through offers to

cooperate received through Multiple Listing Services or other sources authorized by the listing broker, for the purpose of creating a referral prospect to a third broker, or for creating a buyer/tenant prospect unless such use is authorized by the listing broker. (Amended 11/92)

- **Standard of Practice 21-5:** The fact that an agency agreement has been entered into with a REALTOR® shall not preclude or inhibit any other REALTOR® from entering into a similar agreement after the expiration of the prior agreement. (Amended 11/92)

- **Standard of Practice 21-6:** The fact that a client has retained a REALTOR® as an agent in one or more past transactions does not preclude other REALTORS® from seeking such former client's future business. (Amended 11/92)

- **Standard of Practice 21-7:** REALTORS® shall be free to list property which is "open listed" at any time, but shall not knowingly obligate the seller to pay more than one commission except with the seller's knowledgeable consent. (Cross-reference Article 7.) (Amended 5/88)

- **Standard of Practice 21-8:** When REALTORS® are contacted by the client of another REALTOR® regarding the creation of an agency relationship to provide the same type of service, and REALTORS® have not directly or indirectly initiated such discussions, they may discuss the terms upon which they might enter into a future agency agreement or, alternatively, may enter into an agency agreement which becomes effective upon expiration of any existing exclusive agreement. (Amended 11/92)

- **Standard of Practice 21-9:** In cooperative transactions REALTORS® shall compensate cooperating REALTORS® (principal brokers) and shall not compensate nor offer to compensate, directly or indirectly, any of the sales licensees employed by or affiliated with other REALTORS® without the prior express knowledge and consent of the cooperating broker.

- **Standard of Practice 21-10:** Article 21 does not preclude REALTORS® from making general announcements to prospective clients describing their services and the terms of their availability even though some recipients may have entered into agency agreements with another REALTOR®. A general telephone canvass, general mailing or distribution addressed to all prospective clients in a given geographical area or in a given profession, business, club, or organization, or other classification or group is deemed "general" for purposes of this standard.

Article 21 is intended to recognize as unethical two basic types of solicitations:

First, telephone or personal solicitations of property owners who have been identified by a real estate sign, multiple listing compilation, or other information service as having exclusively listed their property with another REALTOR®; and

Second, mail or other forms of written solicitations of prospective clients whose properties are exclusively listed with another REALTOR® when such solicitations are not part of a general mailing but are directed specifically to property owners identified through compilations of current listings, "for sale" or "for rent" signs, or other sources of information required by Article 22 and Multiple Listing Service rules to be made available to other REALTORS® under offers of subagency or cooperation. (Amended 11/92)

- **Standard of Practice 21-11:** REALTORS®, prior to entering into an agency agreement, have an affirmative obligation to make reasonable efforts to determine whether the client is subject to a current, valid exclusive agreement to provide the same type of real estate service. (Amended 11/92)

- **Standard of Practice 21-12:** REALTORS®, acting as agents of buyers or tenants, shall disclose that relationship to the seller/landlord's agent at first contact and shall provide written confirmation of that disclosure to the seller/landlord's agent not later than execution of a purchase agreement or lease. (Cross-reference Article 7.) (Amended 11/92)

- **Standard of Practice 21-13:** On unlisted property, REALTORS® acting as buyer/tenant agents shall disclose that relationship to the seller/landlord at first contact for that client and shall provide written confirmation of such disclosure to the seller/landlord not later than execution of any purchase or lease agreement.

  REALTORS® shall make any request for anticipated compensation from the seller/landlord at first contact. (Cross-reference Article 7.) (Amended 11/92)

- **Standard of Practice 21-14:** REALTORS®, acting as agents of sellers/landlords or as subagents of listing brokers, shall disclose that relationship to buyers/tenants as soon as practicable and shall provide written confirmation of such disclosure to buyers/tenants not later than execution of any purchase or lease agreement. (Amended 11/92)

- **Standard of Practice 21-15:** Article 21 does not preclude REALTORS® from contacting the client of another broker for the purpose of offering to provide, or entering into a contract to provide, a different type of real estate service unrelated to the type of service currently being provided (e.g., property management as opposed to brokerage). However, information received through a Multiple Listing Service or any other offer of cooperation may not be used to target clients of other REALTORS® to whom such offers to provide services may be made. (Amended 11/92)

- **Standard of Practice 21-16:** REALTORS®, acting as subagents or buyer/tenant agents, shall not use the terms of an offer to purchase/lease to attempt to modify the listing broker's offer of compensation to subagents or buyer's agents nor make the submission of an executed offer to purchase/lease contingent on the listing broker's agreement to modify the offer of compensation. (Amended 11/92)
- **Standard of Practice 21-17:** Where property is listed on an open listing basis, REALTORS® acting as buyer/tenant agents may deal directly with the seller/landlord. (Adopted 11/92)
- **Standard of Practice 21-18:** All dealings concerning property exclusively listed, or with buyer/tenants who are exclusively represented shall be carried on with the client's agent, and not with the client, except with the consent of the client's agent. (Adopted 11/92)

Article 22: REALTORS® shall cooperate with other brokers except when cooperation is not in the client's best interest. (Amended 11/92)

- **Standard of Practice 22-1:** It is the obligation of subagents to promptly disclose all pertinent facts to the principal's agent prior to as well as after a purchase or lease agreement is executed. (Cross-reference to Article 9) (Amended 11/92)
- **Standard of Practice 22-2:** REALTORS® shall submit offers and counter-offers, in an objective manner. (Amended 11/92)
- **Standard of Practice 22-3:** REALTORS® shall disclose the existence of an accepted offer to any broker seeking cooperation. (Adopted 5/86)
- **Standard of Practice 22-4:** REALTORS®, acting as exclusive agents of sellers, establish the terms and conditions of offers to cooperate. Unless expressly indicated in offers to cooperate made through MLS or otherwise, a cooperating broker may not assume that the offer of cooperation includes an offer of compensation. Entitlement to compensation in a cooperative transaction must be agreed upon between a listing and cooperating broker prior to the time an offer to purchase the property is produced. (Adopted 11/88)

Article 23: REALTORS® shall not knowingly or recklessly make false or misleading statements about competitors, their businesses, or their business practices. (Amended 11/91)

The Code of Ethics was adopted in 1913. Amended at the Annual Convention in 1924, 1928, 1950, 1951, 1952, 1955, 1956, 1961, 1962, 1974, 1982, 1986, 1987, 1989, 1990, 1991, and 1992.

EXPLANATORY NOTES (Amended 11/88)

The reader should be aware of the following policies which have been approved by the Board of Directors of the National Association:

In filing a charge of an alleged violation of the Code of Ethics by a REALTOR®, the charge shall read as an alleged violation of one or more Articles of the Code. A Standard of Practice may only be cited in support of the charge.

The Standards of Practice are not an integral part of the Code but rather serve to clarify the ethical obligations imposed by the various Articles. The Standards of Practice supplement, and do not substitute for, the Case Interpretations in *Interpretations of the Code of Ethics.*

Modifications to existing Standards of Practice and additional new Standards of Practice are approved from time to time. The reader is cautioned to ensure that the most recent publications are utilized.

Articles 1 through 5 are aspirational and establish ideals that a REALTOR® should strive to attain. Recognizing their subjective nature, these Articles shall not be used as the bases for charges of alleged unethical conduct or as the bases for disciplinary action.

COMPETITION, ANTITRUST AND THE REAL ESTATE SALESPERSON

Congress and the legislatures of several states have enacted laws, sometimes known as antitrust laws, that are designed to protect competition. They do so by a wide variety of prohibitions, two of which are particularly relevant and important to real estate salespeople.

The first prohibition is against any form of price fixing. Price fixing is the formation of an agreement or understanding, express or implied, direct or indirect, between a brokerage firm and one or more of its competitors to fix, control or maintain the price of real estate services to members of the public. A price-fixing agreement is, in legal terminology, illegal *per se.* That means there is and can be no excuse, defense or justification for a price-fixing agreement that the law will recognize.

But real estate salespeople should recognize that similarity or even uniformity in the commission rates of different and competing brokers does not signal the existence of an illegal agreement to fix prices. Price uniformity is a fundamental characteristic of a highly competitive market wherein competitors cannot charge more for their services without losing business to others and cannot reduce the charge for services without impairing their profitability.

Few, if any, real estate salespeople are in a position to fix, control or maintain the prices at which listings are taken, as this is a decision of the broker by whom they are employed or with whom they are affiliated. However, salespeople must know who their competitors are. They must also understand that real estate commissions, like the price of all other goods and services not monopolized or regulated by government, must be established independently by the broker and never by agreement with a competitor.

Real estate salespeople within the same office are not competitors for purposes of the antitrust laws. Likewise, the salesperson's sponsoring broker is not his or her competitor. Thus, it is not contrary to the antitrust laws for a broker to establish independently the real estate commission to be charged for the services of his or her office.

Real estate commissions must always be negotiable; that is, the commission established with respect to any transaction will reflect the most that the property seller is willing to pay for the services required and the least the broker is willing to accept for the services he or she is required to render.

If real estate salespeople believe that the commission required by their broker is unreasonable, they should affiliate with a broker charging a commission rate they deem reasonable.

Real estate salespeople who seek to ingratiate themselves with a potential property seller by suggesting that they are "compelled" to value their services highly because of some agreement among brokers in the marketplace not only devalue their services but expose innocent brokers and salespeople to civil and criminal litigation and liability.

For any salesperson to suggest or even intimate that commissions are the product of agreement between competing brokers or that they are dictated by a real estate board or its multiple listing service is to accuse the brokers or the board of a serious crime—a felony punishable by heavy fines and long terms in jail. Moreover, for any salesperson to honor such agreement, whether or not he or she is the author of it, is to share the guilt and hence become subject to the punishment.

The second prohibition of the antitrust laws that is of particular relevance and importance to real estate salespeople is that against "boycotts and concerted refusals to deal." The antitrust laws prohibit a group of competitors from "ganging up" on other competitors in order to force them out of business or to force them to change the way they do business. Boycotts, like agreements to fix prices, are illegal *per se.*

Real estate salespeople and their brokers are required to respond to the challenges of competition by individual, as opposed to collective, action. The proper response to competitive innovation, be it a different, better or cheaper service, is to meet or beat such competition, one on one. The antitrust laws permit competitors to extol the value of their services and even to question the value of the services of other competitors. They do *not* permit agreements in any form to harass or suppress the operations of a competitor. Salespeople should never suggest or imply that any response they make to a competitive challenge is the product of agreement by other brokers or the real estate board.

Clients who think of a real estate salesperson as a mere MLS catalog clerk and real estate brokerage as nothing more than a guided tour of properties for sale or rent will consider themselves to be overcharged regardless of the commission they pay. On the other hand, clients who recognize the real estate salesperson as a professional qualified and dedicated to securing the highest price and the best terms for their property will also recognize that the "value added" by the services of that salesperson will substantially exceed the cost of those services. It is the responsibility of real estate salespeople to demonstrate that their services more than pay for themselves.

The antitrust laws are intended to establish an economic environment in which the operation of the marketplace determines what goods and services will be produced and the price at which they will be bought and sold. Efforts to collectively restrict supply or artifically control, demand, distort or destroy this marketplace are illegal.

THE CIVIL RIGHTS ACT AND THE REAL ESTATE SALESPERSON

Discrimination in housing accommodations is outlawed by federal law. Many states also have laws prohibiting discrimination, so a wrongful act of discrimination could be a violation of both federal and state law.

The Civil Rights Act of 1866 requires that "All citizens of the United States shall have the same right, in every State and Territory, as is enjoyed by the white citizens thereof to inherit, purchase, lease, sell, hold, and convey real and personal property." In the case of *Jones* v. *Mayer,* decided on June 17, 1968, the U.S. Supreme Court held that the 1866 law prohibits "all racial discrimination, private as well as public, in the sale or rental of property."

The Federal Fair Housing Act of 1968 (Title VIII of the Civil Rights Act of 1968), as amended, prohibits discrimination based on race, color, sex, religion, national origin, familial status or disability.

Any salesperson found guilty of discriminatory practices will have violated not only the law but also Article 10 of the Code of Ethics and Standards of Practice of the NATIONAL ASSOCIATION OF REALTORS®. In addition to civil penalties, that person could face loss of his or her real estate license and expulsion from the board of REALTORS®. In some cases, criminal prosecution would also be possible.

No REALTOR® can afford to employ or have affiliated a salesperson who takes his or her obligation to comply with the Code of Ethics and civil rights laws lightly. The REALTOR® has been held responsible for the salesperson's civil rights transgressions and only rarely has been able to escape liability.

It is not enough that salespeople be familiar with the civil rights laws and take no action contrary to them. They should follow daily procedures and safeguards that will permit them to affirmatively establish their compliance with the law and their innocence of discriminatory conduct. Thus, they should be able to demonstrate that a prospect was offered the same number and range of listings as any other prospect of comparable financial means; that a prospect received the same degree of follow-up and the same level and quality of sales effort. If anything, prospects having protective status should be given more and better service if only to secure the benefit of any doubt that may be raised.

And doubts inevitably will be raised, not only because of the high degree of civil rights sensitivity that exists today for various groups, but also because of the broad range of groups and agencies, public and private, concerned with enforcement of the civil rights laws.

There are two basic theories under which the conduct of real estate salespeople may be challenged as violating the civil rights laws.

The first theory involves the general allegation that they made housing unavailable on account of race, color, religion, sex, handicap, familial status or national origin. The specific complaints supporting this allegation usually take two forms: Sellers or purchasers received less-favorable treatment than that given others, or the salesperson foreclosed the customers from obtaining housing in the community of their choice.

Complaints of less-favorable treatment normally find the salesperson being accused of failing to service the customer as fully as a customer who is not in one of the designated categories for protection under the Civil Rights Act with regard to any facet of the services rendered, or differentiation in the treatment of customers to their detriment in any manner.

Complaints of less-favorable treatment of clients and customers who belong to groups designated for protection under civil rights laws are easily made and can be difficult to disprove because of their inherently subjective and qualitative nature. In dealing with these clients and customers, care and restraint must be exercised and performance on behalf of such persons carefully and accurately documented.

Real estate brokers should prominently display the Equal Housing Opportunity Poster (Figure 2.1) in their offices. Should a federal discrimination complaint be filed, failure to display this poster could shift the burden of proof on the broker and/or salesperson. Proving that they did *not* discriminate is a much more difficult task than defending against an allegation of discrimination where the complainant has the burden of proving discrimination.

The complaint that a salesperson foreclosed purchasers from obtaining housing in the community of their choice is commonly known as a charge of "steering."

Steering, which is specifically prohibited by the federal act, is directing buyers and tenants toward areas or away from areas to maintain homogeneity. Complaints are normally based on race. While steering could be blatant, such as showing black prospects homes in only black or racially mixed areas, or misrepresenting the availability of a property in a white neighborhood to a minority prospect, it could also be subtle. Advertising a property in a predominantly black neighborhood in a newspaper having primarily black readership could be regarded as steering unless non-minority neighborhood properties were also advertised.

Complaints of steering, like complaints of less-favorable treatment, can assume a subjective quality that could make their refutation difficult in the absence of documentation. Such documentation should include, at a minimum, evidence that a prospective buyer or tenant was offered a range of listings available to the salesperson and that such listings encompassed all areas served by that salesperson.

"Blockbusting" is also prohibited by the Federal Fair Housing Act. Blockbusting is inducing panic selling by representing that the entrance of a different group into the neighborhood will decrease property value or result in an increase in crime. Blockbusting, like steering, can be blatant or subtle. Engaging in an intensive listing campaign in an area adjacent to or in transition to minority housing could be viewed as blockbusting when the salesperson or broker did not use a similar approach in areas less likely to undergo ethnic or racial change. "Redlining" is a lender practice of refusing to rent or restricting loans in designated areas. Redlining based on racial composition of an area or racial transition would be a violation of the Federal Fair Housing Act.

The Fair Housing Amendment Act of 1988 added physically or mentally handicapped persons as well as familial status to protected categories. This covers persons under the age of 18 living with a parent or guardian, pregnant women and those in the process of obtaining legal custody.

Exemptions from familial discrimination laws can be obtained for

- units having facilities especially for use by the elderly that have at least one person over the age of 55 living in 80 percent of the units; and
- units solely occupied by persons 62 years of age or older.

FIGURE 2.1   Equal Housing Opportunity Poster*

U.S.. Department of Housing and Urban Development

**EQUAL HOUSING
OPPORTUNITY**

**We Do Business in Accordance With the Federal Fair
Housing Law**

(The Fair Housing Amendments Act of 1988)

It is Illegal to Discriminate Against Any Person Because of Race, Color, Religion, Sex, Handicap, Familial Status, or National Origin

- In the sale or rental of housing or residential lots
- In advertising the sale or rental of housing
- In the financing of housing

- In the provision of real estate brokerage services
- In the appraisal of housing
- Blockbusting is also illegal

Anyone who feels he or she has been discriminated against may file a complaint of housing discrimination:

1-800-424-8590 (Toll Free)
1-800-424-8529 (TDD)

**U.S. Department of Housing and
Urban Development
Assistant Secretary for Fair Housing and
Equal Opportunity**
Washington, D.C. 20410

Previous editions are obsolete

form **HUD-928**.1 (3-89)

*Previous editions are obsolete

Rules against pets cannot be applied to seeing-eye dogs or support animals. Handicapped tenants may modify their units to allow themselves reasonable use of the premises; however, they are responsible for restoration of their unit if a nonhandicapped person would not want the modification. The handicapped are also allowed to alter common areas for access. A handicapped person cannot be charged an increased security deposit because of a seeing-eye dog or support animal or because they altered their unit to obtain reasonable benefits of use.

The Americans with Disabilities Act of 1990 (ADA) is also a civil rights law. It expands the rights of the disabled.

The act provides for equal employment opportunities for the handicapped (applies to employers having 15 or more employees) and prohibits discrimination in any manner that would prevent the full and equal enjoyment of goods, services, facilities and accommodations in any existing "place of public accommodation." The act also applies to new construction.

This act provides that owners of commercial facilities must make their facilities accessible to the extent reasonably achievable. Commercial facilities as defined covers any nonresidential facility that affects commerce. Besides retail sales, this would include service businesses, such as a real estate office.

The words *reasonably achievable* are defined as easily accomplished and able to be carried out without a great deal of difficulty or expense. What is reasonably achievable would be based on costs in relationship to the property value and financial status of the owner or occupant. For a real estate office, it might involve providing a simple ramp to allow wheelchair access, moving furniture to widen aisles, providing a paper cup dispenser at the water cooler, providing handicapped parking and ramps over the curb. It might also require removal of high-pile carpeting and installation of grab bars and a full-length mirror in the washroom.

The act does not require elevators in existing or new structures under three stories with the exception of shopping centers, malls or professional offices of a healthcare provider.

The law states that "any person who owns, leases [or leases to] or operates a place of public accommodation is liable for compliance with the act." This would make property managers and leasing agents, as well as tenants, liable for compliance.

Parties can agree as to who will be responsible for compliance with the act. For example, a property management contract could call for the owner to hold the property management firm harmless from liability for compliance. Similarly, a lease could require the tenant to assume responsibility for compliance. The law is also of importance to appraisers, who might have to deduct the cost of compliance in determining market value. Purchasers of commercial buildings might require that the seller provide a representation of compliance.

ADA provides rather harsh penalties. Failing to correct barriers to handicapped persons could result in up to $50,000 in civil penalties for the first discriminatory act and $100,000 for each subsequent violation. Compensatory damages as well as attorney's fees could also be awarded. Even though the act itself is rather vague and will need to be clarified by court decisions, it seems to be directed at reasonableness.

As a professional, you will have a duty to inform buyers, sellers, lessors and tenants of commercial property about the Americans with Disabilities Act and its basic requirements.

Compliance with the civil rights laws as they relate to the sale or lease of real property requires a thorough understanding of them. These laws look not merely to the intent of a salesperson's conduct but also to its effect. For this reason, salespeople should keep abreast of the developments in the law and should study with care the *REALTORS® Guide to Practice Equal Opportunity in Housing,* which describes in detail greater than this brief summary the obligation and duties of the salesperson under the law.

To support the aim of NAR to make fair housing a reality for all Americans, the NATIONAL ASSOCIATION OF REALTORS® has signed a Voluntary Affirmative Marketing Agreement (VAMA) with the U.S. Department of Housing and Urban Development. The foundation for this agreement is Article 10 of the NAR Code of Ethics.

Individual REALTORS®, by signing VAMA, agree to carry out its provisions. VAMA stresses community involvement and cooperative effort in meeting fair housing goals. It is built around five fair housing marketing principles:

1. The public commitment of REALTORS® to inform clients, prospects and the public that REALTORS® provide equal services to all and comply with fair housing laws. REALTORS® agree to use the equal housing logo and slogan in advertising and to display the fair housing poster in their offices.
2. Local boards shall provide education and training to member REALTORS® as to fair housing.
3. Member firms agree to adapt procedures for fair housing marketing and advertising consistent with NAR-recommended procedure.
4. Persons of both sexes and of all racial and ethnic groups as well as disabled individuals and persons otherwise protected from discrimination are encouraged to enter both the real estate industry and the REALTOR® Association.

5. REALTORS® shall work with community groups in identifying and eliminating barriers to fair housing.

Equal opportunity in housing is an ethical principle to which every REALTOR-ASSOCIATE® must subscribe. It is also the law of the land and good business practice.

Chapter 3

Successful Sales and Listing Qualities

Of all the personal qualities required for success in selling, emotional stamina is perhaps the most important. This is the ability to handle the stress and emotional pressures that inevitably arise in the interpersonal relationships involved in selling.

Everyone has a different tolerance for pressure and stress. However, everyone can learn more about the causes of stress and how to cope with it more effectively. A person entering selling must recognize that emotional tension and pressure is unavoidable. This is called the "law of the situation." It means that it is the duty of the salesperson to understand the customer; it is not the customer's duty to understand the salesperson. Further translated, "the law of the situation" means that to be effective in selling, the salesperson must be well fortified in dealing with the stress factors of interpersonal relations.

The guidelines that follow will help you handle the pressures of emotional stress.

MEETING SALES CHALLENGES

In all interpersonal dealings, ask yourself, "Is the action I am taking directed to meeting the needs of the buyer and/or seller?" This will lead toward acting objectively and not according to whether you feel "justified." Acting as we feel justified usually means actions directed by emotions. Acting objectively means acting logically toward a specific purpose.

Be tolerant of others. Tolerance is the ability to accept other people's capabilities. Frequently we develop stress by trying to push other people to behave as we would like them to. We measure their abilities by our own and become frustrated when they do not make decisions or judgments as quickly as we might under the same circumstances. You must adjust to what others are capable of doing or undue emotional pressures will arise.

Dismiss grudges, grievances and hard feelings. Strong emotions are barriers to good communications; it is essential that you take the initiative in creating a favorable climate for communicating with your customers.

Recognize that you may not get the praise you feel you deserve. The higher up the ladder you climb, whatever ladder you might be climbing, the fewer people there will be around to tell you what a good job you are doing. The more successful you become, the greater will be the need to be able to recharge your own emotional battery without relying on other people to do it for you. It is unfortunate, but some less successful salespeople will not be happy if you achieve greater success than they have been able to achieve. In fact, you might experience resentment. If you let them, they can have a negative effect on your success. On the other hand, associating with highly successful people will serve as a positive motivator for further success.

DEVELOPING POSITIVE ATTITUDES

It takes a good many *aptitudes* to be qualified in real estate sales work, but the process of selling is basically an *attitude.* Your success as a salesperson will depend a great deal upon how well you can build a positive image of what you are trying to do. Beyond putting a dollar figure on paper as a goal, this means visualizing the kinds of activities you will have to engage in to achieve that goal.

The human mind is very much like a computer: it is programmed to go through thousands of actions skillfully, because you have practiced them over and over again until they are performed subconsciously. To become expert at anything requires practice. Mental practice is just as important as physical practice. A positive mental attitude really means seeing things in your mind in a positive manner and seeing yourself succeed in what you are trying to do. These are steps in programming your computer toward success.

Financial goals should be realistic; at the same time, they should challenge you to think beyond routine, to try new ideas and to build selling skills that become uniquely yours.

Positive Company Attitude

Just as you build a positive attitude toward your own success and toward service to your customers, you must build a positive attitude toward your company. It is unlikely that you will succeed without your company being successful or that your company will be successful unless you and other salespeople succeed.

This means teamwork and having and expressing a positive view of your company's reputation. It means loyalty to those with whom you work and an effort to further the objectives of the company and its people. Everything you do to build the stature of your firm enhances your own image as a successful person.

There will be times when company decisions are made with which you do not agree. That is natural, and your broker will welcome your viewpoint and suggestions as the occasion warrants. However, once a policy or decision is made by your firm, your positive attitude must take charge. Think of reasons the new situation will work; don't brood over things that cannot be changed.

A THING CALLED RAPPORT

The word *rapport* is not often used in daily conversation. Instead, we talk about things like "personal chemistry," "different wavelengths" and "getting off on the right foot" to describe how we interact with people. Favorable interaction depends a great deal upon your personal behavior and attitude. There are hundreds of traits that cause people to feel comfortable or uncomfortable with us. Studies indicate there are five traits that appear to be most important in professional selling:

1. *Enthusiasm* means belief in what you are doing, not noise or a cheerleader attitude. It is a spirit that permeates your approach to your customer and client. It is the most contagious of all human traits; if you wish to generate enthusiasm, show enthusiasm.
2. *Perseverance,* a quality of courage, is the ability to keep on trying and testing situations without giving up. It is the trait that causes the successful salesperson to start where other people quit.
3. *Self-reliance* sustains a person through difficult times. It is that part of emotional stamina that helps an individual rebuild confidence when defeat has entered the picture.
4. *Tact* lubricates abrasive situations that are encountered in selling. While you must always be honest, there is never a need to be brutally frank. Speaking softly and helping others feel comfortable is a more rewarding response.

5. *Accuracy* in technical details and information is a must for the successful salesperson. Accuracy is a form of dependability, a most important trait in the eyes of your clients.

UNDERSTANDING HUMAN BEHAVIOR

Some individuals go through life feeling that people are unsolvable puzzles; some simply refuse to try to understand others. No two customers will be alike in their thinking, feelings, attitudes or behavior. Therefore, it becomes important to see each person as an individual and to recognize some fundamental aspects of human behavior that can guide you in getting along with people as they are and not as you might wish them to be.

You cannot "love" people into buying. You must recognize that people buy to fulfill very fundamental needs. When you realize that every question a customer asks and every comment or attitude he expresses is related to one of four fundamental needs, then you can really counsel, guide and assist that customer toward a successful sales conclusion.

A salesperson who lacks a basic understanding of behavior is like a ship without a rudder. Steering people toward achieving needs is the key to personal service in selling.

The four basic needs all human beings seek to fulfill are the same needs every buyer or seller must fulfill in reaching selling or buying decisions.

Physical Needs

These are the needs of a person to feel comfortable; to protect health and improve well-being; to save work, time and energy; and to assure a sense of personal security and independence. Such needs may not be expressed outwardly, but they are inherent in the ways buyers evaluate features of a property or the services of your company. Physical needs are often expressed through concern about the safety of the neighborhood or the house itself.

Social Needs

Every person seeks love and wants to express love; we all want to fulfill the desire to do things for those we love—to make them comfortable, to improve our domestic lifestyle and to enhance the romantic values of living. These needs are strongly presented by customers who express interest in the spouse's satisfaction and the children's comfort, convenience and well-being. The salesperson must listen for these needs.

Ego Needs

All people need a sense of identity, belonging, esteem and approval in the eyes of others. This need is frequently a dominant factor in decisions about real estate that can cause buyers to be unrealistic about what they can afford in a house. The successful salesperson realizes that to deflate a person's ego is tantamount to building an immovable roadblock to concluding the sale. One experienced instructor in selling reminds us that every customer should be seen wearing a sign, "Make me feel important," as a reminder that we should not only see the best in others but express it to them.

Spiritual Needs

These needs are more difficult to recognize. They become active after lower-level needs have been fulfilled. People begin to question if they have realized their full potential. This inward questioning causes many people who have achieved material success to take on responsibilities as teachers or in social service work that pay little in money but much in satisfaction and self-fulfillment. Successfully meeting needs of others will help to satisfy your own spiritual needs. Nothing is more rewarding than the knowledge that you have helped families realize their aspirations.

MANAGING YOURSELF

Some of the earlier advice you will hear in real estate is that you are "on your own" and therefore should discipline your time and your effort. These are wise and worthy words but they really boil down to personal management. Applying management's fundamental aspects to selling real estate will enable you to organize your thinking and increase your effectiveness.

Plan your work for each day and week. Establish priorities to help you achieve objectives. Now, work your plan.

Organize the resources you need to accomplish your plans. Decide if you need help from others and how you will get it.

Serve your customers effectively and with genuine interest and the commissions will take care of themselves.

Evaluate by reviewing both successful and unsuccessful transactions to see what you could have done better. Ask your manager for criticism and accept it in a positive way.

Self-Improvement

One of the most important qualities of a successful salesperson is the ability to recognize that professional growth and development is a continuous process. There are many sources of information on self-improvement, development and the sales process in the programs presented by the REALTORS NATIONAL MARKETING INSTITUTE®, in university and adult education courses, and in published materials that are readily available for your study. Self-development should take place in three areas of potential growth:

Technical Competence   Build your knowledge of real estate and periodically evaluate those areas where you need further information, study and skill. Your customers and clients will not have faith in your advice if your knowledge of your field is not sound and up-to-date. This can also apply to fields that are not exclusively real estate but are closely related, such as banking, construction or architecture, about which you may get questions from your customers. Develop your knowledge according to your interests and capabilities and know where to find answers in those areas beyond your technical competence.

Human Relationships   There is no limit to building insight, understanding and depth in our dealings with people. Much of this comes from the everyday practice you will develop in selling, but much also comes from willingness to assess your understanding realistically and to take steps to improve through further education and learning.

Creativity   Many people let success become a rut. Truly successful people are open-minded to new approaches. Creativity does not have to mean some monumental invention; it can often be a small matter that you have learned to handle in a way that leaves a lasting, positive impression on your customer.

Good Health

Personal health is a highly important part of self-improvement. Without good health, there is little likelihood a person can achieve full potential in anything. If your body does not serve you well, neither will your mind. Never be too busy to have a regular medical check-up and to develop sound health habits.

Good health, vitality and energy are important first impressions to project. In this same light, first impressions are enhanced by good grooming and personal appearance that bespeak quality and concern for self-image. Regular exercise, such as jogging or bike riding, not only helps your body and makes you feel good, it will also help to reduce tension.

YOUR SUCCESS IMAGE

Many people think success is usually a matter of luck—whether one gets the breaks or is in the right place at the right time. Certainly these things can help, but every study of success shows that the individual wanted to succeed and did something to make success happen. Unfortunately, some people have trouble visualizing themselves as a success. These people are found to have a failure image that was often developed early in their lives. Successful real estate salespeople have come to realize that "luck" in real estate is simply the collision of preparation and opportunity.

Building a success image is a matter of recognizing the great value of the service you are bringing to your customers and clients; recognizing that you are truly helping them make one of the most important decisions of a lifetime; and recognizing that you have a positive influence over the thinking, plans and decisions of many people.

The professional in selling never underrates his or her abilities. This does not mean developing a big "I Am" complex. On the contrary, it means never declaring that you are something you do not wish to be! It has been said that the world largely accepts us at our own estimate of ourselves. If so, it is because we usually live up to our own self-estimate. People are successful because they really believe they can be successful.

Much enjoyment from your career in selling will come from the satisfactions that develop as you see your service to other people produce happiness and value. Never was the old philosopher's statement more true than in selling: ". . . as you think—you are."

Chapter 4

Time Management

Setting goals is the first step in effective time management. You need to decide first what you want and how you are going to get it; then plan your time accordingly and discipline yourself to follow the plan. Look at the desks of successful salespeople and executives and you will likely find a written plan or schedule of work for the day and/or week. These people know that time is money and that any time they waste is wasted money.

WHY SET GOALS?

People are basically oriented in two ways: to goals and to tasks. Experienced salespeople in real estate have proved that goal orientation works best for them.

Goals provide the means whereby people make a commitment to themselves. Goals generate the internal motivation to get on with the day's work. Your desire to reach your goal will encourage self-discipline. People do not fail because of lack of skills but because they do not organize their time well and discipline themselves to follow their plans.

Many brokers today are involved in the strategic planning process. Your production goals help your broker establish production objectives for the year.

ELEMENTS OF A GOAL

If your goals are to help you achieve success, they must be attainable, flexible, and measurable, cover a definite time period and be put in writing. They are performance objectives aimed at actions rather than at good intentions.

Attainable Goals

Both salespeople and brokers should be realistic when setting goals. Goals should be neither too easy nor too difficult. For example, if you are averaging $50,000 per year in commissions, a goal of $250,000 for next year may be unrealistic. However, a goal of $75,000 will challenge you to make the extra effort beyond what you have shown you can do. While people will strive to achieve attainable goals, they tend to give up when they believe a goal is impossible for them to reach.

Flexible Goals

The real estate market and the general economy can change a lot in six months, and flexible goals allow for changes. For example, a goal of two exclusive listings per month should permit a variance up or down as financing becomes more difficult or easier to get. Or, suppose you get an exclusive on all the lots in a new subdivision. After a brief celebration, make sure your goals are flexible enough to allow for this change. Don't count on those subdivision lots to get you to your goal for the year. Your goal should still include getting two additional exclusive listings every month.

Measurable Goals

If your goal is "to list 24 exclusives between January 1 and December 31," your goal is measurable. But if you had written, "List as many properties as I can between the beginning and end of the year," that is not a measurable goal. You have no specific number to reach and, therefore, no incentive to work harder to reach your goal. Having a goal that can't be measured is like being in a race that has no finish line. You are likely to give up early.

Time Period for Goals

You should consider short-term goals ranging from several months to a year or more, intermediate-term goals of from three to five years, and career or long-term goals that, depending upon your age, might run from 10 to 20 years. Your daily planning should take into consideration the achievement of your short-term goals. Your short-term goals should be leading toward your intermediate-term goals, which should prepare you to achieve your long-term goals.

The time element is necessary to keep your enthusiasm high. If you set a goal of 24 listings but do not set a time period for getting them, you will not have a target date for getting the job done. Without a target date, goals tend to take second place to what appear to be more pressing matters.

Written Goals

Putting your goals in writing provides a silent reminder of the commitment you made to yourself as well as the means of measuring your progress. This is important to you and your broker as well as anyone else involved in helping you achieve your personal, professional and income goals.

Who Needs to Know

Go over your goals with your spouse or a close friend who will be supportive. Having told someone who is important to you of your goals will motivate you to achieve them. While it is easy to put off secret hopes or plans, once you have written them down and revealed them to another, those achievements become important. Chances are your short-term goals will aid your production and thus make you more valuable to your broker. Let your broker or office manager know about your short-term work-related goals. He or she will be supportive of these goals and can offer positive suggestions for their achievement.

HOW TO SET GOALS

Your goals must be set by you, not someone else. They must be meaningful to you or they are unlikely to be reached.

Your goals might relate to income, savings, property ownership, or educational or professional achievements; or they could be personal rather than career related.

A first step should be to the far future. What do you want to achieve ten or even 20 years from today? You should write these goals down. Now, write a few sentences describing why each of your goals is important to you. By doing this you can quickly eliminate goals that you are unlikely to be motivated to achieve.

The following are examples of long-term goals.

- Within ten years, I will have my own office with a minimum of 20 salespeople working for me.
- Within ten years, I will be in the property management business and manage at least 1,000 units.
- Within ten years, I will own a minimum of 25 rental properties.

- Within ten years, I will have a net worth in excess of $1 million.
- Within ten years, I will own the largest industrial brokerage firm in the city.
- In ten years, I will be living in Beverly Hills.
- Within 20 years, I will be retired with two homes and an annual retirement income of at least $100,000 measured by the present value of the dollar.

Now, a long-term goal does not happen just by wishing for it. Short-term and intermediate-term goals should be chosen that will either help in the achievement of or otherwise be consistent with your long-term goals.

The following are some examples of intermediate-term goals.

- Within three years, I will have met all the requirements for and taken and passed my broker's examination.
- Within three years, I will have achieved the GRI (Graduate, REALTORS® Institute) designation.
- Within five years, I will have received the CPM (Certified Property Manager) designation.
- Within three years, I will buy at least two single-family homes for rehabilitation and resale.
- Within three years, I will have an annual income from commissions of at least $85,000.
- Within five years, I will open my own real estate office specializing in the sale of mobile homes.
- Within five years, I will have received my four-year college degree in marketing.
- Within five years, I will purchase a weekend vacation home for my family.
- Within three years, I will have personal savings in my retirement account of at least $50,000.
- Within three years, I will buy a new Mercedes for my spouse.
- Within five years, I will purchase a commercial rental property.
- Within three years, I will be specializing in the sale of industrial property.

Your short-term goals should lead toward your intermediate-term goals. The goals can be personal or career-related.

- During the month of July, I will take two weeks of vacation with my family.
- I will obtain a minimum of two residential listings per month.
- I will conduct a minimum of three open houses per month during the next year and will contact all visitors within three days of each open house.

- Within one month, I will have prepared a personalized listing presentation manual.
- I will enroll in and complete a community college course in Real Estate Finance with at least a B grade by June 1.
- By June 1, I will have read at least three books on real estate selling and/or listing and will have written a synopsis of new ideas and techniques that I feel will be applicable to my work.
- By June 1, I will be showing homes to at least six buyers each week.
- By August 1, I will have personally introduced myself to every neighbor within two blocks of my home.
- My dollar sales volume for the period of July 1 to January 1 will be at least $3.5 million.
- For the coming year, I will call on at least ten "for sale by owner" ads or signs each week.
- For the coming year, I will write at least 50 listing solicitation letters each week and follow up each letter with a telephone call within five days.
- I will set up a Keogh plan within the next 90 days.
- Within three months, I will be a member of a civic organization.

You will likely discover that you have a great many short-term goals, perhaps three to five intermediate-term goals and one or two long-term goals.

If the short-term goals will help ensure completion of the intermediate-term goals and the intermediate goals lead to the achievement of your long-term goals, you will have developed a plan for personal and/or career achievement. Keep in mind that many personal goals will also contribute to the achievement of your career goals.

CONVERTING GOALS TO A WORK PLAN

To convert your income goals to a daily work program, you will need records. Most salespeople keep monthly or yearly data on the number of listings taken, the number of showings needed to make a sale and the number of sales completed, and a record of both listing and selling commissions.

To relate your goal to the number of showings, let's say you are now making $50,000 a year, that you average ten showings a week and you want to increase your income by $10,000.

$$10 \text{ Showings} \times 50 \text{ Weeks} = 500 \text{ Per Year}$$
$$\$50,000 \div 500 = \$100 \text{ Per Showing}$$

If everything else remains constant (average sales price and commission), you will need to increase showings to 12 per week.

$$2 \text{ Showings} \times 50 \text{ Weeks} = 100 \text{ Per Year}$$
$$100 \times \$100 \text{ Per Showing} = \$10,000 \text{ Additional Income}$$

Increasing the efficient, effective use of your time need not mean working longer hours. It can mean working fewer hours if you learn to make each working hour bulge with productive action.

The trick is to control the 1,440 minutes you have every day and not let the minutes control you. Almost every successful person has some kind of written plan for each day and week. Such a plan is a strength, not a weakness. As these people write their working plan, they also are establishing priorities for what they will do, assigning top place to their most productive activities.

ANALYZING TIME VALUES

The first step toward controlling your time is to analyze exactly what you are now getting out of each hour of your working day. Start by writing down how much time you spend on listing, selling, renting and other activities.

A real estate salesperson's professional time can be broken into four classifications:

1. Class "A" time: spent face to face with someone who can sign a listing or purchasing agreement
2. Class "B" time: spent preparing for "A" time—lining up listings, making appointments, preparing listing presentations and sales negotiation papers
3. Class "C" time: spent on all other real estate activities, such as putting up signs, driving to appointments, writing letters, attending sales meetings and keeping records up-to-date
4. Class "D" time: spent on non–real estate activities like coffee breaks, personal business, recreation and social life

After you analyze your time spent in these four areas, it may shock you to look at the finished analysis and realize how much time you have spent on unproductive activity. However, with this time classification in hand, you can put priorities on what you plan to do each day. The plan will fall into three categories:

1. What you *must* do (keeping appointments to list and show property)
2. What you *should* do (canvassing for new listings)
3. What you *could* do (to give you broader exposure to the market)

Such a plan will provide incentive to eliminate the nonessentials from your working hours. You will soon find yourself establishing a timetable for the day based on who you need to see and when, what calls have to be made and what paperwork has to be done. Planning the workday in increments of half hours has proved best for many successful salespeople.

MAKING EVERY HOUR PRODUCTIVE

Allocate the most productive selling hours to being out in the field. You can do this if you get to the office early every day and get paperwork, telephone calls and other office chores out of the way quickly. That leaves peak daytime hours for work in the field. Lunch hours can be used productively with buyers or sellers or seeing important business and community contacts.

Learn how to cope with interruptions. When people come to you with an unimportant interruption, ask tactfully if it can wait until another time, and if necessary make an appointment to handle it later.

Plan your travel to use minimum time and gasoline. Avoid doubling back by being fully prepared for the job at hand. And while you are in a neighborhood, stop and say a brief hello to former clients. When you are on the road alone, use driving time to listen to cassettes on some phase of the business about which you want to know more or practice planned presentations.

Many successful agents have discovered that having their own paid personal assistant makes economic sense. They have found that having a personal assistant can greatly increase their income far beyond salary costs. Some hire licensed real estate assistants who can handle solicitations and even some sales and listing work, while others have unlicensed personal assistants. The role of an unlicensed personal assistant is more like a secretary and/or personal manager. A great many time-consuming tasks can be delegated to a knowledgeably trained assistant.

You should keep in mind that there are two ways you can increase your income. Besides better utilization of time, you can also increase the effectiveness of showing and listing presentations. You should strive for improvement in both these areas.

Using Your Daily Planner

It is important to have tools to plan your day. You can use a daily planner, although with the growing computer literacy of salespeople, many now use a computer program for planning each day. If they wish, they can readily get a print-out of a daily plan.

You should enter in your planner required personal or business tasks with rigid times, such as office sales or training sessions, board meetings, MLS caravans, personal medical appointments, etc. Many of these can be entered weeks or even months ahead of time. The rest of the time is flexible for your decisions. You should plan each day with the idea of maximizing the effectiveness of your time.

It is best to plan each day at the conclusion of the previous day. You will find that tasks you had set forth for that day were not accomplished. Often an opportunity arises for Class A activity, such as showing a property, and a Class C planned activity is set aside. This is the way it should be. Your daily plan is a guide, but it should not limit you so that you cannot take advantage of opportunities.

If a task was not accomplished, it should be reevaluated. If it is regarded as still important, it should be moved forward to the next day. Otherwise, discard it. Some salespeople like to accomplish early in the day those tasks they find least enjoyable. This affords them mental relief: they can look forward with enthusiasm to performing other planned tasks.

At the end of each day, you should evaluate the way you spent your time before you plan the next day. Ask yourself, "How could I have better utilized my time?" "Were my priorities in order?" Many agents use a pocket recorder to take verbal notes and memos to themselves. These can be especially useful while driving. At the end of the day, one can review the tape and use any comments to help plan the following day's activities. Because so much of your activity centers around use of the telephone, you want this time to be efficient and effective. A telephone schedule should be part of your daily plan.

Use either a commercial telephone log or one of the many computer software programs for your log. You should have a brief summary of the call and any further action required by the caller or by you. Try to make as many calls as possible during the same time frame early in the day. Otherwise, other activities could result in important calls not being made.

Real estate salespeople who don't write down what they need to do seldom accomplish what they intended. A half hour spent organizing activities should mean a more productive day and return far more than the cost in time.

Daily planner books as well as pocket-size computerized planners are available, some of which are adapted specifically for use in real estate. Some include financial tables and telephone indexes. If you have a computer, you could consider one of the excellent planning programs available. Figure 4.1 is an example of a simple daily planning sheet. To save space, an agent would likely use symbols or abbreviations for many activities.

Telephone Tactics

When answering the phone or returning a call, asking "How may I help you?" instead of "Can I help you?" forces the caller to be more specific.

Staying in touch with the office is important. A growing number of real estate salespeople use car telephones or a radio-operated beeper from office to field. Such a service has had some spectacular results in

FIGURE 4.1 Simple Daily Planner Sheet

Tuesday, June 1

Time	Activity	Result
7:30		
8:00		
8:30		
9:00		
9:30		
10:00		
10:30		
11:00		
11:30		
12:00		
12:30		
1:00		
1:30		
2:00		
2:30		
3:00		
3:30		
4:00		
4:30		
5:00		
5:30		
6:00		
6:30		
7:00		
7:30		
8:00		

Phone Calls To Make:

Name	Number	Results

the quick sale of new listings when salespeople are notified of them while showing properties and the new listing falls within the price and style the customer wants. The important point is to keep in touch with the office, whatever method you use.

REGULAR CHORES

No matter what form your daily schedule takes, certain things need to be done. The following list of office and field chores is a memory jogger, a reference for the things you should be doing consistently to create listings and sales. How you do it will be up to you, assisted by your broker.

In the office:

- Arrive on time.
- Review daily plan.
- Read newspaper ads.
- Check message box.
- Check new office and MLS sheets and/or computer.
- Match buyers with properties.
- Promote listings with staff people.
- Prepare property briefs.
- Review escrow sheets.
- Review listing check sheets.
- List follow-up calls to make.
- Get comps for appraisal.
- Verify appointments.
- Call "for sale by owners."
- Call potential buyers for appointments.
- Call criss-cross directory.
- Call expired listings.
- Call old clients for referrals.
- Call escrows for follow-up.
- Address direct mail.
- Follow up prior direct mail with a telephone call.
- Make cold calls.

Fieldwork:

- Check vacant and neglected property.
- Check "for sale by owners" and expired listings.
- Preview new office and MLS listings.
- Show property.
- List property.
- Prospect.
- Get lockboxes and signs.

- Get escrow instructions signed.
- Get loan documents signed.
- Identify yourself to people as a real estate salesperson.

USING FREE TIME

Every working day has some unexpected free time, "found" time, when you are waiting for a customer who is late or a phone call, or when you think there's nothing to do at the end of the day. Put this time to work these ways and you will soon accumulate hours of productive effort.

- Organize sales aids so they are ready for immediate use.
- Reconstruct the last listing interview or showing to determine what needs to be changed.
- Develop contacts with corporation staff people responsible for relocating personnel.
- Read newspapers for transferees, promotions and new businesses moving into the area.
- Make appointments to inspect all listed properties not yet seen.
- Read articles, bulletins and books on real estate and selling.
- Get out and meet new people and hand out business cards.
- Check old listings that may have been taken off the market.
- Call exclusive sellers to report all activity.
- List competitors' expired exclusives and call these sellers.
- Do a little digging for undeveloped land.
- Make a list of the developers and builders doing business in the area and present the vacant property to them.
- Get organized for tomorrow's activities.
- Rewrite ads.
- Evaluate work habits.
- Mail a thank-you to a past client.
- Offer referral assistance to sellers leaving the area.
- Contact sellers who may be looking for another house in the area.
- Concentrate on how to render better service to buyers and sellers.
- Survey neighborhood of a new listing.
- Read the building permit section in the newspaper.
- Offer to help a friend with a tax problem by showing him income property.
- Promote new listings to another salesperson.
- Read engagement and wedding announcements in the newspaper and call to see what their housing needs will be.
- Read the "for sale by owner" ads.
- Call and see some "for sale by owners."
- Maintain a book of owner ads and assist in listing these properties.

The opposite of found time is "time out"—the moments we lose each day in idleness or unproductive business. Think of an eight-hour working day as a bank of 28,800 seconds, each worth $1, given you to invest. Time is a bank from which one can make withdrawals, but one can never make deposits. The withdrawals can be converted into profitable investments or lost through wasteful habits. In a survey of real estate salespeople with average earnings, a list of time lost by a salesperson in an average day included the following:

- Coffee breaks: three per day at ten minutes each equals 1,800 seconds
- Idle talk in the office: 30 minutes, or 1,800 seconds
- Driving the same route to and from the office each day, a non-creative practice that takes away from the opportunity to see new properties available for sale: 40 minutes per day, or 2,400 seconds
- Lost creative time from not having tape cassettes or other training devices in the car to listen to when driving: an average of 40 minutes per day, or 2,400 seconds
- Poor planning, causing a need to double back to pick up signs or secure loan commitments: approximately 30 minutes each day, or 1,800 seconds
- Having to do a job twice because it wasn't done right the first time: about 45 minutes, or 2,700 seconds
- Going to lunch with people who cannot help you in business or in the advancement of your career: about 60 minutes, or 3,600 seconds
- Daydreaming on nonproductive subjects: approximately 20 minutes a day, or 1,200 seconds
- Stopping to use pay phones rather than having a cellular phone available: about 15 minutes, or 900 seconds

If the eight-hour day has 28,800 seconds, each worth $1, a total of 18,600 seconds ($18,600) was lost to this salesperson in time-stealing habits and practices, leaving only $10,200 invested wisely.

Chapter 5

Selling and Listing with Psychology

There was a time when selling was viewed as a manipulative process in which the skillful salesperson could induce a customer to agree to buy or a client to list. The salesperson was regarded as one who had a strong impact on personal relations, could motivate people toward buying and find psychological advantages with which to close.

PSYCHOLOGY BASICS

Perhaps there is some element of these factors in all buy-sell relationships. However, it is far more important in examining the modern science of selling and the professional concepts of buy-sell relationships to recognize some important fundamentals of sales psychology.

First, the salesperson does not motivate other people. Motivation is not something we do to others. Rather, it is something that happens when appropriate conditions are developed, both in personal relationships and in satisfaction of buyer needs, that cause people to pursue a particular goal.

Second, the psychology of buy-sell does not vary from one occasion to another. The fundamentals of buying and selling are immutable and unvarying. No matter what the product or service, a professional salesperson must understand clearly and specifically the three basic elements of buy-sell psychology:

1. What people buy
2. Why people buy
3. How people buy

When these fundamentals are clearly understood, the skilled salesperson can guide, counsel and assist the customer in making favorable decisions, satisfying needs and reaching conclusions that are permanent and lasting buying decisions.

What

What do people buy? Certainly, they do not buy the tangible substance of an automobile, a dishwasher or a home. They are not purchasing the bricks, lumber, plaster and architecture in a house; neither are they buying the steel, rubber and porcelain in the dishwasher. People buy what a product or service will *do* for them. They buy advantages and benefits. Therefore, the successful salesperson learns how to translate all the features of what is being sold into advantages and benefits to the customer. A salesperson who tries to sell something to a customer who does not perceive the benefit of the product, and where no desire for ownership has been created, is likely to be unsuccessful.

Why

To translate features into advantages and benefits, the successful salesperson must understand the basic buying motives—the needs of human beings as discussed in Chapter 3.

How

While it is essential to understand what and why people buy, the real key to successful selling is both understanding and control of how people buy. The sale of any product or service is based upon the positive conclusion of five decisions. Every lister or buyer must make these five decisions—and when the salesperson understands how to assist these decisions, how to develop agreement and how to measure progress, control of selling is assured.

1. The customer must both understand and agree that there is a clearly defined need to buy. This need will be related to one of the motivations discussed in Chapter 3, but it may not always be clearly recognized by the buyer.

For example, a salesperson may not recognize at the start that an important reason for buying a particular property is ease of maintenance and commuting convenience (physical need). The salesperson may also not recognize that a real need is to make the spouse happier in a more spacious home, keeping friction in the family to a minimum (social need). Until the salesperson has clearly identified these needs and helped the customer evaluate them, an important buying decision cannot be made.

2. The customer must decide that this property or service is the one to fulfill the recognized need. A particular home may or may not fulfill the need as recognized by the customer. Accordingly, the salesperson must make sure that time, attention and effort are given to alternatives and questions are answered so the customer will have the information to decide if the property will fulfill the need.

3. The customer must decide that he or she is buying from the right source. You and your firm are the source. You are assisting the source decision when you answer the telephone, making your first impression on the customer and carrying out your sales work.

Many times you have decided to purchase something but somehow the source of supply did not satisfy you, so you went somewhere else. So it is with your customers. They must decide you are the right source. Much of what this handbook is about is how you can become the most reliable and professional source available.

4. The customer must decide the price is right. Sometimes this seems the impossible hurdle in selling, but it doesn't have to be. When price is clearly related to the recognized need of the buyer, it becomes meaningful, realistic and understandable.

When the buyer's need is not clearly defined, price represents a real problem. The greatest bargain ever offered will not attract you if you don't need the thing being offered. (A free appendectomy would hardly be to your liking if you didn't need one.) The successful salesperson learns how to express price in terms of fulfilling needs.

5. The customer must decide the time to buy is now. This decision is really what a closing is about. The theory that there is a psychological moment to close a sale often creates considerable pressure on the salesperson. Closing is a continuous process, starting with the first decisions about need and where to satisfy that need, continuing through your advice and assistance, and developing into a final conclusion when you request a time decision. If the time decision is not favorable, it is evident that one of the other four decisions has not been successfully completed. At that point, the salesperson can confidently go back and review the other four decisions with the customer and find out which one needs further information or guidance before agreement or conclusion can be reached.

ASKING AND LISTENING

You must ask questions in order to understand clients' needs. Unsuccessful salespeople tend to "tell" rather than to "ask." By asking open-ended questions, such as "Why do you want a home on the west side?" or "What other areas interest you?", you can get people to relate their reasoning and you will better understand their needs. The unsuccessful salesperson will tend to ask closed-ended questions requiring a simple yes or no. A question such as "Did you want a home with a fireplace?" is a closed-ended question and tends to limit your ability to meet the best interests of the client.

It isn't enough just to ask the right question. You must listen to the reply and question further if you are unsure of the person's reasoning and motivation.

Your personal attitude toward a lister or buyer influences the source decision. Your ability to "tune in" to the individual, to put yourself in that person's place and try to understand what he or she wants to accomplish are tools in making buy-sell psychology work. These can best be summarized by stressing the importance of listening. When you speak, you talk about what you already know; when you listen, you learn some things you very likely do not know.

A Listening Attitude

When you are talking with a customer or client, make sure that you have chosen a physical environment that encourages expression from the other person. Beware of distractions and any intimation that you are in a hurry or preoccupied. Be careful not to answer questions too quickly. Agree that each question is a good question and ask for some more information before answering. Be careful that you are not substituting your own feelings for those of the persons you are dealing with. When answering a question, you should understand the reason for the question.

Listen with a Purpose

Listen for feelings as well as to what a person is saying. Listen for clues about the needs of the individual. Feelings are essential to understanding the real meaning behind communications. When communications are expressed at an emotional level or come from a highly assertive, evaluative attitude (indicated by words like should, ought, mustn't, ridiculous, foolish, etc.), you can be sure that communications will not be productive. Ask questions that give your customer a chance to come back with facts, logic and reasoning, rather than emotions.

TEST YOUR UNDERSTANDING

It is easy to jump to conclusions about what people say. Avoid this by trying to restate in your own words either the feeling or the content that has been expressed. A customer may state, "I'm very disappointed with the way you have handled this situation; you haven't done any of the things you said you would do. . . ." In this case, it will be futile to come back and argue that you have done what you said you would do or point out how mistaken the customer is.

To test understanding, you might say, "I'm sorry you are upset, but let me make sure I understand; I gather you feel that you have not received all the information you need to go ahead with your personal plans. Is that correct?"

If the customer says, "That's what I'm telling you; I haven't gotten anywhere near the information I expected," you are in a position to ask, "What kind of information would be most helpful to you?"

This approach enables the salesperson to keep communications at the level of logic and reasoning. When they deteriorate into emotional levels, it becomes very difficult to apply psychological concepts to selling.

A-I-D-A

According to the A-I-D-A method, every sale carries the prospect through four psychological steps: attention, interest, desire and action. These must be taken in sequence; it is seldom that any one of the steps can be omitted.

How A-I-D-A Works

Getting the prospect's *attention* is the first step in this process. You cannot get people to buy or even to look at anything unless you are first able to get their attention. This is the first psychological reaction that must occur in prospects' minds. You must make them want to listen to what you are saying.

Attention is a mild form of *interest.* The difference between the two is only in degree. But attention is casual and temporary. It may be broken off at any moment. Hence, you must work to develop a real and sustained interest as quickly as possible.

In bridging the gap between attention and interest, you will find maps, pictures, blueprints and layouts highly effective. When prospects hold in their own hands any object you have given them, they are hardly able to resist some interest in it. This is especially true when it explains something about which they are already interested or presents some constructive new idea that can be of benefit or profit to them.

Arousing the prospect's interest can also be achieved by simply explaining more details about the property and by showing how he or she will personally gain from ownership.

When the salesperson has been able to develop a reasonable amount of interest, *desire* follows. In this stage of the psychological process, the prospect is no longer on the defensive. The prospect and the salesperson are meeting on a common ground. The prospect is willing to listen while the benefits that he or she might enjoy are explained.

If the salesperson does a good job and paints the word picture vividly, the prospect's interest grows until the desire for possession is created. This third step, desire, is very crucial. In many ways, the salesperson has not made any real progress until this stage has been reached.

The last step in the A-I-D-A process is the one in which the prospect says, "All right, I'll take it." From attention to interest to desire to *action* is the course every sale must take. The same sequence of mental reactions takes place when you buy a new automobile or a new suit. These steps have occurred in your mind thousands of times. They are logical steps in selling real estate or any other commodity.

Take It Step by Step

When you understand the A-I-D-A formula, you realize the folly of trying to close a sale before desire has been built in the prospect's mind. Desire is an emotional reaction, and it can spring only from interest. And interest starts with attention. Each step is the result of the previous one; it is impossible to take them in reverse order.

Sometimes you hear a salesperson begin a conversation with, "Would you like to buy a nice new bungalow?" Perhaps he or she should not properly be called a salesperson, yet that is the technique of many who try to sell. They jump to the action step and skip the other three. This frightens the prospect, who jumps to the defensive and promptly answers no. There is no reason why the prospect should say yes, because interest and desire have not yet been aroused.

ADVANTAGES OF HOME OWNERSHIP

In creating desire, you must interject into the conversation facts that are convincing. The following list of arguments for home ownership will be extremely useful. All of these items will not relate to every prospect, but you can select those that seem most applicable to each prospective buyer.

- Financial independence: Many people have started on the road to financial independence through home ownership.
- Cash equity: A well-bought home is like a savings account.

- Credit: Home ownership gives financial and credit rating in the business world, because it is recognized as a fundamental principle of stability.
- Interest in civic and municipal affairs
- Chance for individual expression: A home can be decorated to express the personality of its owner.
- Established environment: Finding neighbors and friends whose friendships last over the years
- Healthful exercise: Pride of possession inspires work in home and yard.
- Character development: Responsibilities of ownership develop business acumen and responsibility.
- Savings: Buying a home encourages systematic savings. Over a period of years, the buyer is money ahead by buying and occupying a home.
- A place for a family's lifestyle
- Appreciation of value
- Peace of mind: Provision has been made for family.
- Interest and property tax deductions
- Protection against inflation
- Protection against rent increases or restrictions based upon a landlord's whim

EMPATHIZE

Regardless of which approach to selling you use, the ability to place yourself in your prospect's shoes is very important. In this position, you can begin to see yourself as a salesperson; you can determine how and why the client reacts in a certain way to the sales presentation and to you.

Do you really act and seem sincere? Is the sales presentation one that you (the salesperson) would believe from someone else if you were the buyer? With empathy, salespeople can answer these and many other questions and adjust their selling according to the kind of answers they give themselves.

ASK THE PROSPECT TO BUY

After spending much time and effort getting to know the prospective buyer, determining needs, talking persuasively and generally bringing the prospect right up to the point of purchase, many real estate salespeople neglect a simple but very important item: asking the prospect to buy. Such salespeople often lack the courage to ask for action. They get the prospect in the mood to buy but do not strike when the iron is hot.

In every sale there comes a climactic moment when the buyer is most likely to react favorably to the suggestion to buy. Knowing exactly when that moment arrives is partly a matter of experience and partly intuition, but it is of the utmost importance.

It often helps to ask questions that, if answered affirmatively, indicate that the time has arrived: "When will you want to take possession of the home?" or "Shall we see if the owner will sell that vacant lot next to the property?" These are often referred to as trial closings.

Either of these questions, or a thousand others like them, may tell you that it is time for the contract to come out of your briefcase. If such questions do not produce a favorable response, you must continue to sell until you feel the time for action has arrived. If you fail in a trial closing, keep in mind that it is not the end of the transaction. You can try again.

Sometimes the salesperson does not realize the state of mind of the prospects when they have to make the final decision. In the middle of a busy period or thinking about his or her own affairs, the salesperson can easily forget prospects' frustration and fear at the moment they are asked to sign a contract. Regardless of the amount of money involved in the transaction, it may loom as large as a mountain to prospects. It is, after all, their money.

Again, the salesperson must put himself in the prospect's shoes; the salesperson must empathize. The element of fear must be overcome if the sale is to be made. You can do much to alleviate the fears of the prospect simply by imagining yourself in reversed roles and assuming an attitude of helpfulness from there.

THE ATMOSPHERE FOR A CLOSING

It is very important that this closing (the moment when the prospect agrees to buy) take place under conditions with minimal interference and interruption. This is an important moment for prospects, because they should be able to participate in the closing in a strictly business-like manner. The closing should take place wherever there will be few interruptions—in the prospect's office if there will be no interference; at the prospect's home if children will not be a distraction; at your office; or even at the home being purchased if the owners are not present.

As you guide the buyer through the closing, you should remain as calm and as confident as you have been throughout the selling process. Continue to take into consideration the feelings and thoughts of the buyer.

By consulting with the buyer about each item of the contract as it is written, by answering questions patiently (even those asked a hundred times before), by having the contract legally amended where needed and by insisting that the buyer read the contract carefully before signing, you can be confident you have sold property that will stay sold. You should work with, and not as, legal counsel in the closing process.

Sometimes the most assured, practiced salespeople will reach what they believe to be the closing with prospects who want time "to think it over." At that point, tell them that you would like to have them think it over to be absolutely certain everything is in order and no mistake is made.

Then keep right on selling as long as there is any hope for an immediate decision. However, be careful not to make an issue of anything that will make the resumption of your sales program impossible if an immediate decision cannot be obtained.

Throughout the selling process, it pays to be aware of the psychological processes going on and, moreover, the psychological needs of the people you are working with. Your own needs are important, but when it comes to working daily with people, the successful salesperson is one who likes people and is genuinely concerned about satisfying their needs.

There are many excellent books and courses that will help you in developing your selling skills. However, keep in mind that reading or being told how to do something is not as effective as actually seeing the technique in use. But no new technique will truly be yours until you have successfully used it yourself. It isn't enough to understand and agree with the theories and ideas of others; you must put them into action.

Chapter 6

Obtaining the Listing

Listings are the key to success in real estate. They are the inventory of the business—the products brokers must have to attract buyers. A real estate sales cycle starts with a good listing that is priced right. The more complete a broker's inventory of well-priced listings, the more buyers he or she can serve and the more money the broker and sales associates will earn.

TWO SALES EQUAL ONE

To sell one property, salespeople must, in effect, bring two sales to a successful conclusion. They must first sell themselves and the firm to the property owner; then they must sell the listing.

Success in the first sale depends on you and your firm having a good reputation in the community and on your skill in persuading an owner that you will do a good job of finding people interested in buying the property and then selling it to them.

Success in the second sale depends on the skills you and the firm have for servicing the listing by advertising it, finding people interested in and qualified to buy it, and negotiating the sale.

Your first objective is to obtain listings, the first sale mentioned above. What are your best sources? How can you cultivate them?

There is no single "best" source. Good sources are everywhere, every day. You cultivate them in ways that fit your personal style, are acceptable in your market and conform to your firm's policy. Your success in obtaining listings will grow as you expand your sphere of influence.

SYSTEMS AND TECHNIQUES

Experienced brokers and salespeople know that certain systems and techniques work successfully to bring listings. Proven methods are highlighted here, but there are always refinements and innovations waiting to be developed as both people and markets change. Your future is as unlimited as your creativity.

A LISTING "BANK"

Build a "bank" of listings. Your deposits consist of all the people who could list their properties with you; withdrawals are the properties sold. If you know 400 or 500 owners in your market area better than any other salesperson, chances are you are the person they will turn to when the time comes to sell.

Your listing bank can be opened when you have made a definite plan and set a goal for a specific number of listings in a certain time period. You can start by getting acquainted with 25 owners each month. This will give you a great feeling of accomplishment as you build your personal inventory of prospects and realize how many people may come to rely on you as their real estate professional. Another sense of accomplishment will come when you know that if you contact a certain number of people every month, your efforts will produce the listings and sales needed to reach your goals.

FARM SYSTEMS

In a farm system, each salesperson is responsible for a specific part of the area the firm serves. A farm system may be structured by the broker, who assigns the territory according to company policy, or it can be an area chosen by the salesperson.

The basic concept of the system is that it is best to specialize in one area rather than running over all the marketplace. Many salespeople prefer to work the area where they live, where they already know some people and where it is easier to become better known to many more. There are geographical and nongeographical farms. A salesperson could specialize in duplexes, mobile homes, vacant lots, horse property, property in a particular price range, etc. Nongeographical farms are more difficult to work, because working such farms means keeping in contact with the owners, who reside over a much wider area than those in geographical farms.

Get to know as many people as you can, and become expert on property values and sales activities in your farm. Develop your own plan to call on owners regularly by phone or in person, sending notes or a newsletter or items of special interest to the people you know and want to get acquainted with. A well-organized plan that is followed carefully will pay handsome returns.

CANVASSING

All owners think about selling their property before they actually put it on the market. Successful listers find a lot of these properties before anybody else knows about them. They do it by cold canvassing. Two methods are used widely: telephoning from criss-cross directories, and door-to-door contacts.

If you use the telephone method, introduce yourself slowly and give the name of your firm. Explain that you are looking for a specific type of property for which you (or someone else in the firm) have a legitimate buyer. Always use real buyers for this approach, and give a few details to show them as deserving of assistance. While people are often reluctant to help people in general, they are much more willing to help a particular family. Describe briefly what the requirements are. Inquire whether the person you are talking with knows of a similar property in the neighborhood whose owner may be thinking of selling. (Never ask if his or her property is for sale. The answer will inevitably be no.)

This canvassing technique has proved successful over many years. Typically, you will average one good lead out of every 25 cold canvass calls. There is at least one person in every neighborhood who will confide in you. Make copious, careful notes. Then follow through.

Call the specified owner, using the same opening. Many will say they are thinking of selling and will invite you to inspect the property.

Face-to-face visiting is the second successful cold canvassing method. If you do it at a specific time every day when you don't have a conflicting appointment with a buyer or seller, you will soon establish a work routine that gets you out where the prospects are.

Canvassing is not a one-time contact; it is a repetitious process. Salespeople who are successful with their farms generally try to contact every owner in the farm at least once a month. Contact might be by telephone, by letter or in person.

Farming requires persistence and regularity. You will need to devote many hours to getting acquainted and becoming recognized in the neighborhood. After your first sign goes up, you will have begun to gain a foothold in the farm.

An average area with 400 to 500 homes will take anywhere from six months to a year to pay off. But once this happens, you should have a permanent and continuing source of listings. Your listing bank will be full.

Some salespeople say canvassing is best done on an informal basis on Saturday in residential areas, when you can meet people as they work in the yard, wash their cars or play outside with the children. The mood and tone of Saturdays is more relaxed, and you are likely to make many good personal contacts this way. Others believe cold, dreary days are best, because owners are more likely to invite you indoors.

If cold canvassing is prohibited or frowned on in the area you serve, you may need to approach it in a different way. Make a list of 25 homeowners and send them a letter of self-introduction. It might read like this:

[Date]

Dear Mr. and Mrs. Smith:
May I take this opportunity to introduce myself to you? I am Jim Searcy, associated with ABC Realty. I will be representing homeowners in your neighborhood and will stop by in a day or two to meet you.

Sincerely,
Jim Searcy

Use your personal envelopes when you mail these letters. Most salespeople find that hand addressing and stamping (not metering) increase the chances of a positive response.

Another approach would be:

Dear Mr. and Mrs. Smith:
I am writing you because I need your help. I am working with a [*young family*] who are very interested in locating a [*three-bedroom home*] in your area. [*They have a seven-year-old son and a daughter six years of age.*] They want to locate in your area because [*it is close to Sherman Park and McKinley School*].

I will be [*stopping by*] [*calling you*] in a day or two to find out if you have any suggestions on how I can help this [*young family*].

Sincerely,
Jim Searcy

When you can call on them, ring the bell and step back a pace or two. When the door opens, your conversation will depend upon the message conveyed in your letter. You should be prepared with a rehearsed introduction that you feel comfortable with. An example of an approach to use with the first letter would be:

"Good morning, Mr./Mrs. Smith. I am Jim Searcy of ABC Realty. Did you receive my note of introduction? It should have arrived today. [They'll usually say yes.] I just stopped by to make your acquaintance. I will be representing ABC Realty in this area and hope you will help me. And for your help, may I please give you this small token of my appreciation?" (Hand the owner some small, useful premium along with your business card.) Usually owners will accept the gift, because they have already received the letter and you have not asked them for anything. You are there only to serve.

Be prepared with a series of pertinent questions:

- Have you enjoyed living in this area?
- How long have you been here?
- Do you feel the neighborhood is improving?
- Do you have children?
- What are their ages?
- Do you have any pets?
- What do you like most about living here?

Having obtained this information, thank the owner for discussing the area with you and go to the next door without mentioning anything about wanting to list his or her house. Twenty-five calls, data on 25 families, and you have started your listing bank. You have your name and association in 25 homes and they now know you.

If your initial letter asked for help in finding a home for a particular family, you should give more information about the family and their needs. Ask the homeowners if they know anyone in the area who might be considering selling their home. Then you can also obtain information about the owners themselves. Always use a real family you are working with when using this approach. An incidental advantage is that prospective buyers will feel greater obligation to work with you when they realize the effort you have expended on their behalf.

Using this approach, you will discover people who are eager to discuss the neighborhood and to ask your views on the real estate market. They may even comment that you are the only real estate person who has not asked them to list their property.

KNOW YOUR COMMUNITY

Most successful real estate people become involved in civic groups and community projects. When they do, they are not only building their own reputation and making social contacts, they are also representing their firm. Community activities often provide a way of finding out what local leaders have in mind for the future of the area. If you are known to these planners and doers, they may turn to you when they need real estate services. You will also find that working with people who are active in business and/or community affairs will positively reinforce your self-image.

CLIENTS

Satisfied clients are a prime source of future referrals. Keep in touch with the sellers and buyers you have served, reminding them occasionally that you would appreciate their referring friends and associates to you when they need the services of a REALTOR®. Clients themselves are potential customers for more business when the time comes to buy another house or when they are looking for income, investment or business properties.

In addition to using direct mail and telephone to keep in touch with clients, a quick, friendly visit when you happen to be driving through the neighborhood can be profitable. Such a visit should not be a hard-sell situation; keep it brief, unless you are pressed to stay to tell them more about something they are interested in.

ADVERTISING

Advertising, both institutional and classified, is used in varying degrees to obtain listings. Follow-up is important and is largely the responsibility of salespeople. Most firms have established methods for recording telephone response to ads. Other follow-up channels include keeping your ears and eyes open for every response or clue that comes your way.

NEWSPAPERS

Local newspapers can be a good source of listing prospects. Their news columns carry information of great value to you as they tell of transfers, promotions, births, marriages, deaths, civic plans and projects, all of which can involve the transfer of real estate. Following up on these leads is profitable.

Legal Notices

Legal records of evictions, foreclosures, code violations, tax delinquencies, divorce, etc., indicate problems. Often a solution to a problem is to free the owner's equity from a property, which is accomplished by a sale.

REALTOR® REFERRALS

Your association with other REALTORS® in your community, county and state is an excellent source of both listings and sales. A REALTOR® in another city or state who knows you through the NATIONAL ASSOCIATION OF REALTORS® or REALTORS

NATIONAL MARKETING INSTITUTE® will feel confident in referring someone from his area to you. Such referrals include not only people being transferred but also investors looking for commercial or investment property in your marketplace.

Your achievement of a designation such as Certified Residential Specialist, or CRS (obtained from the Residential Sales Council of the REALTORS NATIONAL MARKETING INSTITUTE®), can place you in a network of other CRSs who have attained this higher level of proficiency. This designation gives you access to an invaluable directory of CRSs across the country.

OTHER SOURCES

Homes surrounding a new listing are often a good source for soliciting business. Many firms inform the sellers' neighbors of a new listing. This may bring you more new listings and may even provide you with a buyer for the listing you are now promoting (see "Tell 20 System" on page 119).

Expired listings can also create new business. Old listings may seem overpriced or shopworn, when the real reason for failure to sell may have been bad timing (putting a house with a swimming pool and gardens on the market in winter) or financial (a tight mortgage market). Getting a listing of this nature back on the market calls for creative thinking and selling on your part to induce the owner that listing it with you is more likely to consummate the sale.

VACANT HOMES

As you drive through your market area and note a vacant home, find out who owns it. Then contact the owners and let them know you list properties in the area and may be able to sell their property. If it is an empty rental property in need of repair, the owners may want to realize equity without spending money to recondition it. This might lead to a second sale or even a referral to another broker if you induce the owners to reinvest the money realized from the sale of the vacant house.

BUSINESS CARDS

Business cards can be your silent sales tool, and they are one of the least expensive of all advertising items. Put them to work for you every day. Give them to friends and business acquaintances as you stop for a brief hello or as you leave at the end of a business session. The law of averages will work for you in producing results that reflect the number of cards you pass out. An old adage states: "If you see the same person three times in one day, he should have three of your business cards in his pocket."

SEE THE PEOPLE

Busy real estate salespeople spend every possible moment away from their desks, getting out to see people. STP has become a popular slogan that has nothing to do with gasoline additives. It means "see the people," and it works.

As you get out among people and they ask, "How's business?", reply "Good listings are selling great, but I need more good listings. Do you know of anyone who might be considering selling?" Some of the most creative transactions in the business have begun in a casual street-corner conversation between an alert salesperson and another person who had a bit of knowledge the salesperson hadn't yet heard.

When you think you have exhausted all the possible sources of listing referrals, check through the more than six dozen sources that follow.

Financial Leaders
bankers
insurance agents and adjusters
savings and loan officers
trust department officers

Business and Labor
personnel directors
planning departments
finance officers
labor leaders
union officials

Tourists
motel and hotel clerks
airline clerks
car rental agencies
travel agencies
restaurants and coffee shops

Service People and Vendors
gas, electric and water meter readers
mail carriers
door-to-door salespeople
Welcome Wagon hostesses
ice cream vendors
Tupperware salespeople
hairdressers and barbers

Avon representatives
waiters, waitresses
newspaper deliverers

Institutions
school directors, principals and teachers
colleges and universities
Army and Navy post officers
PTAs
librarians
government workers

Media Sources
for-rent ads
newspaper, radio and TV people
printers
For Sale By Owner ads

Merchants and Salespeople
moving companies
retailers
druggists
Chambers of commerce
car dealers, gas station owners and garage owners
heating oil dealers
dry cleaners and laundries
other REALTORS®

Professionals
doctors
management people
lawyers
CPAs
judges
dentists
employment agencies

Civic and Municipal
homeowner associations
municipal officials
county assessors
probate clerks

Social, Church and Charitable
bridge clubs
country clubs
service clubs
garden clubs

block parties
open house hospitality parties
fund-raising committees and canvassers
church groups
lodge groups
veterans' groups
sports and fitness clubs
fraternal organizations
recreation, sports, hobby groups
newcomer clubs

Building
builders' agents
apartment and rental agents
architects
landscape architects
nurserymen
decorators, interior designers
contractors
plumbers
electricians

Miscellaneous
public bulletin boards
community centers
supermarkets
laundromats
barber and beauty shops
garage sales and house sales

GOOD RECORDS

All your efforts need to be supported by useful, accurate records regardless of the sources and techniques you employ to generate listings.

If you work on a farm system, a tickler file of 5 × 7 cards can be used to keep track of your prospects. This card system can serve a broad territory but will require some method of segmenting by neighborhoods or areas. There are a number of excellent computer programs that will aid you in keeping records of owners, personal data and previous contracts. Many agents keep portable laptop computers in their cars and offices so that they have ready access when calling or receiving a call from an owner.

Whether you use computers or cards, Figure 6.1 shows the type of information that should be available in your farm system.

Whatever system you use, keep records and keep them up-to-date.

FIGURE 6.1 Listing File Entry

Address   Owner's Name   Year Purchase

_____   _____   _____

Year built:_____ Approx. Sq. Ft._____ Bds_____ Baths_____

Price Paid $_____

Present Owner's Improvements: _____

_____

Employer: _____   _____

          _____   _____

Children: _____ Ages: _____

Contacts Ph: _____ Price Paid: _____ Letters: _____

    Jan Feb Mar Apr May June July Aug Sep Oct Nov Dec

1994 — — — — — — — — — — — —

1995 — — — — — — — — — — — —

1996 — — — — — — — — — — — —

1997 — — — — — — — — — — — —

Comments: _____

_____

_____

_____

_____

_____

If you note the husband's and wife's businesses and that their companies bring in new people, they can be a source of referrals for you. If you call and there is no one home, note the date and put the name back on your daily calendar for another try soon. Use your records to refresh your memory prior to calling on prospects. They will be impressed if you remember their names.

Every time a house in your area is listed, whether it is your listing or not, mark down the date, listing agent and asking price. When it sells, make a note of that along with the price, type of financing and the new owner's name. If a property sells "by owner," don't be afraid to ask who bought it and at what price. If you have kept in touch with them, they will regard your interest in that area as a natural one. Sales price information is necessary in building your comparable files for listing and appraising. Most of the legwork will be done for you by your MLS service. You will want to know the details of every sale in your farm area sold by owner or through your MLS service.

A complete file of comparables for your farm area will enable you to tell listing prospects the asking and selling price of places that have sold and the asking price of those that did not. Sharing this information with owners who might be considering a possible sale will promote your image as an expert who can help them.

MAKE A CHECKLIST

Here is a list of things to do to expand your sphere of influence. Add to it as you think of new ways to make people aware of your real estate expertise.

- Develop your own centers of influence
- Contact owners of neglected property regularly
- Contact owners of expired listings the day you receive notice of them, unless your local Board disapproves
- Contact owners of foreclosures
- Check local tax records twice a year
- Write absentee owners every three months
- Give your business card to every new contact you make
- Talk and listen real estate wherever you go
- Ask people to tell you about people who plan to move
- Keep in touch with every listing you have sold either by phone or mail
- When an owner signs your listing agreement, ask if he or she knows of anyone else who is contemplating selling
- Drive to and from work a different route every day, looking for listing possibilities

SUCCESSFUL LISTING PRACTICES

However your firm operates, certain elements are essential to successful listing practices. They are presented here with the suggestion that you may want to change the sequence to suit your needs.

Preparing for a Listing Appointment

Successful listers spend time getting ready for this important appointment. Preparation includes researching recent sales in the neighborhood, investigating available financing and knowing as much as possible about comparable properties for sale and that have sold in the area. Use this data to prepare a competitive market analysis.

Listing Kit

You will make points with sellers if you have everything you need with you when you make your first call. Keep a kit of listing materials in your car and check its contents regularly. This is a time-saving arrangement and can save you the embarrassment of having to double back to drop off things you might otherwise forget. Keeping the kit in the car also makes it possible to handle an unexpected listing opportunity.

Listing Kit Tools
50-foot measuring tape and/or an electronic tape measure
listing forms
amortization schedules
hand-held programmed calculator
information on guaranteed sales, if applicable
referral forms for out-of-town transfers
NATIONAL ASSOCIATION OF REALTORS® pamphlets "Selling Your Home," "Selling or Buying a Home," "If You Are Thinking Real Estate—Think REALTOR®" and "Supporting the Heart of Your Community"
company brochures
copies of direct mailings you make on your listing
information on how MLS works
notebook for recording data you will need or a small tape recorder
several ballpoint pens
listing agreements
purchase contracts/receipts for deposit
home warranty forms
copies of home brochures
instant camera

Listing Presentation Book

A listing presentation book needn't be elaborate. Its value lies in the content and the skill with which it is used.

Arrangement of the content is important. The material can be assembled by the salesperson and put in a three-ring binder. Plastic page covers will keep the material clean and make the book more durable. Whole sections or individual pages can be changed as needed. A combination of print and illustrated material is more effective than straight typewritten text. Color adds interest and impact. The listing presentation book is a visual tool that should not take the place of your verbal presentation but should be used to reinforce it. While some owners realize that listing their home is in their best interests, others do not. So the book should include Why List material. The Why List material should cover both Why List with a REALTOR® as well as Why List with your firm.

Material for a listing presentation book should include information about the company, about you, what it means to be a REALTOR® and how your company markets properties. The NATIONAL ASSOCIATION OF REALTORS®' pamphlet titled "Selling Your Home" points out the advantage of working with a REALTOR® and provides homeowners with hints on helping the REALTOR® in the sale of their home.

You should show how your company markets property by using visuals coupled with your verbal presentation.

The firm's marketing program can be explained through forms used to determine how houses are priced to sell (competitive market analysis), sample ads (both classified and institutional), MLS forms, any brochures the company produces on certain types of properties and the company For Sale sign design. You may want to include your personal brochure.

Use news clippings, brochures and/or visuals that tell how long the company has been in business, its growth pattern, the market area served, the number of offices and size of the sales staff, and its qualifications and achievements. Be sure to include pertinent information about yourself, awards you have won, news clippings of your professional achievements and complimentary letters from satisfied clients. It is wise to include any educational courses you have taken to further your career and note your designations, such as GRI or CRS.

Emphasize the following advantages of listing with a REALTOR®:

- Better control over inspection of the property by potential buyers
- No showing without a salesperson
- A schedule of reasonable hours for showing the property
- Sellers not tied down during the listing period

- Sellers kept fully informed on any offer obtained
- In a For Sale By Owner, the commission is usually deducted by the buyer and the seller is left to do all the work for nothing.
- The entire agreement is set forth in writing to avoid the likelihood of costly lawsuits.
- Prospects are prequalified so that you do not waste owners' time with buyers who are unable to buy.
- Owners are protected against sharp operators who use many means to take unfair advantage of owners.
- You aid the buyer through the financing, which usually means a shorter closing period.
- There is a far greater likelihood of a sale for homes listed by a REALTOR® than by an owner selling without this help. This can be readily seen by the number of For Sale By Owner signs that are replaced by signs of REALTORS®.

All this material should be organized in the listing presentation book to give you an unwritten script to follow.

COMPETITIVE MARKET ANALYSIS

Before the listing appointment, complete the competitive market analysis on the specific property. Your competitive market analysis should include

- comparable homes currently on the market.
- comparable homes whose listings expired (unsold).
- comparable homes that were sold (show listing and sale prices).

From the competitive market analysis (CMA), it should be very clear that the higher a home is priced above actual comparable sales prices for similar homes, the less likely it is that it will sell. The CMA will probably also show that higher list prices for comparable homes did not affect market sale prices but did lengthen the time required to sell those homes.

The CMA is a tool that helps owners realize that taking the attitude "we can always come down" is not in their best interests. Chances are you can obtain comparables by logging onto your computer with a password and ordering "comps." The computer needs to know the area desired (often by Thomas Map coordinates), the square footage and other amenities. (Specific data on homes in your area may be available from a computer software service.) You can also get comparables from many title companies. Another method is to use the comp books, but this takes more time. Because your time is valuable, use computer sources whenever possible. Your broker will help you obtain the data and will likely have sample CMAs that you can use as a model.

There are also a number of computer programs that will organize the comp data in an effective visual manner.

A special folder carrying the sellers' names on the cover with your business card on the inside can be an impressive, functional supplement to your presentation manual. By using a laser printer, you can prepare a professional folder cover that conveys to the owners that you not only appreciate their property, but that you are a professional. The folder can hold a market analysis form, some NAR pamphlets, a listing agreement and an offer-to-buy form. This folder can be studied by the sellers at their leisure, acquainting them with how you prepare a listing and the forms they will be asked to sign for both the listing and the sale.

The listing presentation book and seller's folder cause the sellers to look at the marketability of their property objectively rather than emotionally. When the material is accurate and presented professionally, it leaves little to chance.

WHAT DO SELLERS WANT?

A buyer, of course. Beyond that, they want someone to take charge, handle details and help them make decisions; someone to lean on and worry with; and someone to get top dollar for their property.

Your first visit is the time to establish in the seller's mind the fact that you are the real estate expert. Now is the time to take charge and get the seller in the habit of asking you what to do rather than telling you.

YOUR FIRST APPOINTMENT

Arrive on time. Get the conversation started by discussing the real estate business, not the property the prospect has to sell. This helps establish you as the professional the seller wants and needs and opens the way to discuss what your firm can do that the seller cannot do on his or her own.

For example, you know the comparables, you market properties in the area, you screen all prospects, you find prospects the seller could not possibly reach, and you handle negotiations on price and details of settlement. You are selling your knowledge and skills as a real estate professional and persuading the seller that you are the person to handle this important transaction.

Inspection of the property may precede or follow this first discussion. The sequence depends on how you want the interview to proceed.

When you look at the property, remain calm no matter how exciting the prospect may seem. Too many compliments or an overenthusiastic approach on your part could cause the sellers to decide they have understated the asking price. Also make notes about what the property lacks, but do not discuss it at this time. Take your time during the inspection. You want the owners to know you appreciate their home. When the owners tell you about a special feature or something they have changed about the property, make a note of it. You can get the owners involved by measuring rooms and having the owners give you the measurements to mark down.

Discussing Details

After the property inspection, it is time to sit down and discuss details. Try to direct this session to a quiet place where you can sit facing the owners. You must be able to make your presentation without having to turn to glance from one to the other. As you talk, make notes that will help you answer questions.

Learn why they are selling. Listen as they talk about themselves. Interrupt only as needed, to further qualify what they are saying about jobs, children, where they plan to move and when, and what housing they will need. You should be building a family profile and know a lot about the personalities of the owners by the time this interview ends.

Show Your Listing Presentation Book

Now might be the time to acquaint the sellers with your company and the service it offers. As you go through your listing presentation, encourage the sellers to stop you when they have questions. It is said that we retain 10 percent of what we hear, 50 percent of what we see and hear, and 90 percent of what we hear, see and tell. When you engage the sellers in conversation about the listing presentation, you can get them to repeat back to you some of the things you have just told them about yourself and your firm.

Your listing presentation will show that your firm has well-trained salespeople, a reputation for reliability, generates inquiries, qualifies good prospects and eliminates the poor ones.

Explain how your firm qualifies buyers and where buyers come from. Research has proved that 65 percent of buyers are market-oriented—that is, they are referrals to a salesperson or a brokerage firm or are contacted by real estate salespeople.

Stress the safety and convenience of having professionals bring prospective buyers to them, then act as an intermediary in negotiations, financing details and final settlement.

Countering Objections

Objections are the biggest hurdles to getting a listing. An objection is nothing more than a question that should be answered. One good way to answer an objection is to restate it in question form, agree with the sellers that their question is valid and make a statement that answers the question. If they are still not convinced, offer proof. The proof will allow you to expand into more benefits.

The same reasoning applies to the buyer's situation. With a REALTOR®, however, the principals can reach a satisfactory agreement with far greater ease. The REALTOR® negotiates between prospective buyer and seller an offer that can be considered by the seller with all available facts at hand. The sellers have the assurance that if they accept, the sale is consummated; or if they have another possibility in mind, the prospective buyer will be able to consider the counteroffer intelligently and make a prompt, wise decision.

Buyers may be timid and reluctant to talk frankly with the seller. They may shrink from bringing up criticisms that must be answered before a sale can be made. They may be too proud to discuss their financial resources or ask for the terms they need. The owner cannot overcome this timidity, but a good real estate salesperson can.

On the other side of the coin, the owners of the property are inclined to be sensitive. They resent criticism, and their talks with prospective buyers may end in argument. The salesperson, however, can present the buyer's point of view to the seller objectively so problems and stumbling blocks to the sale can be dealt with sensibly.

In relation to the advantages of having the sale handled by an expert, the commission charged by the broker is reasonable. In the long run, it usually costs more for owners to act as their own agent than to use the services of a REALTOR®.

Records show that thousands of people who thought they could sell their property themselves have been unable to do so. Here is where your real skill in selling your services is put to the test. It is also one of the most promising sources of listings.

There are myriad psychological nuances to selling property; all are facilitated by using a third party as a sales intermediary. Owners may be willing to take a lower price but are afraid to appear to concede to the prospect, certain that if they make one concession they will be asked to make two or three. The presence of a third party can solve that problem.

By role playing, imagine the objections commonly raised by owners. Practice your responses. In this way you will train yourself to be able to persuade many of them of the value of a broker's services.

Here are some questions to pose as you talk to people who believe they can sell their own homes.

- Do you really know what your property is worth in today's market? Will you price it too high and discourage potential buyers or too low and lose part of your equity?
- Do you know what A-I-D-A means? Can you write the type of ads that will attract a qualified buyer?
- Do you have a list of prospects and access to numerous buyers? Can you eliminate the lookers from the buyers?
- Can you show other houses as comparables?
- Are you familiar with the techniques of selling real estate? Have you the ability and skill necessary to make a sale?
- Can you show your property as effectively as a broker? Are you prepared to expose your family to any stranger who knocks at the door to see your house?
- Are you available to prospects on a full-time basis until the house is sold?
- Can you answer objections and criticism without losing your temper?
- Do you have the ability to call back on prospects without placing yourself in a poor bargaining position to negotiate an offer?
- Can you draw a legally correct contract and include all the changes and conditions customary in this area?
- Do you understand the disclosures required by law?
- Are you familiar with today's financing? Do you have several sources of financing?
- Do you have the time to handle all these details in light of your other responsibilities?

For a telephone call concerning a For Sale By Owner ad, consider the following approach after introducing yourself as a real estate salesperson for your firm:

"[Mr. Higgins], if I had a buyer for your home, would you be willing to pay my fee?"

If the owner asks if you have a buyer, you could respond:

"I have persons interested in the area, but until I have seen your home I don't know if any of the buyers would be interested. Could I stop by at 3:30 this afternoon, or would 4:30 be more convenient for you?"

If the owners indicate that they would not pay your fee even if you brought them a full-price offer, ask:

"If a buyer agreed to pay my fee, could I show your home?"

This question should result in a positive response. The visit to the home will give you the opportunity to explain that your fee comes from buyer dollars, and buyers dealing direct with owners know this, so they tend to discount any price by at least the amount of the fee saved. Buyers—not sellers—save when the owners sell without an agent.

These same arguments can apply to commercial-investment selling. Indeed, because of the complexities involved in the commercial real estate field, it is likely the services of a well-informed salesperson can be of even greater benefit to an owner or prospective buyer.

Selling the Seller

Once you have persuaded sellers to list the property instead of trying to sell it on their own, you have to persuade them to list it with your firm instead of with another firm.

Talk about your firm's size. There are advantages to listing with small firms as well as large ones. Discuss the points that favor yours.

Stress what your company has that the competition does not—things like a national referral system, good office location and a strong image in the marketplace. If the property is located in your farm area, remind the sellers that this is "your" neighborhood too. Speak emphatically, but do not brag. While you should be positive about your firm, you should not "push" your firm by making negative remarks about other REALTORS®. Article 3 of the REALTORS® Code of Ethics and Standards of Conduct states: "REALTORS® are encouraged to refrain from unsolicited criticism of other real estate practitioners, and if an opinion is sought about another real estate practitioner, their business or their business practices, any opinion should be offered in an objective, professional manner."

Advertising

Many people do not understand the difference between classified and institutional advertising. They do not know the value of the latter in selling real estate or realize the limited effectiveness of advertising a single property (as in classified advertising). Tell how institutional ads strengthen the base of a brokerage's daily efforts and how they attract buyers to the office. This is a good time to mention the convenience of having your firm answer all phone inquiries and how you qualify buyers. If your firm has an established policy on advertising individual listings, explain it fully so the seller knows what to expect. Do not promise more than you can deliver.

Touring the Property

Three things are accomplished by a tour of the house:

1. Rooms are measured and other pertinent data collected.
2. Condition is examined, permitting the salesperson to suggest tactfully what may need to be repaired and what probably should not be done.
3. Conversation will help the salesperson determine why the property is being sold, when it will be available and who makes decisions in the household.

Suggestions for minor repairs are easy to make. Dripping faucets or loose doorknobs are easy to see. They may lead prospects to wonder what unseen defects exist. Overcrowded closets and other storage space may hold nonessential clutter; however, it could suggest to potential buyers a lack of sufficient storage.

A few hours' clean-up and reorganization effort might result in some empty storage space, giving the effect of a plentiful supply. A stained ceiling suggests a leaking roof. Even if the roof-repair job is evident, urge the seller to redecorate that ceiling so buyers will not suspect a still-leaking roof. Cockroaches, moths and rodents are anathema. Call in the exterminators!

On the other hand, major renovations done to the seller's taste might spoil the sale for new owners whose tastes differ. Never recommend spending sums the seller cannot hope to realize in the sale price. To help owners, give them the pamphlet "Speed the Sale of Your Home, Sell It for Every Dollar It's Worth," published by the NATIONAL ASSOCIATION OF REALTORS®. But keep in mind that you should never suggest that an actual defect be hidden or camouflaged. You have a duty of honesty and disclosure to buyers as well as sellers.

DO YOU WANT THE LISTING?

At some point in examining the property and getting acquainted with the owners, you will have to decide whether the listing is a viable one for you and your firm.

The real reason for selling is rarely given in response to the first inquiry unless it involves a business transfer or settlement of an estate. However, it is important to get the real reason so you know if you are dealing with a motivated seller.

Also, many buyers want to know the reason for selling. It may not be important to them, but if a reason is not given, it can trigger suspicion.

Be sure to get the answer to this question in the presence of all owners. Until they agree, you are wasting your time. Find out when the owners plan to move, where to and what their future housing needs may be.

Why do the owners want to sell? Is it imperative that they sell? If the reason for selling is not strong, approaching compulsion, your chances of procuring an acceptable offer are lessened. Because many owners are evasive, getting an honest answer to this question may take more time than some salespeople are willing to give.

Is the property comparable in value to others in the area? An exclusive listing for a home that is not comparable in value to others always presents a selling problem.

Do the owners give the impression of being cooperative? An exclusive agreement is similar to a partnership in which the seller and brokerage work together to accomplish the best results. If one of the owners is opposed to selling, you may encounter difficulties in arranging showings and getting acceptance of a reasonable offer. If you sense you are not developing rapport and gaining the confidence of the sellers, and if you are getting the feeling that these are people with whom you simply cannot do business, it is futile to try further.

Is the market favorable for a mortgage on this property? Availability and cost of mortgage money influence a sale. In an unfavorable market, explore availability of secondary financing from either the seller or some other source.

Will the exclusive run long enough to cover the peak period of the sellers' motivation? Do they need to sell in 30 days or can they take six months? Market conditions can determine the time needed to get the job done. The weaker the market, the more time required or the lower the listing price.

Is the property the kind you believe you can merchandise under the customary exclusive agreement? Limiting characteristics in residential properties include such features as two bedrooms; large, cavernous rooms in older properties; or deluxe houses located too close to properties of much lower value. Such listings often take longer to sell.

Are you genuinely enthused about the property, believing you have a reasonably good chance to sell it during the term of listing? Will your enthusiasm and confidence survive the critical commentaries of lookers and bargain hunters?

Are you willing to be personally responsible to the owners during the term of the listing, to keep them advised of all activity and buyer reactions and to counsel them about price and terms? Informed sellers are receptive sellers. They will be much more responsive to proposals when they know and understand the basis for them and are aware of the effort it has taken to produce them.

Have you made a complete analysis of the property? Many salespeople do not and are unprepared to give professional guidance when the inevitable question is asked: "What is the property worth?" Since many owners have an inflated idea of the market value of their homes, you must be ready with facts to justify your suggested price range. In this regard, your market analysis of the property will be invaluable.

PRICING THE LISTING

Working with sellers to determine the price of their property requires both knowledge and tact. Often the price you believe the property is worth is not acceptable to the owners. They have heard about property values in their neighborhood or what several have sold for. Whether these prices are rumor or fact does not influence the owners' thinking.

If the owners are not convinced by the competitive market analysis that the price you recommended is in their best interests, you might suggest that an appraisal be made by impartial, expert authorities on real estate value. The owners pay the appraisal fee. They usually will not object if it can be demonstrated that an appraisal is to their advantage.

An appraisal may not be necessary if the sellers understand how you arrived at your suggested price and realize the competitive market analysis is accurate and complete as to comparable sales. The sellers can be made to realize that listing at the suggested price is in their best interest.

When an owner is adamant as to a price considerably higher than market data indicates is reasonable, you might want to point out that even if you were to find a buyer at the owner's price, the sale would not be completed. Lenders' appraisers have the same data you have. The result would be an appraisal far below the purchase price, which would preclude the desired loan and leave a buyer who does not want to continue with the transaction.

Some salespeople like to have the listing contract out where it can be seen all through the listing interview but steer conversation away from any talk of price until after they have seen the place and finished their presentation.

In turning the discussion to price, present your research. Show the sellers your competitive market analysis, explaining how reliable these studies have been over many years. Using the market analysis, discuss the comparables sold recently, those now for sale, their pricing and the financing available.

Ask some preliminary finance questions. You will need to know how the property is presently financed. Learn whether or not the owners will carry a purchase money mortgage, either first or second.

You should, of course, know local sources of mortgage funds, such as banks, savings and loans, mortgage companies, insurance companies, fraternal orders and private investors. This information is vital in selling and closing stages and will also increase the seller's confidence in you. Lack of financing know-how has resulted in many a down payment and signed contract having to be returned because not enough time was spent investigating the financial requirements of a buyer in financing or qualifying for a property.

After you have explained what the price range of comparable properties has been for the past 90 days and discussed financing in a general way, stress the importance of pricing properly. Explain the difficulties in selling overpriced properties. For example:

- Homes offered for too long become shopworn and are often difficult to sell.
- Salespeople lose interest after a number of unfavorable reactions.
- Overpricing reduces the response from advertising.
- Also, overpricing helps sell the seller's competitors' properties.
- The property fails to compete with other offerings.
- Buyers expect more at high prices; failing to find it, they seldom become interested again even at a reduced price.
- When a property does not sell after proper exposure for a reasonable period of time, price is the problem.
- When a property has been on the market for an unusually long period of time, buyers will often think the owners are desperate and any offer will be less than reasonable.

Be realistic. Don't allow your enthusiasm for a property to warp your judgment and lead to overpricing. Stress the importance of the time factor and the wisdom of pricing a property realistically at the beginning to avoid the danger of having to take a loss when a listing becomes shopworn. Attracting buyers is the name of the game.

One very successful salesperson suggests an asking price range by saying, "Here, for all these reasons, is the price range within which we believe the average buyer for your house will be. Does that seem logical to you?" The suggested price covers a small price range based on a careful market analysis.

This manner of suggesting a price range tells the sellers you are not appraising their property but want to help them market it. The second part of the statement asks the sellers to accept (or reject) the logic of the calculations. It helps them make their own decision.

Some owners think that if they can convince you to accept a listing at an inflated price, it will mean more money in their pockets. As shown, this is not the case. It is not in the salesperson's best interest to take a listing that is not priced competitively with comparable property. By accepting such a listing, you will only be giving the owner false expectations. Of course, you should never take an overpriced listing with a secret intent to work on the owner to lower the price once the listing is signed. The owner must be part of your team, not an adversary.

Unless the owner is motivated to sell and agrees to evaluate the listing price within a designated period of time based on the reactions of other agents and prospective buyers, you will save yourself time and money by not accepting a listing that is clearly not competitively priced.

IMPORTANT DATA FOR SELLERS

Your pricing figures ought to show exactly how much the owner will realize on the sale. Figure 6.2 is an example of a Seller's Estimated Proceeds form. If an offer is received at less than list price, a new Seller's Estimated Proceeds form should be prepared based upon the price offered. Sellers do not like negative surprises. Therefore, be realistic in your estimates.

The owners may already be familiar with the listing agreement if you showed it to them. As you explain it to them in detail, you are beginning your close. Be sure those who will sign it understand every part of it.

TYPES OF LISTINGS

It is important to understand the basic types of listings.

An *exclusive right to sell* is a listing contract between owner and broker in which the agent is given the sole and exclusive right to sell the property. Under this form of contract, the REALTOR® earns the commission if the property is sold by the named broker, the owner or by anyone else. The commission rate is negotiable.

Under an *exclusive agency* contract, the owners reserve the right to sell the property themselves and not pay a commission to the broker. If the owners sell the property through their own efforts, the exclusive agency ends without any liability for a commission and regardless of the employment period specified in the contract.

A problem with using an exclusive agency listing is that an owner could end up competing with you for a buyer or disagreeing with you as to who procured a particular buyer. Generally, the reason owners would want an exclusive agency listing is that they have one or more parties interested in the property. You should consider suggesting an exclusive right to sell listing with an exclusion for seven to ten days if a sale is made to any of the named parties. If these buyers are at all serious, they will know they must act quickly or they will have to deal through an agent. By these exclusions, you help the owners in making

FIGURE 6.2 Sample Seller's Estimated Proceeds Form

SELLER'S
Estimated Proceeds

Sale Price of Property (Estimated)	.... $	_____
Less Mortgage Balance (Estimated)	... $	_____
Less Other Encumbrances	.... $	_____
TOTAL	.... $	_____
Projected Gross Equity	.... $	_____

LESS ESTIMATED
SELLING/CLOSING COSTS:

Escrow Charges	.... $	_____
Document Preparation	.... $	_____
Title Charges	.... $	_____
Transfer Tax	.... $	_____
FHA, VA or Lender Discount	.... $	_____
Mortgage Pre-payment Penalty	.... $	_____
Real Estate Taxes	.... $	_____
Appraisal	.... $	_____
Survey	.... $	_____
Termite Inspection	.... $	_____
Corrective Work	.... $	_____
Home Protection Plan	.... $	_____
Unpaid Assessments	.... $	_____
Real Estate Commission	.... $	_____
Other:_____		_____

Total Deductions (Estimated)	.... $	_____
Net to Seller (Estimated)	.... $	_____

Compliments of:

NATIONAL ASSOCIATION
OF REALTORS®

REALTOR®   *The Voice for Real Estate*™

EQUAL HOUSING
OPPORTUNITY

116-15
revised 11/89

the buyers decide to buy, and if they don't buy, after the exclusion period you have an exclusive right to sell listing without exceptions.

All exclusive listings should be for a definite period of time. This period will vary according to the kind of property, the activity of the market and the arrangement the salesperson makes with the seller when the contract is executed. In every case, the time period should be sufficient to enable the real estate office to conduct an effective marketing campaign and should cover the period of maximum motivation.

For the broker, an exclusive right to sell listing has many advantages. It justifies spending time and money to locate qualified buyers and to negotiate a good sale. The broker can offer the property through other REALTORS®, thereby giving the owner a special service that includes both individual preferred attention and attention in a wide market. An exclusive listing gives the broker assurance that the property he or she is selling can be delivered at a definite price and on pre-established terms.

Sellers also have advantages in listing exclusively. When they give one broker an exclusive right to sell, the owners have a right to expect a vigorous sales effort. They can confidently expect results, for brokers should never accept an exclusive unless they honestly believe they can sell the property.

An *open listing* is a nonexclusive listing. It can be given to more than one broker. The broker who makes the sale earns the commission. Because other agents are competing, brokers will seldom advertise open listings. Agents will show open listings only when there is nothing else to show buyers, because the agents are often uncertain as to the availability of the property. The axiom "everybody's business is nobody's business" holds true for open listings. Agents who expend time and money on open listings can generally expect failure.

Net listings are not truly a form of listing; they are a method of compensation. The agent receives all above a net sales amount. Net listings are illegal in some states, and even where legal, they are not desirable. The agent wants to get as much as possible for the property, which would affect the time required to sell, while the owner just wants a quick sale at the net amount. Therefore, net listings are considered by many to be unethical.

If the agent earns a greater than normal commission under a net listing, owners often claim they were misled by the agent as to value. Because of the danger of lawsuits as well as ethical considerations, most offices will not accept net listings even where they are legal.

In *option listings,* the agent has an option to buy at a set price coupled with a listing. These listings create serious ethical problems, because the broker has the right to change from an agent to a principal. If the broker exercises the purchase option and then resells at a significantly higher price, he or she could be facing a lawsuit. Therefore, most agents will avoid option listings.

An *oral listing* is really no listing at all. It has been said that "an oral listing isn't worth the paper it isn't written on." People who refuse to sign a listing, insisting that their word is enough, will often accept your buyer but refuse to pay a fee because "it wasn't in writing."

Buyer listings can be exclusive or open listings. Under a buyer listing, the real estate agent acts as a buyer's agent to procure a property for the buyer. The buyer is responsible for the agent's commission. However, the listing agreement might specify that the buyer will have to pay a commission only in the event the agent does not share in any commission paid by the seller.

The advantage to buyers is having their own agent who will assist them in locating and negotiating a purchase in the buyer's best interest. The buyer's agent is not limited to listed property and can show property that has no commission paid by the seller.

Buyer listings are gaining in popularity, and there are many agents who now act as exclusive agents of the buyer. The duties as a buyer's broker are different than those of a broker acting for the seller as a seller's agent or in a subagency capacity. Figure 6.3 will help you understand the difference.

FIGURE 6.3 Customer-Level vs. Client-Level Service

THE SELLING BROKER

Customer-Level Service as Subagent	Client-Level Service as Buyer's Broker

RESPONSIBILITIES

Be fair and honest with buyer but owe greater responsibility to seller, including duty of skill and care to promote and safeguard seller's best interest.	Be fair and honest to seller, but owe greater responsibility to buyer, including duty of skill and care to promote and safeguard buyer's best interest.

EARNEST MONEY DEPOSIT

Collect amount sufficient to protect seller.	Suggest minimum amount, perhaps a note; put money in interest-bearing account; suggest that forfeiture of earnest money be sole remedy if buyer defaults.

Source: *Agency Relationships in Real Estate,* by John Reilly. © 1987 Dearborn Financial Publishing, Inc.

FIGURE 6.3 (continued)

Customer-Level Service as Subagent	Client-Level Service as Buyer's Broker

SELLER FINANCING

Can discuss, but should not encourage, financing terms and contract provisions unfavorable to seller, such as (1) no due-on-sale clause, (2) no deficiency judgment (nonrecourse), (3) unsecured note. If a corporate buyer, suggest seller require personal guaranty.

Suggest terms in best interest of buyer, such as low down payment, deferred interest, long maturity dates, no due-on-sale clause, long grace period, nonrecourse.

DISCLOSURE

Disclose to seller pertinent facts (which might not be able to disclose if a buyer's broker) such as (1) buyer's willingness to offer higher price and/or better terms, (2) buyer's urgency to buy, (3) buyer's plans to resell at profit or resubdivide to increase value, (4) buyer is sister of broker.

Disclose to buyer pertinent facts (which might not be able to disclose if subagent of seller) such as (1) seller near bankruptcy or foreclosure, (2) property overpriced, (3) other properties available at a better buy, (4) negative features, such as poor traffic flow, (5) construction of chemical plant down street that may affect property value.

NONDISCLOSURE

Refrain from disclosing to buyer facts that may compromise seller's position (seller's pending divorce) unless under a legal duty to disclose (zoning violation).

Refrain from disclosing to seller such facts regarding buyer's position (eg, buyer has options on three adjoining parcels). No duty to disclose name of buyer or that broker is lending buyer money to make down payment.

PROPERTY CONDITION

Suggest use of "as is" clause, if appropriate to protect seller (still must specify hidden defects).

Require that seller sign property condition statement and confirm representations of condition; require soil, termite inspections, if appropriate; look for negative features and use them to negotiate better price and terms.

FIGURE 6.3 **(continued)**

Customer-Level Service as Subagent	Client-Level Service as Buyer's Broker

DOCUMENTS

Give buyer a copy of important documents, such as mortgage to be assumed, declaration of restrictions, title report, condominium bylaws and house rules.

Research and explain significant portions of important documents affecting transaction, such as prepayment penalties, subordination, right of first refusal; refer buyer to expert advisers when appropriate.

NEGOTIATION

Use negotiating strategy and bargaining talents in seller's best interest.

Use negotiating strategy and bargaining talents in buyer's best interest.

SHOWING

Show buyer properties in which broker's commission is protected, such as in-house or MLS-listed properties. Pick best times to show property. Emphasize attributes and amenities.

Search for best properties for buyer to inspect, widening marketplace to "For Sale by Owner," lender owned (REO), probate sales and unlisted properties. View property at different times to find negative features, such as evening noise, afternoon sun, traffic congestion.

PROPERTY GOALS

Find buyer the type of property buyer seeks; more concerned with *sale* of seller's property that fits buyer's stated objectives.

Counsel buyer as to developing accurate objectives; may find that buyer who wants apartment building might be better with duplex at half the price or that buyer looking for vacant lot would benefit more from an investment in improved property.

OFFERS

Can help prepare/transmit buyer's offer on behalf of seller; must reveal to seller that buyer has prepared two offers, in case first offer not accepted.

Help buyer prepare strongest offer; can suggest buyer prepare two offers and have broker submit lower offer first without revealing fact of second offer.

FIGURE 6.3   (continued)

Customer-Level Service as Subagent	Client-Level Service as Buyer's Broker
POSSESSION DATES	
Consider what is best date for seller in terms of moving out, notice to existing tenants, impact on insurance and risk of loss provision.	Consider what is best for buyer in terms of moving in, storage, favorable risk of loss provision if fire destroys property prior to closing.
DEFAULT	
Discuss remedies upon default by either party. Point out to seller any attempt by buyer to limit liability (nonrecourse, deposit money is sole liquidated damages).	Suggest seller's remedy be limited to retention of deposit money; consider having seller pay buyer's expenses and cancellation charges if seller defaults.
BIDDING	
Can bid for own account against buyer/customer but should disclose to buyer and seller.	Cannont bid for own account against buyer *client*.
EFFICIENCY	
Don't expend much time and effort, as in an open listing, because in competition with the listing broker, seller and other brokers to sell buyer a property before someone else does.	Work at an "exclusive listing" efficiency, realizing that broker's role is to assist buyer in locating and acquiring best property, not to sell the buyer any *one* property.
APPRAISAL	
Unless asked, no duty to disclose low appraisal or fact broker sold similar unit yesterday for $10,000 less.	Suggest independent appraisal be used to negotiate lower price offer; review seller's comparables from buyer's perspective.
BONUS	
Cannot agree to accept bonus from buyer for obtaining reduction in listed price.	Can receive incentive fee for negotiating reduction in listed price.

FIGURE 6.3 (continued)

Customer-Level Service as Subagent	Client-Level Service as Buyer's Broker
TERMINATION	
Easier to terminate a subagency relationship (as when broker decides to bid on property).	Legal and ethical implications of agency relationship and certain duties may continue even after clearly documented termination.

CLOSING THE LISTING

Ask a question that assumes the listing. For example: "Most of our agency agreements are for 90 or 120 days. Would you prefer a 90-day agreement or should we make it for 120 days?"

Here you have made it easy for the owner to answer. You have not asked for a big decision, only a choice between the two positive options. This is known as "minor point," "alternate close" or "trial close" and is a classic approach.

Another approach to closing is the stair-step arrangement where each objection (question) is met (answered), leading the owner a step closer to the close. Basically, a close is the combination of asking questions, meeting objections and summarizing benefits that are important to the seller.

As soon as the seller has committed to a preferred time period, begin to write up the listing contract. Discuss personal property that is to be included in the asking price. Be sure every item is listed fully in the agreement so there can be no question between you and the seller or between seller and buyer, and so your office forms and MLS sheets are accurate.

PUT IT IN WRITING

A written contract should always be used. The price of the property and the commission rate, which is negotiable, are clearly spelled out in a contract. The seller must understand what commission rate is involved and that the commission is included in the sale price of the property. Be certain he or she understands, for example, that the commission must be paid out of the selling price of the property. This should be stated in writing as part of the contract, along with a specific statement of any other charges or costs to be paid by the seller.

A copy of the listing should be given to the owners at the time they sign. If the listing must be accepted or signed by the broker, another copy should be delivered to the owners when accepted.

Get All the Facts

Every brokerage firm has its own way of keeping all the information on a listing together. It is important to get every detail needed for your own office and the MLS sheet. The more you know about a property, the better job of marketing you can do. Prospective buyers are likely to ask about the following:

- Location of transportation, schools, churches, business and shopping centers, recreation and amusement facilities
- Price asked, mortgage, who holds mortgage and its assumability, interest rate, amortization rates, down payment expected and availability of other mortgages
- Year house was built, type construction, plumbing, wiring and roofing material
- Number and size of rooms on each floor, type basement, garage size and type
- Size of lot
- Heating system, air-conditioning system, utility services, water and sewage systems
- Charges against property—annual taxes, assessments, special tax districts and other liens
- Date of possession
- Attractive special features (lake or river rights, stables, swimming pool, gardens, landscaping, separate living quarters for in-laws)
- Why selling (The reason should not be revealed to other agents or prospective buyers without the approval of the owners. To do so could potentially strengthen the buyer's and weaken the seller's bargaining positions. Because many buyers will want to know, however, owners will generally give the agent permission to reveal why they are selling.)
- Zoning history and present zoning, including nonconforming uses
- Easements granted and deed restrictions
- Insurance information
- Exchange possibilities and kind or value of property considered for trade

Agency Relationship

During the listing presentation, you should fully disclose what your agency relationship will be with the seller or if you will be acting as a facilitator.

As the seller's agent, you represent the seller exclusively. In some cases you could be a dual agent—for example, when your office is the listing and buyer's agent for the same property. Whenever you act in a dual-agency capacity, however, you must make certain both buyer and seller fully understand your agency role.

Figure 6.4 is a sample of Company Agency Policy guidelines, which will help you in understanding the various agency advantages, disadvantages and responsibilities. The NATIONAL ASSOCIATION OF REALTORS® offers a training kit titled "Agency: Choices, Challenges and Opportunities" that will give you a more in-depth understanding of agency choices. However, keep in mind that the seller must fully understand your agency role as a seller's agent or dual agent, if applicable.

The concept of facilitator is that real estate professionals may serve as intermediaries between buyers and sellers rather than as advocates of buyers, sellers or both. Statutes allowing for this facilitator status are being considered in a number of states.

Proponents of the facilitator concept believe that it simply describes what most agents do. You can expect to hear a great deal more about the facilitator concept in the future.

HOME PROTECTION AND WARRANTY PROGRAMS

If your brokerage has implemented or subscribes to a home protection plan, it should be offered to every seller when you take the listing. A home protection plan gives the seller the advantage of offering a "like new" house, because it covers mechanical breakdowns that might occur in central heating and air-conditioning systems, interior electrical systems, plumbing, hot water tanks and built-in appliances, for example, excluding known pre-existing conditions. If any of these systems fail, they will be returned to operational condition by the home protection firm.

When starting a relationship with a real estate company, most home protection firms require a commitment involving either a fee or an agreement to have all salespeople offer the plan to sellers first. If a seller is not interested, the plan is generally offered to the buyer of the house.

Before entering into any relationship, however, your broker should thoroughly investigate and evaluate the home protection firms available. For example:

- What is the firm's financial condition?
- How long has it been in business?
- What are its claims and its service record?
- How much does the plan cost?
- What does the contract cover—and what doesn't it cover?

FIGURE 6.4   Company Agency Policy

SELLER AGENCY EXCLUSIVELY, WHETHER LISTING OR SELLING

Advantages	*Disadvantages*
Common practice: comfortable	Loss of business: agents, buyers
Generally understood policy	High potential for undisclosed dual agency

BUYER AGENCY EXCLUSIVELY

Advantages	*Disadvantages*
No possibility of dual agency	Lose business: seller listings, buyer referrals from listings
No expense of listings	No exposure via advertising of listings
No liabilities as listing broker	Difficult to recruit agents
	Discomfort with new practice

SINGLE AGENCY, WHETHER LISTING OR SELLING

Advantages	*Disadvantages*
Clean agency decisions about both buyers and sellers: simple	Agency must be terminated if a buyer client wants to buy a company listing (risky)
Avoid dual agency by	OR
a) showing company listings first (risky)	Not showing company listings to buyer client
b) showing potential listings as FSBOs first	Feasible only with very small companies
Justification for showing company listings first	

DUAL AGENCY FOR IN-HOUSE SALES, SINGLE AGENCY OTHERWISE

Advantages	*Disadvantages*
Complete flexibility	Extensive training and monitoring necessary
Disclosed dual agency is always better than undisclosed dual agency	Liability of dual agency
	Discomfort with new practice
Less disruptive to current practice	Finding supportive legal counsel

After an agreement has been reached between your brokerage and a home protection plan, each salesperson should be completely familiar with the contract.

Property Profile

It is a good idea to contact a title company and get a property profile (O and E: ownership and encumbrance report) as soon as a property is listed. This will reveal any serious problems that could affect a sale, such as liens. In some cases, judgments filed against an owner could make a sale at the list price impossible. A property profile might also disclose easements you did not know about that could affect value, or even another party who has an ownership interest in the property. Title companies will generally provide computer-generated property profiles at no cost. They will, however, expect your title business when the property is sold. Keep in mind that a property profile is not an insurance policy, and the title insurer has no liability if title defects are discovered later.

COMMERCIAL-INVESTMENT LISTINGS

It is of paramount importance that the most thorough and reliable listing information available on commercial-investment properties be obtained. In listing and selling residential property, a market data approach is most often the basis for determining value and/or price. Income-producing properties are purchased primarily for their ability to produce an income stream after considering all tax aspects and also as a hedge against inflation.

The amenities and physical characteristics of the property, which are of first importance to a single-family residential property, are important to an income-producing property only to the extent that they influence the quality, quantity and durability of the income stream. It is therefore imperative that all of the financial information concerning a property be obtained before marketing it.

CREATIVE SELLING

A good commercial-investment salesperson looks at every parcel of real estate, improved or otherwise, with a critical and creative eye and asks the following questions:

- Is the property being used to its highest potential?
- What other or better use might it have?
- What transaction could bring this about?
- Who are good prospects to participate in such a transaction?

Commercial-investment salespeople listen all day every day for news and rumors involving the market they serve. They learn to filter fact from rumor and know the value of each. They are attuned to business, professional and personal news about people and things, aware that any change might involve possible use of their services. This is creative selling.

You may have heard that your community is thinking of adding a new swimming pool, branch library or neighborhood playground. Then you think of the old house or vacant building in a good location that could be renovated to fill the need or possibly be razed to provide a suitable site. If you have a list of such properties and brainstorm ideas for their private or public use, you may have the beginning of a creative transaction.

Unused industrial buildings offer the same creative possibilities. As post offices, rail stations, warehouses and other single- or multistory business buildings fall into disuse, new shopping and recreation complexes are being designed to continue their useful lifetime. Adaptive uses of historic buildings are a growing challenge in creative selling.

Factual information on every listing should be a permanent record in the commercial-investment broker's office. Besides helping service the seller, this becomes a record of real estate history in the area, valuable when the property is resold, reassessed or appraised.

We have covered only the tip of the iceberg. There are many excellent books and courses that can help you in developing your listing skills.

Keep in mind that, like a house that requires a strong foundation, a real estate broker must also have a strong foundation to have a sound business. Listings are the foundation of the real estate profession, for without listings there can be no sales.

Chapter 7

Servicing the Seller

You have worked hard to obtain this listing. From the initial prospecting to the actual signing of the listing contract, you have handled the objectives masterfully. However, your job is only half completed. Now you must start the marketing program for your new listing and prepare the sellers for what is about to happen so there will be no surprises.

PREPARING THE SELLERS

Preparing the sellers for the marketing process actually begins with your listing presentation; it is here that you set the tone. Explain that the marketing of their house is a joint effort. It is important for the sellers to realize that they will be living in a model home during the marketing period and that they can assist in achieving the highest and best price in the shortest time by following these important points:

- Explain that you don't get a second chance to make a good first impression with prospective buyers. The front door area greets the prospect. Make sure it is fresh, clean and scrubbed-looking. It is important to keep the lawn and shrubs trimmed and the sidewalks free of debris. Plants in bloom add a fresh look and set a positive mood. A fast-greening fertilizer will give a lawn a luxurious look. Birdfeeders also can be a strong plus factor. Place outdoor furniture in a manner that sets off the strongest features of the yard.
- Why try to tell the prospect how the home could look when you can show them by redecorating? Faded walls and worn woodwork reduce appeal. Dripping water discolors sinks and suggests faulty plumbing. Repairs can make a big difference. Loose knobs, sticking doors and windows, warped cabinet drawers, pushed-out

screen doors and other minor flaws detract from the value of the home. In some cases, items that would cost $200 to repair could reduce a prospect's offer by $2,000 or more.

- Display the rooms in their best light and let the sun shine in. Prior to the showing, open the draperies and curtains and let the prospect see how cheerful your home can be. Turn on every light in the house, including closet lights. Dark rooms are not appealing. And remember to display the attic, basement, garage and utility space to their full advantage by removing all unnecessary articles. A possible solution is to temporarily rent a small storage space for these items. On cold days, a fire in the fireplace can set a receptive mood. In hot weather, set the air conditioner just a few degrees lower than normal so that visitors will feel cool when entering.

- Many people are super-sensitive to pets and pet odors. Therefore, pets should be kept out of the way, preferably out of the house. Cat litter boxes should be changed daily and the yard should be checked daily for dog litter.

- Avoid having too many people present during inspections. The potential buyer will feel like an intruder and will hurry through the house. Also, remember to be courteous to the prospects, but don't force conversation with them. It is even better if the owners are not present during the showing. The prospects will then be more vocal about their feelings, which helps the salesperson's job tremendously. Tell the owners that if they must be on the property during the showing, they should remain in one area and not follow the visitors around. Do not volunteer information, but answer any questions honestly. Also, do not have a television on during the showing. You want visitors to be interested in your house, not in a ballgame.

- Let the sellers know how your company sets up appointments to show the property: who will be calling for the appointment and who will be accompanying the prospects. It is important that the sellers understand the need for access to the property and how your company *securely* handles keys or lockboxes. Remind the sellers that one of the reasons they listed with you was to avoid being tied to their home. Also, many homes are purchased by out-of-town buyers who are in town for a limited time; a potential sale might be lost if the house can't be shown due to lack of access. If you use an electronic lockbox, explain that the lockbox provides information as to agents who have visited the property, and that you will contact these agents for their suggestions and to determine the interest of their buyers.

- Explain to the owners that some prospects may come to the door unaccompanied by a real estate agent. Recommend that the owners not let them in, as they are unaware of their motivations and ability to buy. Have the owners call your office, and if you are not available to show the property, another agent should be available to meet with the interested party in just a short while. Leave a supply of your business cards, and ask the owner to give such callers your card so they can call and make an appointment to see the property if an agent is not available to show them the home.

● Explain to the sellers the concept of the multiple listing service and how it benefits them. Explain that as a member of the MLS system, your company will share all the pertinent information on their property with cooperating members of the MLS. Also, tell them
—that the commission will be shared in the event the property is sold in cooperation with a multiple listing member;
—when and how a photograph of their home will be taken for the brochure; and
—the date of your MLS caravan, when local brokers may preview the property.

Review your multiple listing brochure for completeness and accuracy. Remember, this is the first impression that cooperating brokers have of the property; it can be the determining factor for them in deciding whether to show the property to their prospective customers.

SELLING YOUR FELLOW SALES ASSOCIATES

Upon returning to the office, it is important to let your own team of sales associates know of your new listing. This is done in various ways: many offices have a new listing board with pertinent information; others keep a listing "hotsheet" in a central location so all associates can check on new listings, sales, price adjustments or other things of interest happening in the office. Your next sales meeting is an opportune time to share your exciting new listing with your sales associates. It is important for you to be enthusiastic and share with them the high points of the property. In many cases, one of your sales associates will have a potential customer for whom this house is perfect.

The office tour and/or MLS caravan is the next important step in marketing your new listing to your sales team. Again, first impressions are lasting. You should greet the agents enthusiastically at the door, demonstrate the facts and benefits of the property and highlight the outstanding features you believe will be attractive to potential customers. Remember, sales associates must be attracted psychologically to a property in order to promote it. The owners should have the home in "model-home" condition for the MLS caravan. Serving hot coffee and cookies or rolls to the agents will make them linger in the home longer and create a greater impression on them. Additionally, the aroma of home baking at the time of the caravan helps set a positive image. In larger communities, agents cannot physically caravan every new listing. Therefore, they choose listings that they feel have a greater likelihood of selling. One way to increase traffic is to inform agents that you will be serving a breakfast (you can distribute flyers at other offices and the board office). Some agents will offer a buffet lunch. Owners will often agree to pick up or share in the cost.

Property Brief

Most sales offices provide a property brief as a marketing tool to describe a listed property. A multiple listing brochure has limited space for information, and that information is usually in a secret code that is sometimes a mystery even to the sales associate. However, a specially prepared property brief or "home book" (see Figure 7.1) that includes all pertinent data on schools, churches, recreation and shopping facilities, special interior and exterior features of the home, extras that are included and any special showing instructions is extremely beneficial.

Or you can prepare a one-page property brief featuring the home and pertinent details by using your computer and a laser printer. The property brief should also include a photograph or drawing of the property. Some agents use copiers to reproduce the property briefs and the photographs. Some agents attach color photographs to their property briefs.

The property brief is a one-page selling tool containing basic information in a style similar to a classified ad. Many agents use the reverse side for additional property details. The property brief would be given to agents within the listing agent's office, agents on the MLS caravan and to persons who inquire about the property. Copies would also be left at the property for prospective buyers and agents showing the property.

An additional idea that has worked well in the past few years is giving financing methods on the reverse side of the property brief. The listing associate could give four alternative financing methods on the property, including 80 percent conventional, FHA, VA, assumption with second mortgage and adjustable mortgage. In today's market, purchasers are highly sophisticated and experienced and, in many cases, shop with monthly payments in mind. This format not only helps purchasers to see more clearly the alternative methods of purchasing this home, it also aids the sales associate in showing them the initial cash investment needed, their monthly payments and the program structure. Anytime you can give supportive data in the form of a visual aid and also save time for both the purchaser and the selling agent, you are giving additional service to all.

FIGURE 7.1   Home Book

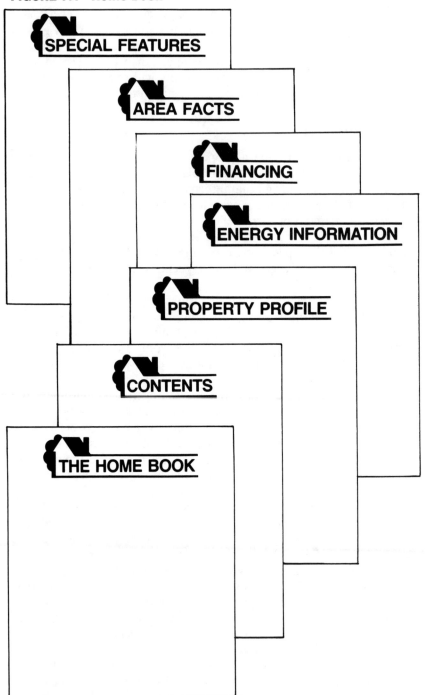

SELLING OTHER BROKERS

In order to give the property the greatest amount of exposure, it is important not to forget the cooperating brokers in your area. Another suggestion for focusing attention on your new listing over all the other listings in the marketplace is to have a special brokers' open house. Explain to the seller that the objective is to make the greatest number of sales associates in the marketplace aware of the property, because many of them have a list of prospects with whom they are working. While some agents serve elaborately catered buffets (generally for high-dollar properties), wine or champagne with hors d'oeuvres is generally sufficient. As an added inducement to attend the open house, often there will be a drawing of agents' cards for special prizes.

In other cases, invited salespeople and brokers go from house to house on a progressive dinner catered by a specialty restaurant in the community. The results are outstanding! You are limited only by your own imagination in this area. Make sure all local offices are invited to the tour, and send a special invitation in the form of a personal note to the most active individual associates. A property brief should be included with each invitation. Afterward, send a thank-you note to all the sales agents who attended your event.

SELLING THE PUBLIC

During the listing presentation, it is important for you to properly educate the sellers regarding the advertising portion of your company's marketing program. The best time to prepare the classified ads on your newly listed property is at the time of the listing. It is also suggested that you involve the sellers and make them a part of the total marketing program by asking for their input when you prepare the ads. "Mr. and Mrs. Seller, nobody knows this house better than you. What do you consider some of the outstanding features of this home?" "What features in this house would you want to duplicate in your new home?" "What type of family do you think your home will appeal most to [retirees, newlyweds, large families, etc.]?" It is recommended that you prepare three ads at this time and use them in rotation during the first 30 days of your marketing process. Ads can be written to emphasize different features of the home in order to appeal to a wide range of buyers.

In many neighborhoods, houses are sold to friends, relatives and business associates of people who already live in the neighborhood. This is called our "Tell 20 System." Anytime anything happens in real estate, you should be able to tell a minimum of 20 people in the immediate area. Using your local cross-index street address directory, find the names, addresses and telephone numbers of the 20 neighbors nearest your new listing. Then send a postcard announcing your new listing to this local center of influence. (Figure 7.2) Postcards are strongly suggested, because they are inexpensive, they eliminate envelopes, the postage is less and they are easier to handle when filling out. Also, a person receiving a postcard always turns it over to read what is on the back but often throws out other unsolicited mail without reading it. The Tell 20 System can be expanded and used when you are preparing for your open house, or when the listing sells. A card called "greet your new neighbor" can go out before a new family moves in, giving their name and new address. It's also a nice touch to add the names and ages of any children in the family.

You can obtain the best results in announcing your listing by calling on these neighbors in person. By delivering the Tell 20 card and property brief, you can gather additional information on the neighborhood and the immediate marketplace. Whether you use a mailout or deliver the cards in person, it is recommended that you make a telephone follow-up shortly after the neighbors receive the cards.

When you have finished your Tell 20 program, a minimum of 20 property owners will know that a neighbor's home is for sale and that you are interested in helping them find new neighbors. Keep track of your contacts either on a form in your listing file or on your computer.

An open house can be a great marketing tool for your new listing. You must plan it, market the open house and follow up on all potential prospects. This includes placing an ad, sending out your Tell 20 open house postcards, sending flyers to cooperating brokers, updating your competitive market analysis and property brief, and having the house in its best showing condition.

SERVICING THE SELLER

The sellers can be an important part of the marketing process, as they have centers of influence in the various parts of their community—friends and school, church and business associates. It is important to get copies of the property brief and a supply of your business cards into their hands as soon as possible. No marketing opportunity should go untapped. People are proud of their homes and enjoy this part of the marketing process when given the proper tools and support.

Once the marketing process begins, the sellers anxiously await your report regarding the impressions of those who have recently seen their newly listed home. It is important for you to call them with the feedback you have received from the sales associates who participated in your office caravan, from the brokers who attended your broker's tour and from prospective buyers who came to the open houses. This can assist you in establishing the proper selling price, making the

FIGURE 7.2   Sample Postcard List of "Tell 20 System"

TELL 20 FORM

Name	Address	Phone	Date Mailed	Date Phoned	Date Personal	Remarks
HUGH E. HARDAWAY	557 Markham	342-8299				
James L. Hansen	558 Markham	344-9403				
Frank Kerns	559 Markham	344-3704				
T.H. Bolton Jr.	561 Markham	344-3637				
William Allen Godwin	563 Markham	342-7936				
J.L. Champion	564 Markham	344-4666				
Kendall Tow	566 Markham	344-5346				
James L. Brantley	568 Markham	342-4627				
Dean A. Berry	569 Markham	344-2609				
Luther N. Davis III	570 Markham	342-3851				
Thomas G. Hart	571 Markham	344-1707				
Major P.R. Hare	572 Markham	342-1435				
H. Burgoyne Taylor	573 Markham	344-3636				
Charles Devan Dicks	574 Markham	342-9154				
Bobby F. Rush	575 Markham	342-6561				
J.H. Freeman	576 Markham	344-4472				
Donald L. Williams	579 Markham	344-1745				
E.R. Williams	600 Markham	342-6176				
G. Murphy Small	602 Markham	344-0715				
D.G. Parvner	605 Markham	344-2099				
William J. Stewart	606 Markham	344-1587				

house more marketable through repairs and decorating and providing additional support for any recommendations you may make.

In order to do the job properly, you must be organized. Keep a separate folder or computer file for each listing that you take (Figure 7.3). In this folder or file, keep all of the forms, information, copies of ads, showing information, your Tell 20 list and a list of all phone calls made regarding the listing. The biggest problem some people have in servicing listings is good time management. A tickler file is a useful means of following up with sellers periodically. Or you might establish a telephone date with sellers, a certain day at a certain time when you will call them regarding their listing. This helps keep you organized and eliminates unnecessary calls from the sellers asking about the progress on their listing.

As the professional, it is your responsibility to periodically review the marketplace and update your competitive market analysis (CMA). Have any of those properties used in the competitive market analysis been sold, expired or taken off the market? What new competition is in the marketplace, at what price, and at what terms? If comparable houses have been sold, why were those homes sold over your listing?

Financing is an integral part of the marketing process. What changes have occurred in the financing marketplace? Are there new rates, new programs, different discount points? Should FHA and VA financing be included? Should the owner contemplate participating in the financing by carrying back a first or second mortgage? This should be done in conjunction with the CMA and with what the competition is doing.

If the property does not elicit an offer from those who have seen it during the first 30 days of the marketing process and was listed at a higher price than you advised when you took the listing, now is the time to sit down with the sellers and counsel them on the advisability of adjusting the asking price. The sellers have a right to expect the benefits of your experience, knowledge and counsel in return for the commission they have agreed to pay you for marketing their property.

COMMUNICATIONS

Many salable listings are lost due to poor communications on the part of the listing associate. It is important to establish good follow-up habits immediately and never to over-promise during your listing presentation. If the sellers want to hear from you after every showing and you agree, then do so. If that is not part of your program, explain what you will do and follow through on it.

As previously stated, you should contact every owner of a listed property on a weekly basis. The reasons most commonly given by owners who fail to extend listings center around failure to communi-

FIGURE 7.3 Sample Servicing Folder

BE PREPARED

Date   Date Taken: _____   Expires: _____   Extended to: _____

          1. **Forms**

_____   a. Authorization to sell
_____   b. Competitive Market Analysis
_____   c. Sellers net sheet
_____   d. What I will do for you

          Other Items:

_____   a. Video presentation
_____   b. Tape
_____   c. Pens
_____   d. Clipboard or folder
_____   e. Scratch pads
_____   f. Business cards to leave with seller.

          2. **Presentation Reminders: In Sequence**
             1. **Never Discuss Price or Tour Property Before Selling Yourself & Company**
             2. Sell yourself and company with Visual Aid presentation.
             3. Discuss "What I will do for you."
             4. Reason for selling.
             5. What are the sellers needs and desires?
                  a. are "net" dollars important
                  b. is seller a buyer
                  c. possession to buyer
             6. Tour the Property - involve the seller. (begin listing agreement with completing measurements.
             7. Discuss Competitive Market Analysis
             8. Financing. Increase marketability with points or 2nd trust deed.
             9. Educate the seller as to unforeseen problems:
                  a. Possible credit problems with buyer - out of town delay, judgements
                  b. Appraisal requirements, price adjustments, repairs.
                  c. Buyers remorse
                  d. Possession requirements
                  e. Permits on additions
                  f. Financing fluctuations
                  g. Buyers who drop by on their own.
                  h. Showing by appointment - have seller be flexible.
                  i. Why a lockbox and sign are advantageous.
                  j. Don't lock the screen door when you leave.
          10. Finalize And Receive Approval On The Authorization To Sell.

WHAT I WILL DO FOR YOU

1. Put your home on the market for sale.
2. Call information to all _____ salesmen for waiting clients.
3. Submit to Board of Realtors to prepare for Multiple Listing Service.
4. Call local Real Estate offices to give them advance information.
5. Present your listing at our Company Breakfast.
6. Advertise locally (this or like properties).
7. Have available at home a list of all features and benefits for the sales people showing their clients your home.
8. Contact 101 neighbors for potential buyers.
9. Open House - between 1:00 and 5:00 if beneficial.
10. Follow-up enthusiastically after Open House to all people who have shown interest.
11. Prepare brochures and distribute to the Multiple Listing Members; if necessary.
12. Communicate all results to you on a regular basis.
13. **Goal**: to continually and always in good taste keep your home in front of motivated salespeople and motivated buyers until Sold.
14. Present all purchase agreements made on your home.
15. Deliver all escrow instructions to you for your approval.
16. Have termite clearance approved.
17. Make certain that loans are processed promptly.
18. Follow up on escrow and title work.
19. Have insurance clearance approved through escrow.
20. Close escrow and deliver your check.
21. Make myself available to help you find a new home.

FIGURE 7.3 (continued)

STAPLE THESE COMPLETED FORMS HERE

1. Listing Agreement
2. Competitive Market Analysis
3. Sellers Net

AFTER SALE SERVICE AND INFORMATION

(Closing) Date of Sale_____ Price $_____ Terms _____

Seller _____ Buyer _____ Buyer Phone _____

Escrow Co. _____ Escrow (Closing) No. _____ Selling Broker _____
(if applicable)

Sales Report No. _____ Closing Requirements _____

Date Close of Escrow or Transaction_____

Loan Co. _____ Date Application Made _____ Approved _____

( ) _____ FHA ( ) _____ Appraisal Ordered _____ Approved _____

Make 100 Contacts "Just Sold" By Phone Or In Person_____

Seller A Buyer?_____ Call Them Immediately_____

After Close Of Escrow Or Transaction—Give Gift_____

ADDRESS_____

SELLER _____ BUYER _____

LISTING NO. _____ SALE NO. _____

FIGURE 7.3 (continued)

SERVICE YOUR LISTING

Calling Twenty Neighbors: <u>THESE CALLS SHOULD BE MADE BEFORE THE SIGN GOES ON PROPERTY.</u>

"Hello, Mrs. . . Please"

"Thank you, My name is . . . . with _____ . Some friends of mine have just listed their home on the market at . . . . Street, and I am calling to let you know it's for sale, and to give you the first opportunity to select your new neighbor. Would you be offended if I asked you a few questions that will help us do that?"

"Have any of your friends or relatives ever suggested they would like to move to your neighborhood?"

"What kind of work does your husband do?"

   "Is there a friend of his at work who might be interested in buying a home in your area . . . or a home other than this one?"

"How long have you lived in the area?"

"Have you ever considered taking some of the equity in your home and purchasing a home in the area as an investment?"

"Do you have any brothers or sisters?" Might one of them consider purchasing a home in this area as an investment?"

LIST OF THE TWENTY NEIGHBORS I TALKED WITH:

1._____   11._____
2._____   12._____
3._____   13._____
4._____   14._____
5._____   15._____
6._____   16._____
7._____   17._____
8._____   18._____
9._____   19._____
10._____   20._____

Prospects From Neighbor Contacts:_____
_____
_____

HOLDING AN OPEN HOUSE:

Tuesday: Call owners and ask that they be gone on Sunday.
          Have Manager place ad in paper.

Wednesday: Canvas - Open House cards or flyers to 100 people in area.

Saturday: Ask seller to cooperate by having everything neat and ready.
           Make a list of amenities with seller to hand out at open house.
           Make signs to sit around house pointing out special features.

DAY OF OPEN HOUSE:

           Call on people where you sent cards, remind them of open house.
           Invite them to bring their friends.
           Don't forget to tell them the owner will be away.
           When putting up flages, don't forget to knock on the doors of property owners and invite them to your open house.
           Have your "Open House" guest book prepared, and ask visitors to sign it.

NEIGHBORS CONTACTED FOR OPEN HOUSE:

1._____   11._____
2._____   12._____
3._____   13._____
4._____   14._____
5._____   15._____
6._____   16._____
7._____   17._____
8._____   18._____
9._____   19._____

FIGURE 7.3 (continued)

SERVICING YOUR LISTING

Date Taken ( )	CALL EVERY WEEK	VISIT ONCE A MONTH
1st Week (date) ( )	Tell Seller of caravan schedule. Contact immediately after caravan. Discuss salesmen's comments. Ask owner to save all business cards. Mail "Thank You" card. Develop "for sale" flyer for canvassing. COMMENTS: _____	
2nd Week (date) ( )	Open house arrangements made if necessary or beneficial. Discuss any suggested improvements to property, i.e., lawns, paint, etc.; Advise on current financing. Check listing book, make certain no errors or omissions. Develop "open house" flyer. COMMENTS: _____	
3rd Week (date) ( )	Discuss reactions of prospective buyers and results of open house after contacting all prospects and visiting sales people. Make suggestions for price, terms, condition changes if needed. Mail "Thank You" card. COMMENTS: _____	
4th Week (date) ( )	New listings and sales in area. Request GI or FHA terms if applicable. Price reduction and any other problem areas. Schedule 2nd Open House if applicable. Develop flyer as to change in terms. COMMENTS: _____	
5th Week (date) ( )	Visit in person. Pick up all business cards and call for opinions. Discuss and review all aspects of this listing. Check property for changes you have suggested. Discuss current finance market. Check condition of sign and lockbox. Mail "Thank You" card. COMMENTS: _____	
6th Week (date) ( )	Discuss current activity in area - sales, listing, etc. Discuss price, terms and conditions. Open House arrangements made for this weekend if beneficial. COMMENTS: _____	
7th Week (date) ( )	Review results of open house and response of other salesmen to listing. If price change is required, BE FIRM but polite in asking for it. Review comps again. Mail "Thank You" card. COMMENTS: _____	
8th Week ' date) ( )	Visit owner this week. IF NOT SOLD by now you definitely need some changes. DO NOT PROCRASTINATE...DO NOT SHIRK YOUR OBLIGATIONS. Does owner really want to sell? MANAGERS INSPECTION (check condition of sign and lockbox). Develop flyer - change terms. COMMENTS: _____	
9th Week (date) ( )	Arrange caravan for new salesmen, and forgetful old salesmen. Get written opinion from salesmen. Mail "Thank You" card. Arrange for Open House if beneficial. COMMENTS: _____	
10th Week (date) ( )	Review last week's caravan - in person. Pick up all company and other Broker cards and get these salesmen's opinions on saleability. COMMENTS: _____	
11th Week (date) ( )	Discuss company and other broker comments. Discuss price, terms and conditions; sales and new listings in area; marketing; current financing, etc. Mail "Thank You" card. COMMENTS: _____	
12th Week (date) ( )	Discuss activity - local and general. COMMENTS: _____	
13th Week (date) ( )	Consider another Open House. Review with broker and salesmen. Mail "Thank You" card. COMMENTS: _____	
14th Week (date) ( )	Advise seller on results of open house - reaction of drop-in buyers, visiting brokers. Discuss price, terms, and conditions of this listing. COMMENTS: _____	
15th Week (date) ( )	Strongly present and recommend changes you feel will increase saleability of home - price, terms, conditions. Mail "Thank You" card. COMMENTS: _____	
16th Week (date) ( )	VISIT OWNER THIS WEEK: KEEP UP YOUR COMMUNICATIONS WITH SELLER - CONTINUE TO CALL WEEKLY.	

cate. By contacting every owner on the same day of the week with a status report by letter as well as by telephone, you need not worry about keeping owners informed. Many agents fear contacting owners when there is no activity on the property for several weeks. Actually, it is a problem that should be viewed as an opportunity. The problem might be in the condition of the property and/or the price that can be remedied with work on the property and/or a price adjustment.

All owner contacts and comments should be entered into the property file folder or computer file. Your weekly contacts should cover advertising, open houses, responses to ads and showings, as well as other marketing efforts, such as contacts with neighbors.

Discuss open houses with the owners. Let them know your strategy and how they can assist. Send copies of your property briefs for other listings, new MLS brochures and updated CMAs so they know what is happening in the marketplace. Is the sales activity in the marketplace going up or down? What is happening in the area of financing? Is their house competitive with comparable houses for sale? Let them know.

By keeping in touch, you will have a salable listing as well as a good center of influence for future business. Remember, your success is in direct proportion to the quantity and quality of service you give the public.

Chapter 8

Advertising and Public Relations

ADVERTISING OBJECTIVES

While the quantity and kind of advertising differs from firm to firm, the reasons for real estate advertising are universal. Good advertising gets the name of the firm into the public eye and mind, helps create goodwill and prestige, leads to listings, attracts prospects, helps market specific properties and informs the public about real estate.

Although any and all of these objectives could be accomplished through personal contact, advertising is the most efficient and effective way to get the job done.

SCOPE OF AN ADVERTISING PROGRAM

In most residential real estate firms the largest percentage of the company dollar is spent on advertising. In a small office advertising may be limited to For Sale signs, classified ads and occasional direct mailings prepared by salespeople or the broker. A large, departmentalized firm is likely to employ a wide range of media and may either have its own advertising department or retain an advertising agency to handle the work. No matter what size the firm or how much money is spent, it is important that all salespeople know about the campaign so they can tell clients what is being done on their behalf.

Two Kinds of Advertising

Real estate advertising can be divided into two categories: marketing and institutional.

Marketing advertising, aimed at obtaining listings and finding buyers, consists of classified and display ads in print media to promote specific properties, radio and television commercials, direct mail and outdoor advertising.

Institutional ads, which also use display ads, commercials, direct mail and outdoor advertising, put the firm's name before the public and explain the services it offers or the philosophy of the real estate business. This kind of advertising promotes the name of the firm, tells the public about the quality of the firm's operation and reinforces logo recognition. A logo is a distinctive design or symbol used by a firm. It could even be a particular type style for the company name.

The primary difference between these two kinds of advertising is the purpose for which they are used. If an ad is used primarily to promote the firm's reputation, the advertising is generally institutional. When it is geared toward attracting buyers and sellers, it is usually considered marketing advertising. However, marketing advertising will also have some institutional impact if it repeats and reinforces the public's recognition of the firm's name and logo. Real estate salespeople advertise themselves in an institutional manner through business cards (often with photographs), name tags and magnetic car signs. In these formats, they let others know they are engaged in the real estate profession and their affiliation. A REALTOR® designation should be included to show that they are members of the NATIONAL ASSOCIATION OF REALTORS® and subscribe to its Code of Ethics.

Consistency in Advertising

Logos, slogans and company colors convey your company's image whether they appear on For Sale signs, stationery, direct mail pieces, premium giveaways or in classified and institutional ads. Changes should be made with great care and should not be made too frequently lest they interrupt the continuity of the message. Colors and logos should be consistent and should be used in signs and ads so that the public will recognize the firm. People inside a company often tire of a theme or program long before it has made its maximum impact in the marketplace.

Evaluating Effectiveness of Advertising

Most firms follow regular routines to measure response to their classified and display ads and then use these data to determine the program's effectiveness. Each time someone calls or comes into the office, the salesperson or office staff member asks how he or she came to contact the firm. If it is in response to an ad, the person is asked the name of the newspaper or radio or TV station and the date of the ad. By keeping this and other written records, the broker and the sales staff know which media generate action and which days of the week ads pull the best response. Firms can ascertain the response to ads in a particular medium, a particular ad and a type of ad. This knowledge is valuable in preparing ads to maximize the effect of a firm's advertising dollars.

It is more difficult to measure the effectiveness of institutional campaigns. REALTORS®, their salespeople and office staff have to keep attuned to public reaction to advertising that does not draw measurable response.

CLASSIFIED ADS

Classified newspaper ads are the REALTOR®'s most common advertising tool. A good classified ad serves a variety of purposes:

- Brings buyers to a broker who has properties to sell
- Helps the broker obtain more listings
- Builds familiarity with a real estate firm
- Brings traffic to a real estate office
- Keeps firm name in the public eye
- Stimulates word-of-mouth advertising
- Promotes individuals when their names appear in ads
- Increases staff loyalty and pride in the firm
- Helps persuade people with down payment money to spend it on real estate
- Tells the public the range of services a firm has to offer
- Helps persuade sellers that your firm can market property better than they can
- Lets the owners know you are working to sell their property

Writing Classified Ads

Since the listing salesperson is most familiar with the property to be advertised, it is up to that salesperson to describe the property, whether he or she writes the ad or gives someone else the information. Whoever writes ads, it is important that the style conforms to the firm's image and the ongoing advertising program.

The classified ad should not tell the whole story but should leave some question or curiosity in readers' minds so they will want to inquire further. If the ad tells readers everything they want to know about a property, chances are they may not call. When you omit certain essential information intentionally or use a technical term to describe a property's unique feature, inquiries are generated.

When you write ad copy, the major objective is to create a visually appealing ad with good descriptive copy that embodies the points you would make if you were selling the prospect in person.

Keep in mind that advertisements do not sell real estate; salespeople sell real estate. The purpose of your ad is the same A-I-D-A approach described earlier. Get the reader's attention, then interest, followed by desire that will culminate in action, which in the case of a classified ad is either a telephone call or a visit to either the real estate office or the advertised property for more information.

Some Do's

Collect all the facts. Once you are well acquainted with the property, think about what it has to offer the different members of a family, a person living alone or someone who wants to use it as a business investment. Then write the ad.

Get the main benefits in the first five to eight words. Start with the headline. It should dominate the ad and highlight the single most salable feature—location, view, price, emotional appeal, architecture, condition or size. Examples of headlines that get a reader's attention would be "Four Bedrooms," "Zoned for Horses," or "Under $100,000." A particularly desirable area could also be a headline feature, such as "Orchard Ridge." In many areas view is an important feature, and it could be expressed as "Magnificent Mountain Vistas."

When there is no strong feature that buyers are seeking, you should consider an attention-getting headline to compel readers to read the body of the ad. Although readers may read every ad in smaller markets, in large markets your ads may be in competition with hundreds of others for comparable properties. Examples of attention-getting headlines would be "Like a Fine Wine," "Nuts," "Remember When," etc. The ad body must flow from the headline and use adjectives that provide the reader with a positive mental picture of the property. However, it is important to be honest in your portrayal of the property.

While an ad that mentions mechanical problems could keep car buyers away, negative advertising can be very effective in real estate. Many agents report the highest number of responses when they advertise "fixer-upper" properties. Problems with a property attract callers who sense a bargain.

Your ad should be bold, dramatic and original. The 12 most persuasive words in the English language, as determined by a group of researchers at Yale, are: save, need, easy, discovery, money, results, safety, proven, you, health, love and guarantee.

Make the body copy easy to read. Give important details only, such as number of bedrooms.

A Newspaper Advertising Bureau survey of people planning to move indicates that each homebuyer has one lifestyle element as a primary deciding factor. The most popular ones are spaciousness, a showplace, good place for children, solid comfort, easy maintenance, safe neighborhood, ease of commuting, privacy, place to swim or keep fit, lots of conveniences nearby, pushbutton living (inside is most important) and natural surroundings (outside is most important).

Ask for action. Make it easy for the prospect to respond. Create a clincher that stimulates the reader to do something positive, like call your office or attend an open house.

Give your firm prominent identification. Provide readers with an easy-to-spot phone number, address, office hours or even directions to your office (or the property advertised, if it's an open house).

Plan a good layout. Let the headline stand apart from the rest of the copy. If you list more than one property, leave a little open space between each one.

Be truthful.

Some Don'ts

Don't use vague generalities, worn-out phrases or too many superlatives. Words like *cute* and *cozy* have been overworked.

Don't use too many abbreviations. They make an ad look more like a puzzle than an invitation to buy.

Don't write an ad to fit a predetermined number of lines. Ads that are 20 percent longer might increase responses by 50 percent or more.

Don't use headlines that tease or bully. They could turn readers away.

Don't paint an untrue word picture. It will destroy your credibility with a prospect who comes to look at the property.

There are, of course, many more techniques to good classified advertising. Study all the real estate classifieds in your papers and decide what makes a good ad and why.

There are a number of excellent books that will aid you in understanding how to write effective classified ads. In addition, classified advertising personnel at your local paper may be able to assist you with ideas on effective ad layout, headlines and wording. However, always keep in mind that you want your ads to stand out from all the others.

DISPLAY ADVERTISING

The big plus in display advertising is the use of pictures, showing what a REALTOR®'s best properties look like. Word descriptions under the pictures may not be complete; but because most people are basically interested in looking at the property pictured, a brief description sometimes helps. If it leaves several questions unanswered in the reader's mind, it can generate a call for more information. Besides newspapers, display ads are frequently used in homebuyer magazines. It is important to have a high-contrast photograph or it will not reproduce well.

Display ads can be used to describe several properties, even when only one is illustrated. Display ads are often used for new subdivision or builder sales.

DIRECT MAIL

Small firms find direct mail campaigns particularly effective in telling their market audience about properties they have for sale, whether residential or commercial-investment. When possible, the mailing piece should provide a place for a salesperson's signature or a pocket for a business card enclosure to lend a personal touch. Direct mail is the costliest advertising in terms of cost per contact, but it nevertheless can be effective both in obtaining listings and in attracting the interest of prospective buyers in properties that you have for sale.

An excellent approach is to combine the direct mail piece with a telephone call. The mailer will indicate that you will be calling the recipient.

Direct mail pieces can include a return coupon or card the recipient can use to indicate further interest in the promotion. A record of responses will provide the firm with a measure of the effectiveness of the program.

Direct mail brochures are often quite effective in selling commercial-investment property. Brochures describe only one property; but if that property is worth a half-million dollars and the brochure helps sell it, the money has been well invested. Such a mailing would be directed to a carefully developed list of private investors, syndicators, corporate investors and others chosen for their natural interest in a specific property.

INSTITUTIONAL CLASSIFIED

Classified ads can carry a firm's institutional message by brief mention of special services the firm has available, worded to generate phone inquiries for details.

An editorial column advertisement is effective when done well. Written by a REALTOR® or a member of his or her staff or agency, it looks like a regular news feature or other editorial column except that it must be marked "Advertisement" or "Paid Advertisement." Such a column can feature tips on investment real estate, the climate of the local real estate market, suggestions on buying and selling homes and other real estate topics. Regardless of the content, the fact that the column appears regularly with the firm's name on it (and perhaps a picture of the person who signs it) adds to the REALTOR®'s advertising impact. But it must be produced by someone who writes well and can meet a regular deadline. The cost of such a lengthy regular feature may be high, but in many instances the returns in sales and goodwill more than compensate for the dollars spent.

RADIO AND TELEVISION

Though the initial cost is high, electronic media ads often bring results equal to newspaper classifieds at the same time they serve a strong institutional purpose. Effective radio and television advertising requires special competence in both choosing outlets and preparation of text and visuals. Televised real estate showcase programs can be effective in advertising more expensive properties as well as for subdivision sales. Many firms have experienced excellent results from cable television bulletin board channels. Besides pictures and text, many bulletin board channels now provide verbal descriptions of properties as well. Firms using these media should get the best professional counsel available.

SIGNS AND BILLBOARDS

Your firm's For Sale and Sold signs serve as strong institutional advertisements, telling the local public how active you are in the marketplace. Colors, typeface and design are important.

Signs should carry a minimum of text. Their visual strength is in your color and a good logo, the identifying mark of your company.

Billboards also keep the firm name in the public eye. Giant versions of small property signs, they literally shout the firm's name and logo to people as they drive by.

There is a rule of thumb that billboard text should be limited to no more than five words that can be read in four seconds. Billboards require the services of an ad agency for both design and placement. They are used most frequently to advertise a residential development or commercial-industrial complex. Some large firms now use them in an institutional way in large cities, keeping their name in the public eye.

In rural areas, for a modest fee, a broker might be able to obtain permission to erect his or her own large sign. Such a sign might be cost-effective. However, billboards on major traffic routes around larger cities can be very expensive. Costs can exceed $2,000 per month for just one large bulletin sign. These high costs make billboards too expensive for institutional advertising for the majority of brokers.

Smaller versions of outdoor ads are used in public transportation spaces—airport corridors, buses and trains. Some taxi companies sell display ad space inside their cabs. These display ads not only catch the eye of local people but also get a firm's name before newcomers quickly.

TRUTH-IN-LENDING

The provisions of the Truth-In-Lending Act of 1969 are important in all kinds of advertising. Anyone in a real estate firm directly or indirectly responsible for advertising should be completely familiar with the act.

Basically, the law restricts the language that can be used in advertising relating to terms of purchase or financing unless all financial information is included. REALTORS® can advertise the annual percentage rate but not the pure interest rate, or they can avoid mentioning any financing terms in their advertisements. Your broker will advise you how his or her advertising program conforms to the act.

PUBLIC RELATIONS, PROMOTION AND PUBLICITY

Public respect, goodwill and faith in your firm must be earned. Everything every member of the firm does becomes part of its public relations, creating an image that cannot be bought. Good public relations are "deeds first, words last." Implied in this is the public's trust in the firm, its people and its ethics, and its concern for the well-being of its clients.

How can salespeople earn the respect, goodwill and faith of the public they serve? They can carry out their firm's policy by both actions and words.

Actions include everything from a positive attitude toward the job, the firm and the community they are selling. Enthusiasm for the job includes being on time and doing what you promised. Positive thinking about the firm can be conveyed all through the working day as you let people know you believe you are working with the best company in the business.

Belief in the community begins with the job and carries through to devoting some free time to taking part in business, civic, service or other organizations that need help and support.

Promotion and publicity are the "last words" of public relations. The firm promotes its public image when it publicizes its actions and achievements. Promotion includes helping a worthy cause or project succeed by taking an ad in a benefit program, lending window space to publicize a project, donating premiums or prizes for benefits, sponsoring sports teams, having a float in the town parade or perhaps providing balloons for everybody who attends.

Promotion and publicity are bound only by what a company can do in good taste within the limits of its budget.

There are other things real estate firms can do that are a combination of promotion, public relations and what amounts to institutional advertising.

Working with news media people is one. Most newspapers and radio and television stations have a reporter assigned to cover real estate news in the local market. While you as a salesperson may not be assigned to work with these reporters, you can help your broker identify possible news stories to suggest to them.

Some REALTORS® encourage their staff people to get acquainted with reporters and editors, knowing that it pays to be a reliable source of real estate news and facts. Media news people and real estate professionals share a common interest in promoting the attractiveness of a town or market area as a good place to live and/or work.

In order to increase newspaper coverage of your firm's activities, you should make it easy for the newspaper. Provide the newspaper with a completed press release article with appropriate headline as well as a 5″ × 7″ or 8″ × 10″ high-contrast glossy photograph. With masking tape, attach photo caption identifying any persons in the photo.

Ideas for press releases could include new hires, promotions, educational achievements, professional designations earned, sales achievements, listing achievements, interesting sales or listings (dollar amount, well-known seller or historical property), interesting or celebrity buyers, new office opening, change of office, change of ownership, and so on.

Radio talk shows offer another unique opportunity to cooperate. Some shows have guests who discuss their area of expertise with the host and accept telephone queries from the listening audience. Such exposure is a fine way to widen the public's acquaintance with your name and your firm.

Listen to these shows and become familiar with their format. Then list several suggestions for real estate topics you believe would interest their audience. Call the show's producer for an appointment and discuss briefly why you think real estate would be a good topic for the show. The producer may accept any of your good ideas or may ask you to develop one you had not thought of. Cooperate. It could be the beginning of a profitable relationship.

Chapter 9

Finding and Working with the Buyer

Once you have listed a property, you have made that first sale mentioned in Chapter 6. Your next challenge is to find a buyer, consummate the second sale and earn your commission on both.

PROSPECT SOURCES

It is just as important in selling as it is in listing to let as many people as possible know you are in the real estate business. You should also be thoroughly familiar with every listing in your firm and well-acquainted with other listings in your farm area. Study the classified and display ads so you will be prepared to talk intelligently to whomever calls in response to them. You should consider other properties that a caller on a specific ad would be interested in. In this way you will be prepared if it becomes apparent the advertised property is not suited to the caller's needs.

You should have a street map that clearly shows properties with your firm's For Sale signs. You can do this with stick-on markers. Often callers will have the right area but the wrong street and/or address; a readily available map will help you quickly locate which property the caller is interested in. There are several computer programs designed for this purpose. An area or street and general features will identify the appropriate listing.

Your inquiries will come from a variety of sources. Ads locate some buyers and make the phone ring. The Tell 20 system mentioned in Chapter 7 is a good source to cultivate either in person or by phone. The breadth and depth of your acquaintance in your market can be a rich source of prospects.

The long list of contacts in Chapter 6 (see page 84) will be just as valuable in cultivating buyer prospects. Open houses attract prospects, especially in areas that do not have multiple listing services. There will be some casual walk-ins at the office, inspired by properties displayed in your windows or a spontaneous decision to start looking for another place to live. An especially promising source is referrals who call or come into the office because you or your firm was recommended.

All these sources are reasons to take floor time because it keeps you on the scene where important activity is taking place and gives you a turn at telephone inquiries.

Other sources will depend on your generating interest in specific listings. Keep a good file of potential buyers and go through these names regularly to try to match their needs to your listings. Keeping in touch with these people will help you think of them when new listings are put into the system. And you will build their confidence in you by letting them know you remember them.

GETTING READY FOR TELEPHONE CALLS

Ads make the phone ring. So do referrals. So it is very important to handle telephone inquiries with skill.

If you do not have a computer file to update daily, clip the classified ads for your market from your daily newspaper. Paste each on a separate 3 × 5 card, leaving room to list similar properties you know. With these cards, you are ready to talk about any advertised property being called about as well as suggesting similar listings the caller ought to see.

Callers have probably marked other ads to call about besides your property. If you are unable to obtain an appointment from a call about your property, ask if there are other ads of interest to the callers. You should volunteer your help and try for an appointment to show the callers properties listed by another agent.

When you have made an appointment from a call, you don't want your prospects to remain on the phone calling other agents about their advertisements. You might consider asking the callers to go through the classified ads and mark other properties that are of interest and bring the paper with them to your office. You then can provide additional information and arrange to show any properties of interest.

This makes it easy for the buyers and helps to keep them with your office.

USING THE TELEPHONE SKILLFULLY

People skilled in telephone communications say that if you smile as you pick up the phone, you convey an immediate feeling of goodwill to the caller.

Successful salespeople also say they think "sell" as they pick up the phone. Whether you are smiling, thinking "sell" or doing both, answer the phone on the first ring if possible!

Your objective when answering a telephone inquiry is to get an appointment. You need to determine whether the person calling is an interested buyer or just a curious neighbor. Don't automatically dismiss calls from neighbors as a nuisance. Neighbors might be calling because they have some friend or relative they feel will be interested in the property. A few questions could reveal a prospective buyer.

Do not try to sell the property over the telephone. You want to create an interest and establish rapport with the caller-prospect, get to know something about him or her and get an appointment to show the property or other property. Of course, you will want to qualify prospective buyers prior to any showings.

Callers' emotions are at a high level. If they are serious prospects, they are thinking about a very important purchase. It is your task to keep their enthusiasm high and satisfy their curiosity about the property while you establish rapport and persuade them to make an appointment to see you in person. Open the conversation by giving your name slowly and asking for the caller's name. Use the caller's name several times during this initial conversation. It will help to fix it in your mind, and people like being addressed by their names. Get the caller's address and telephone number as quickly as possible so you will be able to follow up. Learn how to give some information in response to questions and end your statement with a return question, thus forcing callers to respond with information you need. Many experts on telephone technique say that you should actually be giving more information than you get. You must avoid giving trivial details. After you have the appointment, end the call on a positive note by telling the prospects that you look forward to meeting them and you feel certain that you have a property that will meet their needs.

Most companies have a prospect profile form to remind salespeople of every point to cover in telephone qualifying. You begin to qualify during the initial contact. For example, if someone calls your office about an ad or in response to a For Sale sign, ask a few basic questions to establish rapport, then attempt to set up an appointment to show the property and/or discuss the prospective buyer's needs.

Ask questions that elicit a response that is more than a yes or no. Stimulate conversational replies, then listen carefully. And, of course, arrange the appointment as soon as possible. The positive choice technique works well in arranging appointments; for example, "I can arrange to show you and your husband this lovely home today at 3 PM, or would 4 PM be more convenient for you?"

Phone Problems

The following are a few problem situations you may encounter in your first telephone call from a prospect and suggestions for handling them successfully.

The caller will not give a name. It may be a nosy neighbor, in which case there is no way you can get the name. On the other hand, if the caller is sincere (you will develop an "ear" that can distinguish between the two), offer to send something—a map, a packet about the area or information on another property. To do this you will need the name and address, which you can usually get. It's a good idea to get the phone number, too.

The caller is "just checking" or "calling for a friend." Continue the conversation until you know if it is authentic interest worth pursuing. Where did the caller hear about the listing? Is he or she familiar with the area? The answers to these questions should help indicate the caller's sincerity.

The caller names another salesperson he or she is working with. If you know that other person, you can say that the caller is in good hands. You might suggest they ask the other salesperson to show them the property, in case it is a firm that concentrates on its own listings. It is courteous to call the other salesperson, telling him his client called about a listing and that you urged him to see it. The other salesperson may sound embarrassed, but he is likely to be pleased and may someday return the favor. Often the "other salesperson" is nonexistent. Some salespeople say, "If you will give me the salesperson's name I will call and tell [him/her] about the property so [he/she] can arrange to show it to you. Or, if you prefer, I can show it to you today at 3 PM—or would 4 PM be more convenient?" If they make an appointment with you, you can be sure that they do not consider themselves obligated to any other agent.

Callers say they are not ready to look just yet. Probe a little to learn the reason. If they say they simply don't want to be bothered with calls, assure them you will leave them alone and that your main interest is in trying to help. If they seem to just be procrastinating, you may persuade them to see you by offering alternate hours for a house call: "I could come out at either two or four o'clock on Tuesday. Which would you prefer?" That way you both sound like busy people trying to find a little time to discuss an important matter.

The caller wants to drive by the property. If you do not want to give out the address, your reply could be "It wouldn't be fair to you or the owner to give you the address. By just a casual exterior inspection you will miss a home that I really believe will excite you. I can arrange to show you this exceptional property at 3 PM today—or would 4 PM be more convenient for you?" Another valid reason could be the owner's instructions not to give the address to anyone not accompanied by a salesperson. It might also be against company policy. Both reasons can be presented as a means of protecting owners, and may persuade callers to let you show them the property.

Telephone Courtesies

Good telephone manners are not only important in dealing with clients, they also affect your relationships with other sales associates. Here's a checklist of questions to remind you what not to do.

- Do you let the phone ring three or four times before answering?
- Do you forget to take a message or take a garbled, incomplete one?
- Do you interrogate the caller with questions like "Who's calling?" and "What do you want?"
- Do you leave callers hanging several minutes while you look up some fact without asking if they would rather you call back?
- Do you carry on a conversation in your office while talking to someone on the telephone?
- Do you talk with a cigarette, gum or pencil in your mouth?
- Do you talk too fast?
- Do you fail to have handy the information you are likely to be called about?
- Do you repeatedly interrupt your caller in mid-sentence?
- Do you speak so indistinctly that you are asked to repeat yourself several times?
- Do you continue to talk after you have tied down an appointment?
- Do you sign off abruptly without giving the caller a chance to finish?
- Do you bang down the receiver?

QUALIFYING

Qualifying is the who, what, when, where, why and how of the customer's needs. You have to know the questions to ask, then listen carefully to the answers. Full communication is necessary if you are to select the right properties to show.

Why qualify? It is your obligation to yourself to determine whether or not your prospect is a qualified buyer. If he or she will not or cannot buy, you have not only lost time, you have also lost money. If you do not take time to qualify carefully, you could find yourself in an embarrassing position at or near the time of closing with both a seller and a buyer who are frustrated and angered by your carelessness.

Where Does Qualifying Begin?

Qualifying should start with the initial contact and should not cease until a contract is negotiated and signed. If the buyer is under pressure to find a property quickly (as in the case of sudden transfers), you will have to work more quickly and spend more time in an intensified qualifying check. But accuracy and thoroughness are essential no matter what the circumstances.

The qualifying interview should take place in a quiet spot where you can visit openly and frankly—a place as free of interruption as possible. Some salespeople prefer to arrange the initial meeting on their own ground, the office, feeling it puts them in the most favorable position to create confidence, and because all the tools of the trade are available there to assist in the presentation. Others prefer to meet prospects in their home so they can see the prospects' living style and gauge more accurately the type of people they are dealing with.

What Qualifying Determines

Qualifying will tell you the following:

Who the buyers are; who their friends are or will be; whom they work for or will be working for; who they want to impress or are impressed by; and who referred them to you.

What type, style and size home they need; their income, debt and debt service; their hobbies; their motivations; their children's ages; and what they do not like about their present home.

When they have to move; when they started looking for a home; when you can meet with them.

Where they are now living; where they worship; and where they plan to go from here.

Why they are making this move (transfer, desire to move up or down, financial reasons, divorce, change of location).

There are really two separate qualifications—one is needs and the other is financial.

You should not start showing homes that prospective buyers have expressed an interest in until you know that they are financially qualified for the purchase.

Qualifying Interview

Begin the interview with a request for the prospect's permission to ask personal questions, so that midway through your interview the climate is not destroyed by an objection to a question you pose. (One way to get permission is to suggest that your desire to help solve housing needs is similar to a doctor's need to know patients' symptoms before the doctor can prescribe treatment.)

Clues

You have a beginning clue to their needs in the ad to which the prospective buyers responded. You have even stronger clues if they called in response to a For Sale sign. (You know a house size and style that appeal to them and a neighborhood that interests them.) However, don't assume that prospects can afford to buy the home they call about. You will have to determine their financial capability. Similarly, the way prospects dress or the cars they drive are poor indicators of their financial qualifications. Avoid acting on your initial impressions.

Ask pertinent questions about family size and the number of people who will be living in the new home. Encourage the prospects to talk about their social and business expectations and ambitions and the importance to them of community and civic life. In answering these questions, buyers reveal a lot about themselves; but you will still have to do some reading between the lines.

Urgency

Urgency can be an important qualifying point. Are the buyers' needs urgent enough for you to clear your schedule and give them your full attention? For example, people who have sold their former home and are living in a motel deserve your undivided attention. You want to explain to them that you will be giving them 100 percent of your time for the next few days to solve their housing problems, but in exchange you expect 100 percent of their time. This shows prospects that you value your time, understand the urgency of their needs and will accommodate your busy schedule in a professional way.

THE "4-7-3" FORMULA

The "4-7-3" formula is a series of qualifying questions. The sequence in which they are used is flexible. Many variations will produce the results you want. The strength of the formula is that your qualifying questions are structured. This structured approach will produce useful information rather than just conversation, and you won't fumble and stumble through qualifying interviews.

Four Questions

Four preliminary questions should be asked during your first contact, which most likely will be by telephone. They help you determine if the prospect is a looker, a professional shopper or a real buyer.

These are the questions to ask:

1. Do you own your own home now? (If the answer is yes, proceed to the next question.)
2. Are you planning to sell it before you buy another?
3. Is your property already listed with another broker? (If the answer is no, proceed to the next question.)
4. Are you planning to list it?

Seven-Days-a-Week Test

Another question helps separate the wheat from the chaff, the motivated buyer from the nonmotivated one. The question is structured as follows: "If you'd like me to help you find a home, I'll be working for you seven days a week. I'll contact you whenever I find a property I think is right for you. How does that suit you?" Serious buyers will be pleased to learn that you want to work diligently for them; prospects who are not really ready to buy will not welcome such a commitment from you.

You can also ask prospects to call you about ads that interest them (even ads from other agents) or about any interesting homes that have For Sale signs. In this way, you are enlisting them as active helpers.

Three Follow-Up Questions

1. How long have you been looking for a house?
2. Have you looked with any other brokers?
3. Which property appealed to you most?

These three questions usually produce better results after you have met your prospects and can discuss their preferences in person. You will find out if they are hard to please, unsure of what they want, confused from having seen so many properties, whether the looking has been haphazard or planned, or if they have come close to making an offer on any property. Successful salespeople ask questions to get answers that serve as beacons, showing them the way to a sale.

Financial Qualifying

Successful residential salespeople say financial qualifying seeks the answer to these questions:

How much cash is available? Is it in the form of cash or equity in property? What jobs will support the purchase and what net income do they produce? How much other debt has been incurred?

Can the buyers write a contract today? Can they make a deposit? How large a deposit can they make?

FINANCES

Finance questions should tell you quickly whether buyers can invest in a property immediately or whether they must first sell another place. Questioning along this line should reveal their financial situation in general, what down payment is possible and what their outstanding obligations are.

If you win their confidence as the interview proceeds, prospects are likely to show no reluctance to share details of their financial situation. Determine the amount of any current mortgage balance and an estimate of the equity they have in their present home. Add these two figures to determine what value the prospects have placed on their present home. This opens the way to discuss financing options.

In many areas, you can contact lenders by telephone and get a quick conditional commitment as to the amount of loan that buyers will qualify for. You should also be aware of the lender ratios used for conventional, FHA and VA loans. If you understand ratios, you can determine with a fair degree of accuracy the ability of prospective buyers to borrow. Lenders customarily use both a front-end and back-end ratio. The front-end ratio is the percentage of total monthly income that the borrowers can use for housing costs (principal, interest, taxes and insurance). If the lender's front-end ratio is 28 percent and prospective buyers have a monthly gross income of $3,000, they can spend $840 per month for principal, interest, taxes and insurance payments. Estimating taxes and insurance and deducting this amount from $840 will tell you how much they can pay for principal and interest. By using a loan amortization book at current interest rates for different types of loans, you can determine how large a loan the buyers will qualify for. Borrowers must also meet the requirements of a back-end ratio, which is the percentage of gross monthly income that can be spent on principal, interest, taxes and insurance (total housing costs) plus long-term debt service. (Long-term debt might include car payments and credit card payments as well as other loans generally made for one year or more.) This ratio might be 36 percent. If the gross income is $3,000 per month and the back-end ratio is 36 percent, then the purchasers can spend no more than $1,080 per month for housing costs plus payments on the long-term debt. Down payments will vary by lender, if there is private mortgage insurance, and by type of loan. The prospective buyers' down payment could limit the type of loan available. The down payment plus the loan that the prospects qualify for determines maximum total purchase price.

Even though you have gone through the ratios, you still want prospective buyers to be prequalified by a lender. If the prospects fill out the prequalification forms at your office, they will feel a greater obligation to work through you. The lender could also discover problems that could save you a lot of wasted effort and redirect any effort toward owner-financing situations.

There are loan calculators available that will allow you to quickly compute what buyers will qualify for. Even better, there are computer programs that not only compute the data but will give buyers a printout showing how they qualify for the various types of loans at current interest rates.

At some point in discussing finance, you should explain the costs of settlement on a property. Many buyers have been dismayed to discover on the day of closing that they must put up more cash than they had planned to cover legal fees, taxes, insurance premiums and other items usually adjusted to the date of closing. If the buyer will be a first-time owner or is coming to your area from another state, this discussion is especially important.

Once you have the facts on a prospect's present financial status, you will want to discuss mortgage financing and monthly payments, making full disclosure of all the costs involved in owning the subject property.

First-time homebuyers may have no concept of what they can afford. And experienced, conservative buyers may not realize that their income justifies monthly payments higher than they plan. However, many buyers are knowledgeable in regard to what they will pay or can afford. Housing may be only part of what they are interested in acquiring or enjoying.

It takes courage to tell people what they can or cannot buy. Salespeople who are afraid to ask financial questions and to tell people their limits generally can expect to have many sales fail to close.

The Investment Property Buyer

It is particularly important to qualify buyers of investment property. Many brokers use a counseling session technique to determine what people in the market for investment real estate need, want and can support financially. Are buyers looking for income today or appreciation? Are they looking for tax benefits? Can they maintain the property themselves? Are they really interested in buying? What degree of risk are the buyers willing to accept for the possibility of greater return? Is the investment planned as a long-term or short-term investment? What other investment properties have the prospects owned? What properties do they presently own?

Your skills in understanding people are also needed to help confused buyers express their real needs. Many who know what they want appear incapable of expressing their needs until an intelligent, sensitive salesperson helps them formulate their ideas.

Are Others Involved?

Finally, regardless of buyers' ages use the qualifying interview to find out if anyone else will be assisting them in their decision on a new home. Many older people ask the advice of children and relatives; young couples often want parents or a contractor uncle or friend to pass judgment on the place of their choice. When this is the case, you will want to include this person in the showing sequence, particularly if he or she is not familiar with your market area. Otherwise, you risk lost time and perhaps a lost sale.

The New Home

Now you can begin to discuss the features your prospects want in a new home. By saving this part of the interview until last, you are in a position to direct the discussion toward the amenities available in homes in the prospects' price range.

If, at the beginning of the interview, you have encouraged the prospects to expound on all the features they want in a new home, you may have to end the discussion by taking away half their dream ideas to fit realities. You can spare all of you that embarrassment by thoughtful guidance. Having established the general price range, ask what features of their present home the family enjoys most and what they feel it lacks. Then listen carefully. This is the time you must learn what they are thinking. Master the art of asking questions, not answering them.

If prospective buyers say they want particular features, ask why. You might find that there are homes without this feature that will serve the prospects' needs.

Disclosures You must make certain that the buyers fully understand your role in the sale. Are you a sellers' agent, buyers' agent, dual agent or facilitator? Before they have the opportunity to disclose personal information to you, they should understand what it means to act in your specific capacity and that they have the right to choose. Some agents use a disclosure form that prospective buyers read and sign. Some states mandate such disclosure.

Closing the Qualifying Interview

As the qualifying interview comes to a close and you are setting an appointment to show properties, you can initiate a positive selling climate by asking, "If we find a home that meets your needs, will you be in a position to make a favorable decision that day?" This is a powerful question—a tested shortcut to success; time and again it has spotted the "I want to sleep on it" syndrome.

A well-conducted qualifying interview is expected by today's sophisticated buyer. Common sense dictates a professional approach that gathers information first, fits listings to buyer qualifications and saves the time of buyers, sellers and salespeople.

Many agents like to give prospective buyers a blank copy of a purchase contract before they finish the interview. They explain that when they find the home the prospects want, this is the form that will be used. By getting familiar with it in advance, buyers are less likely to be fearful of the form when it is time for signatures.

You should also consider giving prospective buyers a copy of *Buying a Home,* published by the NATIONAL ASSOCIATION OF REALTORS®, which points out the advantages of working with a REALTOR®.

SHOWING

From the moment you ask the first question in a qualifying interview until you believe you have all the data you need, your main purpose in asking questions is to build the buyers' confidence in and reliance on you. Asking questions and listening carefully to the answers will help persuade them that you are genuinely interested in serving their needs.

Sometimes it can be difficult to determine through qualifying what kind of property is most likely to attract buyers. There will be times when you simply cannot analyze a buyer's tastes and inclinations or learn in advance what his or her reaction is likely to be. You must ask prospective buyers questions about every house you show. You will want to know which features they liked best or didn't like, and why. What features did they wish the house possessed, and why? How did they react to the neighborhood, and what were the reasons for their feelings? You also want to know how each house compares with other homes they have seen. If the buyers tell you the other homes don't compare to the first house shown, they could be in a position for a natural closing. Keep in mind that you want the buyers to be doing the talking, and you should be doing the leading with your questions. Salespeople who tell are not nearly as successful as salespeople who ask.

Some salespeople deliberately show homes other than the one they hope to sell. Getting the buyer's reaction to these places gives you a better idea of what to say and show when you finally reach the property where you expect to put your real sales skills to work. This technique can be dangerous, because it can give prospective buyers the idea that you are not really listening to what they are saying.

Caveat It is essential that you keep firmly in mind that every person, regardless of race, creed, color, sex, national origin, familial status or disability is entitled to equal opportunity in housing. The law in this regard is discussed in Chapter 2.

Showing Routines

Plan your entire showing routine. Decide the sequence in which you will show properties. Don't choose properties based upon the fact that they are your own listings. If you choose properties based on what you believe are the buyers' needs, you are more likely to gain their trust. Call ahead and make showing appointments with the sellers, keeping the arrival time as flexible as possible. If you can get the sellers to agree to "sometime this morning" or "afternoon," that's fine. They may ask for a time limit of an hour or two; or you may suggest taking along the key or using the lockbox in case the seller is not at home—that is preferable anyway, giving you total privacy.

Do not become inflexible if buyers' reactions to a home make you realize that other homes you intended to show are not appropriate. Instead, notify owners that you will not be showing their property today. Then call to make new appointments.

Who Is Coming Along?

Know in advance who will be coming along to a showing. This is especially true in residential sales. En route to the property (or even before, if possible) you should find out if one spouse makes the decisions or if it is a mutual process. Or, if the prospective buyer is widowed or divorced, will a third person "going along for the ride" really decide whether the prospect should buy?

The third person may be lending money for a down payment or may be a knowledgeable friend on whose advice the sale may hinge. It is a mistake to ignore this individual, or to express annoyance at his or her presence. Instead, direct some leading questions to that person.

Most salespeople can recall sales they lost because they concentrated on the wrong person.

Try to avoid having the owner of the property accompany you during the showing. If possible, get the run of the house, since an owner's sales effort may undermine yours. Furthermore, if the owner brags about the property, the potential buyer may think the owner is overanxious to sell and conclude that the property can be bought at a much lower price.

Showing Techniques

Buyer confidence can be won or lost quickly by a salesperson's method of showing a home. No two showings are identical, but the following basic principles can be applied in most cases.

Show the house in relation to the area. Choose your route to the house so you take the prospects over pleasant streets, passing school, church and park or golf course on the way. Keep in mind that you have a duty to disclose any adverse material facts about property uses or features in the area that could affect buyer desirability. If it is impossible to take the buyers in your own car, suggest that you ride with them. This means they will have to return to your office after the showing. Meeting prospects at a property is a last resort. Make certain they have clear directions; you will reduce the likelihood of a drive-by without stopping if you have their name and telephone number.

If the property has good "curb appeal," park across the street so that the prospects can appreciate the property and its setting. Then walk to the front door with the thought of creating an "at home" feeling, which might not be possible if you enter the house too abruptly.

Point out the exterior features so the prospects will remember whether they are in a brick or frame house while you are showing them the rooms inside. Explain who the neighbors are and tell about other homes on the street, but do not stop for a detailed discussion. Walk directly to the door.

Introduce the prospective buyers to the owners if they are present. Personalize the visit to show that you feel that both the prospects and the owners (or tenants) are important and that you respect them. Introduce them properly by name and add a brief identification (their business connections or other appropriate information), if advisable, to show that you recognize their standing. You might think of yourself temporarily as their host.

Chat briefly, avoiding lengthy conversations. Take leave of the owner and proceed with your planned trip through the house as expeditiously as is polite and graceful.

Show the buyers what they want to see. Guide the way, but let your buyers take the lead in selecting the features that interest them most.

When you know what they want, focus on it. If prospects have already stated a preference for a large living room, be sure that they know the dimensions. Measure it to dramatize your statement that it is 35 feet long. If they mentioned sliding glass doors or a preference for vaulted ceilings or hardwood flooring, direct attention to what they said they wanted to see.

Let them visualize their family right there in the room. Remain quiet and give them an opportunity to mentally place their furniture and get the feeling of the room. Sell the prospects their own ideas, not yours. Let them indicate what they are looking for and help them feel they have found it.

Make each room mean something. Notice something about each room so that if the occasion arises, you can add something convincing to what the prospect says. For example, point out that the wall space in the bedroom will accommodate either twin beds or a king-size bed. You might ask "Whose bedroom will this be?" or "How would you use the extra bedroom?" Questions such as these make prospective buyers think in terms of ownership.

Suggest new uses—especially when the house does not contain facilities they have mentioned as desirable. If prospects want a den or office and no room is fitted for that purpose by the present owners, show a room that would serve the purpose.

Show the full possibilities of the property to be sure they understand its maximum value. For example, call attention to a dramatic view, an opportunity for a conversational grouping of furniture in the living room, or the clear space and headroom for table tennis in the basement.

HANDLING OBJECTIONS

Turn objections to positives whenever possible. Point out faults so that a minor flaw doesn't become a major objection. Turn faults into selling benefits by being ready with an intelligent answer. A property fault can become an effective selling point if you know the remedy, particularly when you have a written estimate of the cost of necessary work.

Anticipate objections. Before the buyers say the kitchen is too small, describe it as a step-saving kitchen. Point it out: "The functional kitchen allows for a much larger family/dining area."

Make the buyers feel at home. Relax, don't hurry. Pause when they want to look at some feature closely. Don't keep the pace at a nervous tempo.

Let the buyers get the feel of the house. After prospective buyers have been shown through a house, it is an excellent idea, when the owners are not present, to invite them to sit down in the living room, den or a room with an especially attractive view so that they can feel at home there.

Or, let them recheck alone, while you wait. Say something like this: "If you'd like to go back by yourself, I'll sit down and read the paper. Take your time, I'll be right here to answer any questions you have." The fact that you are not hurrying the buyers will put them more at ease. It also gives them a chance to talk together in private. Failure to allow buyers this opportunity to communicate feelings has resulted in many lost sales opportunities.

Some agents like to use a prospective buyer evaluation form for each property viewed. They give the prospective buyers a form on a clipboard with a pen. For each property viewed, they attach one or more photos of the property to the form.

A typical form would look like Figure 9.1.

By having the parties independently complete their forms and then evaluate the forms together, you open up communications between the buyers as well as among the buyers and you as the salesperson. Use of this form avoids the possibility of buyer hesitation because of uncertainty as to what his or her spouse really thinks of the property. The form can also lead to a very natural closing.

If your prospective buyers are interested in a property, you should be enthusiastic about it. Make them feel as if they are the only ones in the world who should own this home. Keep in mind that buyers tend to be hesitant. When you find a house that meets your buyers' needs and they feel comfortable with it, you should reinforce their positive feelings. Like everyone else they need reassurance. This is the time to give it.

Keep their interest and confidence. Listen respectfully and do not argue. A buyer may advance an uninformed opinion, but you can turn it tactfully or ignore it altogether. Never talk down to prospects even if they ask questions that seem foolish to you. Meet them on the common ground of confidence and understanding. Be patient and avoid high-pressure tactics. Lead them along until they are ready to make up their minds.

ESTIMATING COSTS

Paint a true picture. Don't underestimate costs. It is best to prepare the buyer for the correct amounts. If you say that taxes are "about $800" and they turn out to be $2,000, or that closing costs "may amount to $250" and the actual figure is $600, you are in an adverse position with the buyer. At the time of any offer, you will wait to give the buyer an estimate of buyer costs. Figure 9.2 is an example of such an estimate, also include closing costs shown in Figure 6.2 (page 102).

If you are not sure of the exact costs, it is better to estimate high. If taxes and settlement costs are lower than you quoted, the buyers may find they have saved a few dollars and will be grateful. If costs run higher, they will resent your inaccuracy.

FIGURE 9.1   Home Evaluation Form

```
┌─────────────────────────────┐
│                             │      Address _____
│        Photograph           │
│            of               │             _____
│         Property            │
│                             │      Price _____
└─────────────────────────────┘
```

Features of this home I like: _____

_____

Why? _____

_____

Features I wish this home had: _____

_____

_____

Why? _____

_____

☐   I like this home better than the other homes I have seen.

☐   I preferred the property at _____

   over this home because _____

   _____

☐   I would not be interested in owning this home.

☐   I would like to own this home.

☐   I would be interested in owning this home if it had _____

   _____

☐   I would be interested in owning this home if it were priced

   at $_____

FIGURE 9.2 Sample Buyer's Estimated Costs Form

BUYER'S
Estimated Costs

PRICE:

Purchase Price.................... $ _____

Down Payment .... $ _____

Balance .... $ _____

GROSS MONTHLY COSTS:

Principal & Interest .... $ _____

Real Estate Taxes (Estimated) .... $ _____

Fire or Homeowner's Insurance
Premium .... $ _____

Other_____$ _____

_____ _____

_____ _____

Monthly Cash Outlay (Estimated) ..... $ _____

MONTHLY TAX DEDUCTIONS:

Mortgage Interest (Estimated) .... $ _____

Real Estate Taxes (Estimated) .... $ _____

Total Monthly Tax
Deductions (Estimated)............. $ _____

NET MONTHLY COSTS:

Monthly Cash Outlay (Estimated) ..... $ _____

Monthly Tax Savings
(Assuming_____% tax bracket) ...... $ _____

Net Monthly Cost (Estimated) .... $ _____

Compliments of:

NATIONAL ASSOCIATION
OF REALTORS®

REALTOR® *The Voice for Real Estate*™

EQUAL HOUSING
OPPORTUNITY

116-365
revised 11/89

KNOW THE ANSWERS

During a showing, you may be called upon to answer any kind of question about the community in which the property is located. You should be familiar enough with the community to answer such questions. Here are some things a homebuyer might want to know:

- What elementary and high schools serve the area, and where are they located?
- Where are the nearest churches, theater, shopping center?
- What public transportation is available, and how close is the nearest stop?
- What are the annual taxes? Are there any special assessments?
- Is the house completely insulated, and with what material?
- When was the house built and by whom? What kind of heating system does it have, and what condition is it in? What are the annual fuel bills?
- Why is the owner selling?

A commercial or investment buyer will want to know these things:

- Rental information on a building—Types of leases and when they will be up; what rent increases are in order?
- Structural information—When was a new roof put on? Is the plaster still good? What is the size of the air-conditioning plant?
- What were maintenance and/or utility costs for the prior year?
- What financial options are available for the purchaser?
- What improvements have been made in recent years?

Answering questions like these with confidence strengthens your position as the salesperson. They cannot be answered unless you have researched them in advance. Your sales kit should contain maps, charts and reports on all phases of the community.

TIE-DOWNS

The idea behind tie-downs is to obtain a yes answer from buyers to questions or statements that reaffirm their needs or wants. Four techniques are suggested for using tie-downs.

Ask only those questions that will elicit a yes answer and will remind the prospects of something they like about this property. Be specific.

End your statements with tie-down phrases, such as "Don't you?" "Can't you?" "Isn't that right?" "Don't you agree?" "Wouldn't you?"

Keep your objectives in mind. Ask your questions with the expectation of a certain outcome. Don't just rattle out irrelevant questions to keep the conversation going; be selective.

Avoid glibness; don't sound like you are making a pitch. It is easy to sound phony and mechanical. Think about this and develop your skill in tie-down conversation to a natural way of speaking.

Be sure to help your prospects overcome their objections tactfully, logically and firmly but not in a high-pressure way.

MEETING FINAL OBJECTIONS

Suggest that buyers develop a "needs" list. This may help later in overcoming objections. No home is 100 percent perfect; there are always some disadvantages, and a degree of compromise is always necessary. If you are helping the prospects buy a home that meets their requirements, it is sometimes necessary to keep reminding them of the positive features.

If you remind the buyers, point by point, of all that they found to their satisfaction, you will calm their fears, restore a measure of confidence and preserve the negotiation.

What do you do if they balk again when the purchase agreement is ready for signature, saying they want to think it over? Some of the following techniques for meeting final objections may work for you.

As always, do not argue or challenge. Accept the objection and offer a benefit. If you can offer the benefit as a tie-down question, it will be stronger.

There is often a "hot button," some unusual feature that is particularly attractive to the buyers. If there is such a button, push it hard. Describe its rarity or uniqueness. Dwell on the pleasure and satisfaction it promises. If they want it badly enough, they will usually compromise on other issues.

If price is the problem and your research among comparables shows it to be fair, emphasize that fact as many times as necessary.

If you are in a rising real estate market, make the significance of this clear to the buyers.

You might agree that they should fully consider the property before they make any decisions. Then you should suggest going through the property again, even if it is a third or fourth visit. Reviewing the property will assuage their fears, and you should again be closing the sale.

It is not wise to recommend haste through fear of other imminent offers unless you actually know of any. It is legitimate to point out that while the buyer thinks things over, the house remains on the market and may be sold at any time, and that there are showings scheduled by other agents. Most salespeople recall clients who missed a property through delay, to their subsequent and genuine regret. It will strengthen the point if you can relate such an experience that you know occurred.

The closing process begins with the qualification process. You want the prospects to be with you in a "buying mode" and not just a "looking mode." Actually, you are closing every step of the way. There is no magical moment when salespeople know that prospects want a particular property, but there are some signals.

The buyers may introduce new objections simply to give themselves time to think, so they will not make an unwise decision. That is why many objections are insincere or self-defensive in nature. Such objections are generally easy to counter.

The REALTORS NATIONAL MARKETING INSTITUTE® publishes several leaflets that have proved helpful to salespeople working with first-time buyers.

THE CLOSING

The closing is a series of agreements, exchanges and discussions during which you should be ready to ask for the buyers' offer. Now is the time to keep your mouth closed and your ears open, listening for the signals that indicate the prospects are ready to buy.

Most prospects buy; they are not sold. Stop talking and start listening when buyers agree with your sales talk, begin to boost the property and say their family likes it. Nod in agreement, reaffirm the interest expressed by one family member and move to close the transaction. Be content to answer questions but stay on track. Do not introduce strange subjects or wander off on a tangent. The buyers have begun to make an important decision. Let them. This is not the time to start talking about other properties they have yet to see.

Some successful salespeople like to involve the buyers in the calculations of the sale by giving them paper and pencil and having them make their own notes of financial details along with the salesperson. This not only requires concentration on the purchase but also prevents the buyer's mind from wandering, perhaps generating new objections while the salesperson's attention is diverted.

Closing the sale is a matter of doing the right thing at the right time. If you have taken care of all the factors leading up to the close, the close itself should be a natural end to the transaction.

Timing

Timing is extremely important for the close. Trying to close too early, before there is reasonable evidence that a closing technique will work, can make the prospects feel unduly pressured. They will either shy away or question your motives.

On the other hand, talking too much can bore the prospects. Keep in mind that while your prospects want you to be interested in them and their needs, they are not that interested in you. The time for small talk is not when a closing could be imminent. If they have reached the point of decision, further efforts on your part can sometimes bring up subjects that will create objections or doubts that will make your task more difficult.

The good salesperson observes prospects, watching for signs that the time has come to close. The time to employ a closing technique is when those signs are revealed, whether early or late in the presentation.

When you feel the time has come to ask the prospects to make an offer, you can use any of several effective closing techniques. In each case, choose the one that seems most suitable for your particular prospect. Keep in mind that if one closing fails, you can try another later. It is better to try for a closing that fails than to not try at all.

Closing Techniques

Ideo-Motor One approach to closing is the "ideo-motor." The principle of this approach is that if you put an idea in a prospect's mind and keep it there against all extraneous and opposing ideas, it will produce action.

Minor Point Close The minor point close is another approach. After the prospective buyers have finished inspecting the house and you are walking down the front walk, stop, turn and silently observe the front door of the house.

Soon the prospects look to see what you are staring at. When their curiosity is at a peak, ask: "Don't you think the door would look better painted black?" If the people say that they like the color as it is, say, "All right, we'll leave it that color." You have sold them the front door and the home that goes with it. You have closed on a minor point and a major point is carried along with it.

Assumptive Close Another very effective close is the assumptive close. One way to initiate this is to make sure the buyers come to the office so that you can drive them to see the house. After the showing, the buyers can't say that they will think it over and get in their car and leave.

As you approach the office upon your return, use an assumptive close by saying, "Let's go into the office and see if we can work this out." If the buyers accept the invitation, they are getting close to buying.

By-Pass Close Making a final decision is a painful and difficult process for many people, because they fear making a mistake in something as important as buying a house. The by-pass close breaks the big decision into little ones.

Find out which property the prospects like best, how many bedrooms they will need and whether they would like the house to face east or west. By getting the answers to these and other questions, you can select the proper location for your prospects, match its features with their preference and leave them with no sensible alternative but to buy. However, don't tighten the qualifications to the point that no home available will fit buyers' needs.

The Positive Choice Close The positive choice close is simply asking a buyer to choose between two choices, either of which means a sale. For example: "The owners indicate they could give occupancy by March 1. Is that satisfactory, or would you prefer April 1?"

Some salespeople like to take photos of prospects in front of and/or in the homes they are interested in that show off positive features of the property. They will use these photos as a closing technique when there are two homes that buyers are interested in. They will lay the photos out and ask the prospective buyers, "Which one is your new home?"

A good technique to use when prospective buyers are unsure between two properties is to ask, "If the properties were both priced the same, which home would you prefer?" You should be selling the benefits of the home they prefer. They want to buy it, and they want you to convince them that they should.

Adviser Technique Some prospects are so lacking in confidence in their own decisions that they need someone to lean on for advice, someone in whom they have confidence and respect. This calls for the adviser technique.

To use this closing method effectively, you must gain the confidence and respect of the prospects in the early stages of the presentation. You must convince them that you understand and appreciate their needs and desires in housing. If you can establish this rapport, the prospects will be inclined to accept your advice and to let you help them make the decision. They are, in effect, deferring to an expert in whom they have confidence.

When using the adviser technique, be sure to tell the prospects what would be wrong for them as well as what would be right. Help them exclude those houses or locations that would not suit their needs, and then show them why others would work for them. This will convince them that you are advising and not just selling.

Urgency Close   The urgency close is one of the most effective tools for closing a sale and one that can be used with a little imagination in almost any situation. Any excellent or unusual feature of the property, such as proximity to shopping centers or schools, can be used to emphasize the quality of the house and the urgency of making an offer.

It would help in these cases to have a map or diagram indicating available properties. This makes it easier to show the prospects why one location is superior to another. If your prospects want some special feature, such as a tennis court or rose garden, point out that the number of such houses is limited and that they sell quickly.

Urgency can also relate to price. When prices are rising fast, the safest way to get what you want is to make an offer without delay. Never base urgency on a phantom buyer. However, if other prospective buyers have seen the property and you know they have an appointment to view it again, then it would be proper to point it out. You could also properly point out that a recently listed property has had exceptional activity and will likely be sold in a relatively short time.

Ask for the Offer

You cannot approach the sellers without a viable offer in your hand. At the point when you know the prospects are very likely to become buyers, ask them to make an offer. If you do not get an answer, be silent and wait. Make the prospective buyers answer, even though the silence seems eternal.

If you are representing the owners, it would be a breach of agency duty to recommend an offer below list price, although it would be proper to ask the prospective buyers how much they are willing to pay.

Do not encourage prospective buyers to believe that an unrealistic offer will be accepted. Consider asking how they arrived at that figure and if they believe it is fair based upon the values you have shown them.

One technique is to fill out the offer form except for the price and hand it to the buyers with a pen, telling them "You obviously like this house better than any other home you have seen or you wouldn't be making an offer. If you want this home, I recommend that you raise the offer so it will be yours." To convince the buyers to raise their offer, give them comparable sales data.

Many agents rush to get an offer at any price and then hope for a counteroffer to be accepted. Unfortunately, unrealistic offers often harden a seller against a buyer and hinder such negotiations. It is far better to get a good offer so you can honestly recommend to an owner that it be accepted.

When a buyer is offering less than the list price, you should explain that a larger earnest money deposit will increase the likelihood of the sellers' acceptance.

Earnest Money Deposit

As evidence of good faith, buyers should always make an earnest money deposit when they sign a contract. The amount should be substantial and depends upon the value of the property.

Earnest money makes the offer bona fide to the owner. When the time comes to ask for this deposit, the buyers usually inquire, "How much do you want?" The reply should be, "It is customary to make an earnest money deposit of ＿＿ percentage of the purchase price," (whatever is customary for the area). Also, explain that the deposit is part of the required equity money (down payment), which will have to be posted soon.

Ask Them to Buy

Ask them to buy and perhaps they will. Whenever it seems logical in the course of your conversation, let the prospects know that you want them to have this house. This can be done without undue pressure, and it is flattering to a customer who may never have made such a big purchase before.

You may not be able to sign a contract on the spot, but you can still make the sale. Reach an understanding and part as friends.

If you have done your job well and the house really fits, arrange to talk with the buyers again as soon as possible.

Leave something tangible with them. A card filled out with pertinent facts will serve the purpose; a property brief is even more effective. It should contain an exterior picture, floor plans, description, all financial data and, on costly homes, a few interior views. The information given will keep on selling and answering questions and, because you might want to recover it, you have a good reason for a return call. If you have taken photos of the prospective buyers outside or in the house, these are even more effective. They will help to create a desire for ownership.

If the prospective buyers do eventually buy the property, you can be certain they will be showing the photos to friends and relatives. This will reduce the likelihood of "buyers' remorse," where buyers want to back out of the purchase.

It should be noted that the closing techniques we've just discussed are most appropriately used by sellers' agents and subagents who are working with buyer customers. Buyers' agents work for their buyer clients by giving clients their best professional advice, assisting clients in making decisions that serve the clients' wants and needs and then advocating for those decisions.

Advise the Buyer Realistically

No sale is really good unless both sellers and buyers benefit. If the buyers' income doesn't qualify them for a property, resist the temptation to try to sell it to them.

Don't try to stretch the limits of the lender's prequalification estimate. You are likely to have buyers whose hopes have been shattered and sellers who feel that you failed them.

In order to get the listing, you told the buyers that you didn't waste owners' time with buyers who couldn't qualify, and now you have done just that.

On the other hand, some buyers arbitrarily set a price limit on a real estate purchase that is lower than they can really afford. Good salespeople sense this and point out the advantages of a higher-quality investment that is within the buyer's reach.

WHEN THE SALE SEEMS TO BE LOST

You have shown a house that you believe meets the qualifications of your buyers and they show no reaction. Your instinct may tell you this is a house they will never buy.

Do not trust such instinct. Do not despair. Call the buyers later. They may be people who believe a poker face will keep the price down, or it may simply be their nature not to show enthusiasm. If yours is one of the first properties these buyers saw, they may have decided not to respond until they have seen some others. After looking at them, they may appreciate the qualities of the house you showed them.

Make that follow-up call. The buyers may still not buy the place you showed them, but your continued interest may elicit the response you need to help you suggest other properties.

Where You Can Go Wrong

If you wonder why you did not sign a prospective buyer, perhaps the answer is here. You may have

- failed to understand what the prospective buyers wanted and showed them unsuitable property.
- neglected the prospective buyers too long—they became friendly with another salesperson and gave him or her their business.

- become involved in an argument, won the argument and lost the sale.
- lost the buyers' respect because you couldn't answer their questions.
- tried too hard to get their signatures before you sold them on the benefits of a purchase.
- talked too much about the great buy they would get and too little about what it would do for them and their family.
- kept waiting for them to say they would take the property, but the interview was interrupted before they ever got around to doing that.
- talked yourself into a sale but kept talking and talked yourself out of it.
- overstressed your technical knowledge of the contract—you realize now that the buyers weren't interested in knowing all you knew about it.
- accepted the buyer's objections too readily.
- pressed for a sale without knowing enough about the buyers' actual needs.
- failed to call.

THE CONTRACT

The initial contract of sale between buyers and sellers should set forth, in detail, the entire agreement entered into between these principals. It should scrupulously conform to the requirements and customary practices of your state and locality.

In addition to the standard provisions, you will want to include special provisions, such as specific mention of all chattels or removable fixtures, warranties or certifications that may cause misunderstandings between the two parties.

The contract should also include any other elements legal counsel suggests. It is highly advisable to have available a list of previously drafted and approved clauses, stipulations or provisions necessary to add to or modify your standard contract form.

Avoiding Contract Problems

A law professor once told his class that if ever real estate salespeople started to write good contracts, half his students would have to start looking for another profession!

He was being facetious, of course, but the fact remains that most legal disputes in real estate have their origins in contract flaws—errors that could have been avoided easily when the contract was drafted. To avoid trouble, have everything in writing, including personal items of relatively low value. When left to oral agreement, they can be the basis of future controversy.

Some general rules to follow include the following:

- Don't try to tailor a residential purchase contract for commercial or industrial property or for the sale of a business.
- Don't try to cut and paste several forms to create a contract. If a standard contract will not fit a situation with relatively simple modifications and/or additions, seek legal advice.
- If you find it necessary to delete printed matter or paragraphs in a contract, have all contracting parties initial the cross-outs, because the changes originate with the offer to buy.
- If you are not sure of the interest rate a lending institution will apply to a loan assumption or a new loan, write in the highest interest rate that the buyer is willing to pay, using the phrase, "not to exceed___percent per annum."
- If there is not enough space on the form for the personal property list included in the transaction, itemize the personal property in the form of an addendum and have all parties initial it.
- If the deposit seems too small because the buyer's checking account balance will not cover the appropriate amount, accept the buyer's check for the smaller amount but write the contract so that an increase to the full amount is required within 24 hours of the seller's acceptance, or use a promissory note if acceptable in your area.
- If a husband and wife are buying property and are unsure how they should take title, refrain from advising them and insert the words "instructions to follow" in the appropriate space on the contract form. If you advise people on title matters, you may find you are inadvertently offering legal recommendations.

Disclosures Make certain that you have fully disclosed to prospective buyers any information you have about the property that could reasonably be viewed as negative. Make certain that the buyers fully understand your agency role and your relationship, if any, with the property owners. Make certain that any state-mandated disclosures have been made. (Many purchase contracts include mandated disclosures.)

Chapter 10

Negotiating and Closing

With an offer from a potential buyer, a good salesperson doesn't rush immediately to the seller. First, think the offer over. Is it a reasonable one? Do you understand all the financial terms? Do you honestly believe this offer will benefit the property owner? If you have been conscientious, you will be able to answer these questions affirmatively and you have a reasonable offer that will mutually satisfy buyers and sellers.

When you represent the sellers, you should be prepared to recommend acceptance of an offer you believe to be reasonable. To do otherwise would not be serving the sellers' best interests. Many advantageous sales have been lost by trying to get just a little bit more. Similarly, if you believe an offer is not in the best interests of the owners, you should be prepared to recommend the offer be rejected or a counteroffer be made. Keep in mind that you can only recommend; the decision is made by the owners.

You should always point out dangers in offers, such as when the buyers will not be making any down payment or will actually net cash from the purchase transaction. You should also be prepared to point out the dangers of sellers carrying back a "subordinate" mortgage as well as trades in which cash value of the trade property has not been properly ascertained.

If the buyers' offer is on a form you are not familiar with, you should make certain you fully understand all provisions before presenting it. With computers and laser printers, some buyers have prepared forms that appear to be standard forms but don't actually say what you would reasonably expect them to say.

DO YOUR HOMEWORK

If the offer is reasonable, now is the time to do your homework so you take as much information as possible to the seller along with the signed offer. You should prepare a new estimated sellers' proceeds form (see Chapter 6) based on the offer received, so the sellers fully understand the net effect of the offer. Have data on comparable sales as well as other benefits besides price that this particular offer has to its credit.

For example, if the suggested possession date fits in perfectly with the seller's plans, this may be a good reason to accept an offer that is slightly below price expectations. Point out that a convenient moving date could save your client money in the long run. Whatever good reasons you give the client for accepting an offer, back them up with solid facts.

When you have analyzed the positive and negative points in the offer, planned your presentation accordingly and are satisfied that the transaction will be fair and beneficial to both parties, you are in the right frame of mind to make a convincing presentation. As a final thought, recall the buyer's motivations. Think of trade-offs that could be developed that will bring buyer and seller into agreement.

SET UP AN APPOINTMENT QUICKLY

Meanwhile, if you are not the listing salesperson, get in touch with him or her and ask to set up an appointment with the seller. If you are the lister, have someone in your office call to make the appointment promptly. Having another person arrange the meeting not only allows you time to prepare for it but also helps avoid a premature discussion of the offer with the seller. In either case, you have important preparation work to do prior to the meeting.

Go to the sellers with the thought that you could be bringing them the solution to a series of worries, decisions, apprehensions and sometimes false hopes. Use the first few moments with the sellers to help ease these tensions, engaging in small talk.

CONVEY THE OFFER

When you present the offer, you want to be relatively close to the sellers. When sellers are physically close to you, they find it more difficult to maintain an arbitrary or argumentative position. The sellers' kitchen table is an excellent place to present an offer, as the nonthreatening environment helps in the communication process.

As you settle down for your presentation of the offer, be sure you are seated facing the sellers. This arrangement is important so you can observe their reactions (especially if there is more than one seller), so you can see how they respond to each other with both spoken and silent communications, and so you can be sure which is the dominant one, the decision maker.

Try to get the sellers to discuss their reasons for selling (if they have not done so already) so their motivations will be clearer to you and any urgency in their situation can be reinforced.

Tell the sellers what's been happening in the market. Keep them involved in the conversation by asking some related questions, such as did they know a certain property in the neighborhood has been taken off the market, and why? Now, with the sellers' attention and interest locked in, bring out the purchase contract. But don't hand it to them just yet!

If it is your office listing and the property has been on the market for some time, you should consider going through a brief history of the listing. If an agent had recommended a list price less than that at which the property was listed, this should be pointed out. Any difference in price can later be related to the difference between the offer and the suggested list price. Tell the owners how you marketed their property, explaining the number of agents in your office and in the MLS service who had access to the property. If there were open houses, property briefs prepared and ads for the property, this information should be included in the history.

Now tell the sellers about the buyers. Personalize them as people the sellers would like to have living in their home. If the offer differs significantly from the list price, explain the buyers' reasoning for their offer. Sellers may become belligerent if they feel buyers are arbitrary or trying to take advantage of them.

The main items of sellers' concerns are likely to be price, terms, closing and personal property.

Explain the offer in plain, simple language. Start out with the positive factors (their possession date may fulfill the sellers' need to move quickly). Review the possible objectionable points, but do not stop to defend or even comment on them. Remember, they are negative only in your estimation. If you defend them, it might create doubts in the minds of the sellers that didn't exist before. State the entire offer plainly, then hand it to the sellers to read.

Be wary of the sellers' first question or comment; it could lead to a rambling discussion of the merits of the offer if you are not careful. For example, the offer may involve a second mortgage and the sellers don't want to get involved in that. Acknowledge the comment, but as you do, bring out a scratch pad and use it to resume control of the presentation. Do this by focusing the sellers' thinking on how much cash they will end up with, getting them to check your figures as you note them on the scratch pad.

The next step could be the presentation of the sellers' net sheet. They may have seen figures of a general nature when they listed their home; you can now show them exactly what their position will be at the offered price and terms on a certain date.

When an offer is received shortly after a property is listed, some owners tend to think that the price they set was too low, so they become immovable as to any concessions. You should explain that quick offers are common when a new listing is received, because new listings create both agent and buyer interest. The first 30 days of listings that are priced competitively tend to be the most productive period for sales. Explain to the owners that many sellers, to their regret, believe their house can easily be sold when they get an early offer, so they refuse to give even minor concessions. The result is that the buyers are often lost and the owners eventually sell for far less than they would have received with the early offer. Many agents tell owners about this psychological problem at the time they take the listing to avoid owners becoming unreasonable when a quick offer is received.

Diplomacy Is Important

Throughout this period of presenting an offer, going back to the buyers with a counteroffer and perhaps going through it again or starting the whole process over, you must use all your skills to work constructively and diplomatically with people concerning one of the most crucial topics to anyone: money. You must be sensitive to the feelings of people at the same time that you must be more logical and reasonable than ever before during the selling process. Never show anger, frustration or annoyance with either buyers or sellers, no matter what you may feel.

When talking to the owners about the offer, for example, emphasize what the buyers like about the property instead of the negative factors. Explain to the sellers that the buyers see one or two drawbacks, but on the whole they are pleased enough with the property to make a reasonable offer. In this way you can explain the buyers' rationale for making their offer without, at the same time, attacking the sellers' property. You may also point out the competitive market for similar properties, how many others the buyers have seen and how hard you worked to obtain a reasonable offer.

Don't start writing up a counteroffer as soon as the owners object to an offer. If you honestly believe that acceptance is in the owners' best interest, do your best to gain that acceptance. Point out that by their signature they can obligate the buyers, but a counteroffer is really a rejection of the offer. The buyers are free to look at other properties. Ask the owners if they are willing to risk what has been offered for only a little more. You might point this out by saying, "Right now you have 96 percent of what you want. Are you willing to gamble this 96 percent in the hopes of gaining just 4 percent more?"

You should also point out that a counteroffer will be greeted with relief by many buyers who suffer "buyers' remorse." They are overwhelmed by what they have offered and are having second thoughts about the purchase. A counteroffer is often seen as a chance to get out.

If a counteroffer is necessary, the sellers should be persuaded to give in on at least one point of contention. Buyers want to feel that they have gained something by their shrewd negotiating. When sellers simply counter with the list price and terms, buyers are likely to walk away unless they have formed a strong desire to own that particular property.

If you cannot reasonably bring the buyers and sellers together on a sale, chances are the buyers do not really want this particular property. It may be too expensive, or there may be something about it that does not suit their needs or tastes. Although you should have discovered this well before nearing the closing of this transaction, you can continue working with the prospective buyers until the appropriate property is found for them.

Do They Really Want To Sell?

There are times, however, when the stumbling block is not with the buyers but rather with the sellers. Suspecting this, have an honest talk with the sellers and find out what the problem is. Are their objections to price adjustments so rigid that there can be no compromise with any prospective buyer? Has something happened to make the owners change their minds about selling—something they themselves don't even realize has happened to make them less serious about the sale? Were they ever really serious about selling? Find these things out before further embarrassing, destructive situations develop with these sellers and potential buyers.

THE ART OF NEGOTIATION

Counteroffer

Frequently, the best you will accomplish is a counteroffer in which the sellers agree to accept a price somewhat above the offer but less than the listing price. Be certain this counteroffer is the lowest figure obtainable from the sellers at this time before taking it to the potential buyers. Explain to them in depth and unemotionally the rationale of the sellers.

Often, this process will bring the matter to a successful close. However, experienced salespeople tell interesting stories of negotiations requiring several more trips between sellers and buyers. Negotiation is truly an art requiring tact, patience and perseverance.

With some buyers and sellers, it pays to let them sleep on it rather than having them reject the agreement. Compromises impossible to get tonight are often obtainable tomorrow, after one or both parties have had a chance to cool off and appreciate the significance to them of the loss of the sale or purchase.

A short counteroffer may be set forth, written to conform to your own local laws and regulations. However it is written, it must be neat, concise and clear. A lengthy or complicated counteroffer should be written on a separate addendum sheet or, if available, on a form printed for that purpose. Be sure that a reference to the counteroffer is included in the acceptance clause on the face of the contract.

On the way to meeting the buyers again, analyze the counteroffer from their point of view. If you honestly believe it represents a fair solution to their problems, your attitude can be positive and constructive.

First, state the points of the original offer you succeeded in getting the sellers to accept. Then explain the counteroffer that resulted from hard bargaining. Present the counteroffer as a positive rather than a negative. With their original low offer, they succeeded in saving $____. Ask for the buyers' acceptance.

If they express reservations, remind them of all the reasons they have for wanting this property. The best way to do this is to have them restate their reasons as responses to your questions. Then reduce the difference between offer and counteroffer to X number of dollars per month or state as a percentage: "For only *2 percent* more you will have purchased a really fine home." This is the dollar difference technique. Remind them, too, that the house remains on the market while they are thinking about it and could be sold to someone else.

If The Counteroffer Is Not Accepted

Don't assume the transaction is dead if the counteroffer is not accepted at once. Sometimes buyers regret earlier decisions and phone the next day to close the agreement.

Turn-Down

If the sellers turn down the buyers' first offer without a counteroffer, it becomes your challenge to narrow the differences by further negotiation with the buyers. If they understood at the outset that they had not bought the house but had only made an offer to buy, they understood from the beginning that their offer might be rejected. However, they probably expected you to return either with an acceptance of their offer or with a counteroffer. Go back to the buyers in person; try not to handle this over the phone. Explain the sellers' reasoning in the rejection. Explain also that the price is firm because it was set low to sell, and the low price was very likely a significant reason for the buyers' interest in the home.

LEGAL COUNSEL MANDATORY

Salespeople should know what goes into a contract for a real estate transaction. The real estate salesperson is a professional in the real estate field and in that field only. You should never attempt to practice law along with real estate, and legal counsel should always be recommended. In some states, use of legal counsel is mandatory.

Many real estate firms use contract forms or blanks approved by the legal counsel of the local board of REALTORS® or by the broker's own attorney. Either way, the contract used should be drawn with adequate legal advice and in strict accordance with local laws.

All principals in the transaction should have legal counsel. The legal rights of the buyer and seller must be protected throughout the transaction. The salesperson and his or her firm are largely responsible for this.

Many court controversies over land ownership are the result of rushing transactions through without adequate legal counsel. To be a contributing agent in such cases is gross negligence on the part of the real estate salesperson or the broker. If a legal interpretation is needed, it should be provided by an attorney, not a broker or salesperson.

The way to be sure a sale is properly closed is to have reliable legal counsel. If there is uncertainty, it is never safe to proceed in a closing without the assistance of a competent attorney. Both the broker and the attorney have important functions in the transaction; there should never be any conflict of interest between them.

To conclude the transaction, when the buyers or sellers have accepted the offer or counteroffer, convey the acceptance back to the buyers or sellers immediately. Give the parties their ratified copy of the agreement at the first opportunity.

WHEN A SALE IS MADE

In most cases, the serious buyer and seller will get together on price, financing and other considerations. You may have to work with buyer and seller through several offers and counteroffers, but if the principals are truly interested, an agreement will be reached.

With this agreement, a sale has been made. The prospect has agreed to purchase the property on terms acceptable to the owner. However, there is a difference between making a sale and closing the transaction.

The transaction is not closed until there is payment of full price, the deed is delivered and all technical details of the sale have been handled and completed. Good salesmanship is as important while you close the transaction as at any time in the course of listing, showing and selling the property.

Replace the For Sale sign with a Sold sign as soon as all contingencies have been removed from the contract in writing. The sellers will be glad to be finished with inquiries and showings.

Follow through with information on what the sellers should do about financing, tax and other payments until closing day. Have the sellers get together all the documents and memos that will expedite the closing. Get the current tax bill, the deed to the property and a loan statement or loan payment book. Ask for the title insurance policy, other insurance policies that will be germane to the closing, and any other information the sellers can provide on encumbrances, unrecorded deeds and reconveyances. These are needed to expedite the settlement and to establish a factual report of the sellers' net cash position.

The culmination of your successful sales effort should be an exercise in efficiency. Use your daily planner to note important follow-up details preliminary to the final closing. Keep buyers and sellers fully informed, conforming with uniform settlement practices. Give them copies of settlement papers as far in advance as possible so they can become familiar with them and, if they wish, discuss details with their legal counsel. Do everything in your power to have all parties to the final settlement fully prepared for closing the transaction.

Expert procedure during this time can settle any misunderstandings that may develop and can maintain the goodwill of buyer and seller, both of whom may represent future business through referrals.

RESPA

Your legal responsibilities regarding disclosure of settlement costs are covered under the Real Estate Settlement Procedures Act (RESPA), which became effective on June 20, 1975. Under this law, a number of new procedures and forms are required for settlements involving most home mortgage loans, including FHA, VA and loans from financial institutions with federally insured deposits. Most of the RESPA requirements are the responsibility of the lender. Some of them, however, directly affect the REALTOR®. It is important that you become familiar with the law, in terms of both its direct requirements of you as a REALTOR® and the effects it will have on the lending and settlement process in your area.

Following is a summary of the RESPA provisions that are most important for REALTORS® in their roles as brokers and salespeople. If you perform other roles, such as lending and closing, you will need to check further on how the law affects you. For more detailed information, please consult your local board.

RESPA deals with the following concerns:

- The coverage—types of transactions affected by the law
- The booklet—settlement (closing) cost information booklet
- The process—timing and procedure for advance disclosure of closing costs and waiver provisions
- Unearned fees—prohibition against kickbacks and unearned fees
- Title insurance—prohibition against sellers requiring buyers to pay for title insurance from a company selected by the seller
- Seller or agent disclosure requirements—requirement for disclosure of ownership information and, in limited cases, previous sales price on existing homes

FIRPTA

The Foreign Investment in Real Property Tax Act (FIRPTA) was passed to prevent foreign sellers from selling real property in the United States and then failing to pay taxes on their profits. This law requires a buyer to withhold estimated taxes equal to 10 percent of the sale price when the seller is foreign. This money must be paid to the IRS within ten days of the sale. If the buyer fails to withhold taxes and the seller fails to pay income tax on the sale, the buyer could be subject to a penalty of 10 percent of the purchase price or the seller's tax liability plus interest and penalties, whichever is less.

Exempt are personal residences purchased by the buyer for $300,000 or less or sales in which the seller has obtained a waiver of withholding from the IRS.

The burden of determining if the seller is foreign falls on the buyer. The buyer can rely on a statement of the seller's nonforeign status made under penalty of perjury coupled with a U.S. taxpayer identification number. The agent should make certain that the buyer is protected against FIRPTA tax liability.

THE SETTLEMENT

In some areas of the country, the settlement is handled by an independent escrow. The parties to the transaction sign escrow instructions. The seller deposits a deed and the buyer deposits the purchase price in cash and/or signed mortgage documents. The closing becomes an escrow procedure without the presence of buyer, seller, agent, lender or legal counsel.

If a closing agent is used, keep in touch with the agent on a weekly basis. Make certain the documents are prepared, received and signed on schedule. Many agents use computer programs to keep track of contracts. If there is a closing problem, immediately contact the parties and explain the problem and what is being done to solve it. Always disclose, even when it is information that will upset one or both of the parties.

If the broker is handling the closing, he or she should make certain that both buyer and seller have the opportunity to obtain legal counsel. Even if a person is not represented by counsel, the broker must ensure fair treatment. In some areas, attorneys handle the closings. The broker and the attorney both have important functions in the closing. There should not be a conflict of interest between them.

Forms for Settlement

When you have a binding contract between buyer and seller, your broker will have a form to be filled out and kept in the permanent file of the sale. Closing forms vary from firm to firm, but they include most of the following information (depending on the kind of property involved):

purchase price
earnest money deposit
mortgage history
mortgage institution
tax information
closing date
location of property
insurance information
title expense
service charges
sales commission
attorney's fees

escrow fees
rental information
list of tenants
utility information
possession date
guarantees on any equipment or improvements

Checklist for Settlement

A great many details are involved in a closing. Many real estate offices use a computer program to either handle the settlement or to keep track of it when it is being handled by an attorney or an escrow. Such a program may include the following items:

Title
abstract guarantee
correcting affidavits
quitclaim deeds
judgments, liens
mortgage satisfied
survey
estate-guardianship matters
title insurance
certificate of title
vendor's affidavit
warranty deed
Financing
lease with option
payment book
loan application
extra propositions
notes—mortgage to vendor
second mortgage to vendor
Taxes
property tax bills
receipts
personal taxes paid
FHA tax credits
exemption receipts
state and local taxes (deed)
intangible tax
gross income tax
Insurance
cancelled
new

prorate
endorsements
assignments—interest
company consent
deliver to mortgagee
FHA credits
Statements
insurance
loan
rent
commission
proration
closing
Assignments
leases
loan book
FHA tax-insurance credits
lease with option
roof guarantee
notice to vacate
letters to tenants
management contract
service contracts
utility contracts
Bill of sale
refrigerator
automatic heater
furnace
air conditioners
other equipment
personal property
Warranties
home protection plan
any additional warranties
Keys and miscellaneous
doors
automatic garage opener
appliance and systems manuals
Disclosures
seller disclosures (if required)
agency disclosure (if required)
FIRPTA requirements
statement of nonforeign status
withholding of 10 percent unless exempt

Broker Settlement Methods

There are several methods of handling broker settlements. Some brokers prefer to get buyers and sellers together at the same time. Others prefer to have the papers signed in advance by one of the parties and then to obtain the other signatures.

The closing, whether with buyers and sellers present or done individually, should take place where all the necessary records, facilities and clerical assistance are available. The principals should be able to study the statements without distraction. If the buyers are financing through a mortgage, the closing may take place in the offices of the lending institution.

The salesperson should follow through to the very end of the transaction, assisting in every aspect and seeing things through to a satisfactory conclusion.

The real estate firm, optionally, may perform such services as transfer of utilities to the name of the purchaser, agreement of leases and endorsement of insurance policies. Many brokers provide buyers with information on whom to contact for utilities, information on special homeowner tax credit applications, information on school registration, and so on. Such services, plus a cooperative, interested attitude on the part of the salesperson and the broker, will be remembered by buyers and sellers.

KEEP IN TOUCH

Even when the transaction is closed, you are not finished in your dealings with buyers and sellers and you never should be.

Many salespeople get in touch with the new owners shortly after the transaction is complete. Some bring a gift; some send a congratulatory letter; some just drop in for a friendly talk. Anniversaries of moving into a new home are remembered by real estate firms with a card each year. When you show continued interest, you build confidence that pays dividends in additional sales.

Don't forget the sellers either. It may not be long before they have need of a real estate firm, and you want them to remember you at that time.

Salespeople who keep the respect and friendship of their buyers and sellers are always a step ahead of the others. They will speak well of you when someone asks them whom to consult on a real estate matter. A satisfied client is a precious asset in the real estate business. At least half, and in most cases more, of the sales made by most real estate firms can be traced to referrals from satisfied buyers and sellers.

BUILDING FUTURE SALES

Whether selling new homes or old ones, the salesperson who does a good job in locating young couples in small homes is building for the future. Before long, as families grow, they will be in a position to buy larger homes. Equity built up in a small home can be the down payment on a larger one.

If you render good service for the first home and keep in touch after the sale, you can expect to be well received in the future when you offer your services to them and their friends.

Make it a point to call on buyers shortly after you sell them a home. In addition to being sources of leads, many of them will soon be in a better financial position and ready for a better home.

Many first-home buyers outgrow their new quarters faster than more seasoned buyers, who not only know with certainty what their likes and needs are but also know what their income is likely to be in the future. These new homeowners recognize that their own limitations rather than any pressure from salespeople led them to purchase homes that are now inadequate. Some may wish they had waited or bought a different style of home. By showing concern for their welfare, you will make friends who may someday list their homes with you.

Chapter 11

Financing

The sale of real estate involves a large financial commitment. The average buyer is seldom in a position to finance a purchase with cash but must borrow the difference between the sales price and whatever cash he or she has available.

HELPING THE BUYER

You cannot complete a sale until the buyers are in a position to obtain the funds needed. Successful salespeople maintain good working relations with several lending institutions in their area and do all they can to assist buyers in obtaining real estate financing. Lenders can be helpful in providing financial details and in keeping the agent up-to-date on the lender's financing requirements and loan terms being offered.

On project or new development home sales, lenders will provide you with complete and accurate mortgage information. On income property sales, they will furnish you with a mortgage financing description that should answer every question raised by the buyer.

While much financing information can be obtained in advance of your offering, it is important that salespeople not try to assume the role of lender. Do not be afraid to say, "I don't know, but I will find out." Many loans could be worked out if brought to the lending institution rather than having the salesperson attempt to handle the problem.

You should, however, find out the alternative mortgages available and the differences in terms, down payment, monthly payments, costs, etc., from area lenders and either provide the buyer with lender loan application forms (and help him or her fill them out) or set up an appointment for the buyer with the lender. Tell the lender to have its appraiser contact you for access to the property. Have a current competitive market analysis that you can provide to the appraiser.

In most instances, a client will place considerable trust and confidence in a salesperson who can offer sound and timely counsel on financial arrangements. It pays to be as informed as possible on real estate financing methods and the practices of lending institutions.

MORTGAGES, TRUST DEEDS AND LAND CONTRACTS

The mortgage is one of the basic instruments in real estate finance—it is what the average person identifies with the field of real estate finance. A mortgage is a pledge of property to secure a loan.

In and of itself, the mortgage does not represent a promise to pay anything. The promise to pay is contained in the note (often called a promissory note) that usually accompanies the mortgage. Thus, the mortgage comprises two separate items: a mortgage (pledge of the real estate to secure the loan) and a promissory note (the promise to pay). A mortgage is essentially a contract, and as such must possess the legal characteristics of a contract dealing in real property. Those characteristics are as follows:

- Competent parties
- An offer and acceptance
- Valuable consideration
- Legality of object
- A written, signed document

While many people refer to all financing arrangements as mortgages, trust deeds and land contracts (also known as land sales contracts or contracts for deed) are also widely used. Under a trust deed, the buyer or borrower (the trustor) gives a deed (trust deed) to a third party (trustee) to secure the lender (the beneficiary). When the note has been satisfied, the trustee gives the trustor a reconveyance.

Trust deeds can have advantages over mortgages for lenders, because foreclosure is generally less costly and quicker than foreclosing on a mortgage.

A land contract is a two-party document by which the seller actually retains legal title as security and gives the buyer possession. Title is not transferred until the entire contract or a designated portion is paid off. Land contracts are usually used for seller financing with low down payments. Foreclosure is generally simple, because the seller has retained title; however, the buyer has an equitable interest in the property, and what *appears* simple may not be so in reality. For the purpose of explaining loans, we will refer to all types of financing as mortgages.

Mortgages fall into two basic categories: amortized and straight-term.

Amortized mortgages are the most common and provide for payment of the entire principal and accrued interest in periodic (usually monthly) payments. Several varieties of amortized mortgages are available today and are explained individually and in detail later in this chapter.

In a straight-term loan, the principal is not repaid until the end of the mortgage term. Interest payments may also be deferred until the end of the term or may be paid at specified intervals (monthly, yearly, etc.). Few straight-term mortgages are negotiated for residential property.

TYPES OF MORTGAGES

The basic mortgage loan can be tailored to fit many needs and serve a variety of purposes. Each type may have advantages or drawbacks with respect to the borrower's needs. You should be familiar with the basic characteristics of each.

Conventional Mortgages

Originally, the term *conventional mortgage* referred to any mortgage that was not insured or guaranteed by a third party. Only the credit standing of the borrower and the property offered as collateral supported the promissory note.

In recent years, however, this term has referred only to the absence of federal involvement—whether or not the mortgage is insured. Several private companies now insure conventional mortgages.

While terms vary, some conventionals are available with as little as a 10 percent down payment. However, anything less than a 20 percent down payment usually necessitates the purchase of mortgage insurance to protect the lender from default. In some cases the insurance can be dropped after the loan-to-value ratio becomes sufficiently large.

Many lenders prefer to write conventional mortgages for several reasons. First, conventionals allow more flexibility in the specific agreements and terms of the loan. Second, conventionals avoid the profusion of paperwork and delay typically associated with federally insured or guaranteed mortgages. Third, the cost of loan administration is minimized.

Conforming Vs Nonconforming Loans   Lenders, after making a loan, can either keep the loan or sell it in the secondary mortgage market. Conforming loans are loans that meet the standards for purchase by the Federal National Mortgage Association (Fannie Mae) or by the Federal Home Loan Mortgage Corporation (Freddie Mac). These loans have strict qualifying guidelines and loan limits. Nonconforming loans do not meet these qualifications.

Because lenders do not have the option of readily selling a nonconforming loan, they will charge a higher interest rate than for conforming loans. When a borrower is unable to qualify for a conforming loan, lenders who are making loans for their own portfolios should be considered.

Federally Insured or Guaranteed Mortgages

Frequently, borrowers without funds to cover the down payment on a conventional mortgage will apply for a federally insured or guaranteed loan on which the equity requirement is minimized.

Federal Housing Administration (FHA) insurance requires rather stringent borrower eligibility and property requirements. However, because FHA loans are designed especially for first-time buyers, the down payment is low: 3 percent on the first $25,000 of purchase price, 5 percent on $25,000 to $125,000 and 10 percent on the remainder. FHA sets a maximum loan amount that varies by area.

The property must be appraised by an approved FHA appraiser. The purchase price may be more than the appraised value of the property, but the purchaser must sign an affidavit stating that he is aware that he is purchasing the property at a price above the appraised FHA valuation.

No secondary financing of any kind is permitted when obtaining a new FHA loan. FHA loans made prior to December 15, 1989, are fully assumable; loans made after December 15, 1989, are assumable by owner-occupants who qualify for the loan.

The Department of Veterans Affairs (VA) mortgage guarantee program is open only to qualified veterans.

Qualified veterans may obtain loans up to $184,000 with no down payment. The amount of a veterans' loan is not regulated, but the VA guarantee is limited.

Veterans' loans made prior to March 1, 1988, are fully assumable. Loans made after this date are assumable only if the buyer qualifies for the loan. The property must be appraised by a VA-approved appraiser. VA guaranteed loans are based on the appraised value rather than the selling price.

Buyers can find out if they qualify for a VA-guaranteed mortgage by writing or calling the nearest VA office and giving them their Social Security number, military serial number, date of birth, date of entry into the military, date and place of separation, the name of the unit at the time of discharge and the type of discharge.

Blanket Mortgages

Developers of large parcels of land (as in a single-family housing development) frequently utilize blanket mortgages. These allow the borrower to sell subdivided parcels, pay off the portion of the loan that parcel represents and obtain a release from the mortgage.

The retention of financing on the remaining unsold parcels makes this type of mortgage perfect for development and subdividing purposes. A usual lender stipulation is that the borrower must pay off more than a pro rata share of the loan. In effect, if a tract of 10 parcels is developed, the lender may require that in excess of 10 percent of the loan be paid off as each parcel is sold, in order for the parcel to be released from the mortgage, until the entire loan is retired.

Buydowns

Buydowns are used most often by developers of single-family or condominium housing to increase buying activity when interest rates are exceptionally high.

For example, if the market interest rates are 8 percent and the developers are advertising a 6 percent, 30-year mortgage, they have "bought down" the interest rate by two percentage points for a specified period (usually one to 10 years) of the 30-year term. To do this, the lender computes its return on the 2 percent for the buydown period and charges the developers the present value of the difference as a front-end fee.

It is extremely important for the buyers to know the length of the buydown period because, at the end of that time, their interest will jump to the higher rate. Their monthly payments will then increase to reflect the new interest rate.

Actually, anyone—including the buyer—can buy down the interest rate of a mortgage loan. And because the buydown fee is prepaid interest, it is tax-deductible.

Wraparound Mortgages

A wraparound mortgage (sometimes called an all-inclusive deed of trust) is a mortgage encompassing any existing loans and is subordinate to them. The existing loans remain on the property as unsatisfied, outstanding obligations, with the wraparound becoming a second, third or fourth (etc.) loan. The face amount of the wraparound is the total of all existing mortgages plus the amount being loaned by the wraparound mortgagee. The term of the wraparound is generally the time remaining on the original loan.

In order for a wraparound loan to be used, the underlying loan(s) must be assumable. Wraparound loans offer some interesting advantages to sellers. Assume a property has a 6 percent assumable first mortgage for $50,000 and the current interest rate is at 8 percent. If sellers were willing to carry financing at 8 percent and had a buyer with $10,000 down willing to pay $110,000, the seller would have two choices:

1. They could let the buyers assume the 6 percent mortgage and carry back a second mortgage for $50,000 at 8 percent interest. By assuming the below-interest loan, the buyers would take advantage of the below-market financing.
2. The sellers could write a new loan (wraparound loan) for $100,000 at 8 percent interest. The buyers would make payments on the $100,000 loan at 8 percent and the seller would make the payments on the $50,000 first mortgage at 6 percent. The seller would thus take advantage of the interest differential and earn the equivalent of 10 percent on equity.

Fixed-Rate Mortgages

Fixed-rate mortgages are fully amortized loans and are repaid in equal (generally monthly) installments spread over 15, 20, 25 or 30 years. The interest rate stays the same for the life of the loan, so only a change in taxes or insurance, if included in the loan payments, could change the amount of the payments.

Because the lender risks locking in a long-term loan and having the cost of funds rise above the rate of return from the loan, short-term fixed-rate mortgages generally have lower interest rates than long-term loans.

Renegotiable-Rate Mortgages

A renegotiable-rate mortgage is a fixed-rate mortgage for a short term, such as five years, but the payments are generally based on a 30-year amortization. When the loan period expires, the loan must be paid in full or the payments and interest are adjusted to reflect the current interest rates.

Because lenders have relatively low risk as to interest rates rising, they are generally willing to offer a significantly lower interest rate than for fixed-rate 30-year loans. The lower interest rate, and sometimes lower loan costs, could make the difference in the ability of a borrower to qualify for a loan.

Adjustable-Rate Mortgages

The adjustable-interest-rate mortgage (ARM) is one in which the interest rate periodically increases or decreases based on the financial market index to which the loan is keyed. The loan interest is set at several points above the index, called the margin. Interest rates are based on a prearranged contractual agreement. Monthly payments also may be increased periodically.

Many ARMs limit (cap) the percentage of interest rate increase or decrease at each adjustment period. Some cap the percentage of increase in the monthly payment adjustments if the borrower so desires. Most ARMs have a lifetime cap on the loan. Some ARMs allow negative amortization (the principal owed increases, because a cap on payments does not cover the interest due). Other ARMs prohibit negative amortization. Some cap neither interest nor payment adjustments. Therefore, it is extremely important that the borrower fully understands what changes will occur during the term of an ARM loan.

Because of relatively low lender risk as to changing interest rates, lenders offer lower rates for ARMs than for fixed-rate loans. They also generally offer lower loan origination costs. Because the lender is protected against rising interest rates, ARMs are generally assumable by qualified buyers.

In order to attract borrowers to ARMs, lenders offer "teaser" interest rates. These rates are less than index and margin would otherwise allow. The teaser rate could be for a specific period, such as six months or one year. A cap on interest increase could allow a borrower to have a below-market interest rate for several years. The low initial interest rates allow borrowers to qualify for an ARM loan who might otherwise fail to qualify for other types of loans. The worst-case scenario for a borrower would be that interest rates would rise to the loan cap, which would necessitate a significant increase in payments.

Seller Financing

When there is a ready, willing but not quite able buyer, the seller may offer to sell the property and take a purchase money mortgage as partial payment or sell under a land contract. The buyer's equity or cash down payment makes up the difference. The urgency to make the sale may encourage the seller to offer mortgage terms below the current market rates. Purchase money mortgages are subordinate to any existing mortgages on the property. When a seller does not need the cash and certificate of deposit rates are low—for example, 3 percent—that seller might consider carrying a 6 percent loan to have advantages over a cash sale.

In order to carry back a second mortgage or sell on land contract, the prior existing loans must be assumable. Otherwise, the lender could call in the loan under the due-on-sale clause.

Second Mortgages

If a lender is unwilling to lend the full amount borrowers need, the borrowers may seek additional funds from other sources if their credit standing is good. Funds obtained in this manner are subordinate to the original mortgage, which represents the first lien on the property. Loans obtained subsequent to and in addition to the primary mortgage are called second, third or junior mortgages. Any number of these lower-level liens may exist, but it is unlikely that a borrower will negotiate more than a second or perhaps a third mortgage. Home-equity loans made by banks and thrifts are really second mortgages.

A point to keep in mind, however, is that because of the added risk, the interest rates borne by these junior mortgages run considerably above loans that represent first liens on a property.

THE MORTGAGE MARKET

The mortgage market comprises an array of lenders (institutional and individual), borrowers and both public and private regulatory and financing agencies. The transactions and interactions among these participants in the market dramatically affect the viability and the very nature of real estate finance.

Savings and Loan Associations

Savings and loans associations, or thrifts, were once the largest source of home loans. With deregulation, S&Ls were able to make large commercial loans offering greater returns. A market decline resulted in loan defaults and the costly failure of a great many of these institutions. Because of more strict regulatory surveillance, S&Ls are now more conservative in their loans, but they are still a significant source of financing in many areas. The distinction between savings and loan institutions and banks has become blurred, and in many cases former S&Ls have become banks.

Mutual Savings Banks

MSBs are perhaps the most conservative thrift-type financial institution. While the average MSB holds somewhere between 60 and 70 percent of its loan portfolio in one- to four-family-home mortgages, conservative attitudes toward risk management have produced portfolios containing much higher proportions of government-insured or -guaranteed loans than are found in other financial intermediaries.

Real estate financing at MSBs takes place under low loan-to-value ratios and maturities of the most conservative while still practicable length. However, as an offset to these conservative terms, MSBs generally offer to lend at rates below those of institutions offering more liberal terms. Thus, MSBs offer an interesting complement to the policies of S&Ls.

Commercial Banks

Commercial banks traditionally have been lenders of short- to medium-term business loans. They have, however, increased their percentage of outstanding mortgage loans. Commercial banks make a great many home-equity loans (second mortgages) as well as construction loans. These loans have a higher rate of interest than home purchase loans.

Today, many commercial banks also play a significant role in home purchase loans, making conforming loans that they can resell to Fannie Mae or Freddie Mac. Banks will make nonconforming loans (usually to customers of the bank) for their own loan portfolio.

Lending policies at commercial banks are regulated by state banking commissions and the Federal Reserve System. Some commercial banks are more liberal than others in respect to real estate loan policies.

Life Insurance Companies

Although life insurance companies were at one time a substantial force in the residential mortgage market, they have since relinquished heavy involvement in residential real estate in favor of large commercial loans and the securities markets. Life insurance companies prefer large loans. Because there are few lenders for these loans, life insurance companies often demand an equity position in a project as a condition of the loan. This is known as a participation loan.

Life insurance companies are unlikely to become involved in single-family home loans unless they are involved in the financing or development of a large project.

Mortgage Companies

Mortgage companies are a major player in the mortgage market. They make both conforming and nonconforming loans that they resell in the secondary mortgage market. While they may resell loans to Fannie Mae and Freddie Mac, they also sell packages of loans to lending institutions, pension funds, trusts and even insurance companies.

Although mortgage companies may use their own funds to originate loans, they do not generally hold a large portfolio of loans for their own investment purposes. They make their money on loan origination costs and possible price premiums when they sell the loan.

They generally service the loans they sell and charge a servicing fee to the lenders holding the loan.

Mortgage companies may act as a "mortgage correspondent" for another lender, in which case the loan funds may come directly from the other lender.

Mortgage Loan Brokers

Mortgage loan brokers are middlemen who arrange loans by bringing together borrowers and lenders. They seldom use their own funds for the loans and, unlike mortgage companies, they seldom service the loans they arrange.

Mortgage loan brokers frequently can arrange loans where conventional financing is not readily available, such as for raw land or lots. However, the security for the loan must satisfy the lender's criteria.

The mortgage loan broker's fees are usually paid by the borrower. Loan costs and fees tend to be higher than for other lenders. In some states a mortgage loan broker must have a real estate license and is regulated by the state real estate regulatory agency.

Other Institutional Sources

Real estate investment trusts (REITs) provide a funnel for individuals' funds into the real estate mortgage and sale markets. Although not very important in the one- to four-family-home mortgage market, their importance as a lender in other categories of long-term mortgages and construction financing, as well as in investing in large properties, has become quite noticeable.

Credit unions and pension funds are also sources of real estate finance. Neither has a particularly large impact on the primary mortgage market, but their potential merits warrant including them.

Credit unions are a relatively accessible source of home-improvement loans. Some of the large credit unions are involved in the mortgage market, but their impact has not been significant.

The size of pension fund assets and their importance in the financial market is substantial. One would expect pension funds to be active in nearly all investment areas (particularly those that meet the safety of principal, liquidity and yield requirements), but a survey of distribution of these assets reveals that investments in mortgages are insignificant.

Pension funds have experienced several shifts in investment policy. In the transition from archconservative to moderately liberal, mortgages gained some favor, but most pension fund activity had been through the secondary market. They had increased their involvement in commercial projects, but because of losses are now investing primarily in conservative securities and have abandoned higher-risk investments.

Noninstitutional Sources

Individuals and trust funds are two major noninstitutional sources of real estate financing.

Individual financing has always represented an alternative source. In many cases, individuals are willing to assume much greater risk than institutional financiers. Most individual mortgage investments have been either seller carryback financing or cash investments made through loan brokers. Relatively few individual investors arrange their own loans.

Trust funds are a second noninstitutional source, accounting for far less than 1 percent of outstanding mortgage loans. Trust funds are more likely to purchase mortgages in the secondary mortgage market than to make the loans as a principal.

AVAILABILITY OF MORTGAGE FUNDS

Real estate financing is not always readily available on terms and conditions one might wish. Government regulation and agency activities, fluctuations in the capital market, attitudes toward risk and a variety of other considerations affect the availability of mortgage funds.

Government Influences

While the importance of the FHA and VA have been discussed, other important government agencies also affect the mortgage market. Some of these, such as the Federal Reserve System (FRS) and the Federal Home Loan Bank System (FHLBS), are primarily regulatory agencies that oversee the operations of commercial banks and federally chartered savings and loan associations. The Federal Reserve Board (FRB) establishes the "discount rate," an important monetary policy control of the interest rate at which members may borrow from their local district Federal Reserve Bank.

Other government and quasi-government agencies, such as the Government National Mortgage Association (GNMA), the Federal Home Loan Mortgage Corporation (FHLMC) and the Federal National Mortgage Association (FNMA), operate an extensive secondary mortgage market. These secondary mortgage market activities originally extended primarily to FHA and VA loans but now include conventional mortgages. By increasing and decreasing their purchase of mortgages from institutional lenders, these government agencies are able to contract or expand the amount of mortgage funds available in the market.

The Department of Housing and Urban Development (HUD) also affects the housing and mortgage markets through its housing subsidy and urban renewal programs.

Many other smaller agencies also have an impact on the availability of funds for real estate financing. The Farmers Home Administration (FmHA), the Small Business Administration (SBA) and even the Department of Transportation have noticeable, however small, effect on mortgage and capital markets. The general credit policies of the U.S. government can have persuasive effects on interest rates and overall economic conditions as well.

Perhaps the best that can be said is that government influence on and over the availability of mortgage money, while indirect, is both widespread and of great magnitude.

Lending Risks

Both institutional and noninstitutional lenders of funds must face and assume various types of risks. Institutional lenders, in particular, have developed rather formal and definite policies and procedures in evaluating the risks associated with real estate mortgage loans.

Both the borrower and the lender assume risk in financing arrangements. The borrower risks the property pledged as security and perhaps other assets as well. The lender faces the potential loss of principal and the attendant yield on it. Thus, the risk in lending is not borne exclusively by any single party to the contract.

Both borrower and lender face interest rate and purchasing power risks. Rates may rise, making the lender's yield below market; or they may fall, making the cost of borrowing higher than necessary. Inflation affects the purchasing power of the dollar to the benefit of the borrower, since the borrower is able to repay the loan with cheaper dollars. Deflation, on the other hand, benefits the lender.

From the lender's standpoint, the borrower and property also represent sources of risk. Thus, the lender will always conduct a careful check of the borrower's credit standing and have an appraisal of the property done to make sure that it represents adequate security given the size of the loan.

If risks seem too great, the lender may deny the loan or request that mortgage insurance be provided. Most lenders have standardized guidelines concerning the acceptability of mortgage applications. If the risks associated with the proposed mortgage do not conform to these standards, the application is usually denied.

Other areas of risk involve the legality of ownership interest, zoning and subdivision prohibitions, and a host of legal considerations. Thus, risk in lending affects the overall availability of mortgage funds—particularly with respect to the individual's circumstances. As with other counsel the broker may give clients, information concerning the risks associated with mortgage financing is of great importance and should be understood clearly from the outset.

SPECIAL TYPES OF FINANCING

There are occasions when standard mortgage financing provisions do not provide the borrower with the incentives or investment return that is sought. In these situations, special types of financing have evolved to cope with unique needs and circumstances. The needs of the borrower often demand that special lending packages be constructed. The following are some of the more common special arrangements.

Construction Loans

Because of their short-term maturity, construction loans are not generally considered to be mortgages. Unlike a typical mortgage in which proceeds are paid out in a lump sum and repaid over a 20- to 30-year term, a construction loan is disbursed slowly as the construction proceeds. It requires a seasoned lender to administer the disbursement properly and is rarely written for maturities in excess of three years. Because of the high risk involved in speculative construction, lenders typically require high interest rates on these loans.

Commercial banks and, to a lesser extent, savings associations and mortgage REITs are the most common sources of construction loans. In many cases the construction lender may also pick up the permanent loan on the property, as its early involvement with the project necessitates little added expense to underwrite the final mortgage.

Developers and lenders take risk in committing to permanent financing at the time the construction loan is written. If the interest rates subsequently fall, the developer is committed to a high-interest loan. If the interest rates rise, the lender is committed to a below-market loan. If permanent financing is not arranged, the borrower could be faced with a market situation where an acceptable loan is not available.

Bridge Loan (Gap Loan or Swing Loan) These are relatively short-term loans and are usually written at relatively high interest rates. They are generally straight loans, interest payment only, with the principal due on the due date. They are often taken out by developers between the construction loan and permanent financing, or when a buyer will have money coming in from a pending sale of another property.

Participation Loan   These loans, which are usually for commercial property, give the lender an equity position in the property in addition to the interest. The equity position is sometimes given in exchange for a lower interest rate that makes the investment viable. Insurance companies are the largest lenders involved in participation loans.

Shared-Appreciation Mortgage   This is a type of participation loan. Under such loans, a private lender advances a buyer money toward the down payment of a home. After an agreed period, the property is to be appraised or sold and the lender is to get back his or her investment plus a share in the appreciated value.

The lender in a shared-appreciation mortgage is often a relative who wants to help the buyers but is unwilling to do so in the form of a gift at the time the loan is made. Some sellers will provide for shared-appreciation features in carryback financing when the buyer has little or no down payment.

Reverse Mortgage   These loans are typically made to elderly homeowners who have substantial equity in their homes. The lenders make periodic, usually monthly, payments to the homeowners. Because the homeowners make no payments on the loan, the interest compounds. Upon the death of the homeowners or sale of the property, the loan is repaid. These loans allow homeowners to maintain their standard of living without having to sell their homes.

These special lending/financing situations can hardly be considered an exhaustive listing. Land leases in lieu of purchase, syndications, the use of non-realty collateral for mortgage security and mortgage bonds are other special types and methods of real estate financing not discussed here but with which you may at some point become involved.

Chapter 12

Expanding Your Services

The majority of real estate firms are involved primarily in the listing and sale of residential property. Some firms specialize within the residential area. Specialties could be mobile homes, condominiums or homes within a designated price range or subdivision.

As the real estate industry broadens its scope, brokers are challenged to develop or enter new services and fields of selling.

IMPROVING EXISTING PROPERTIES

The shortage of vacant land within city limits has increased the value of ground under existing homes. Unearned increment of land value in many cases actually increases the sale price of used homes. A study of land values under older homes in districts where streets are paved and sewer, water and other utilities are in and paid for may reveal their sales advantage over unimproved lots in a subdivision.

Rehabilitation and redevelopment, not demolition, may be the most practical way to renew old neighborhoods. Present owners may be persuaded to modernize for profit. Their activities may be part of a broad program backed by the local board of REALTORS®, the local government and, in some cases, the individual entrepreneur working singlehandedly to get such campaigns under way.

Many brokers and real estate salespeople counsel buyers or personally invest in property needing rehabilitation: After rehabilitation the property is either rented or sold. In selling your own inventory, care must be taken so that buyers realize that it is your own property and you are thus acting as a principal and not in any agency capacity.

SELLING TO BUILDERS

Some agents specialize in lots and land, selling to builders. They work closely with builders to fully understand their needs. They then locate properties for these builders.

SELLING FOR BUILDERS

Most new homes are the products of builders who make their living supplying housing to meet public demand. To complete their program of development, construction and sale, builders must either have salespeople in their organization or use the services of real estate brokers and salespeople. Some brokers work with builders from the start of a subdivision project. They help find the site, handle the purchase, arrange financing and handle the advertising, marketing, sale and settlement of the finished properties. And when buyers have old homes to dispose of, the brokers sell them too, sometimes offering a trade-in.

While some large real estate firms have new-home specialists sell builders' houses, many treat new-home sales like other listings, and their salespeople sell both new and preowned homes.

In some cases, you will be unable to meet the needs of a buyer with an existing property. Some salespeople work closely with designers and builders and arrange for a custom home to be built for the buyers.

BUYER AGENCY

Most real estate agents have been seller agents or dual agents. In the past few years, we have seen the emergence of buyer agency, which opens up a new window of opportunity for real estate professionals.

As a buyers' agent you act *for* the buyers rather than *with* them. Your obligation is to best meet the needs of your buyers. This would include helping the buyers to negotiate the best purchase price and terms from the buyers' viewpoint. Some buyer agents act exclusively as buyers' agents, while most have added buyer agency as an additional service to the more traditional listing of property and, hence, representing sellers.

Under a buyer listing agreement, the buyers' agent usually shares in the fee paid by the sellers, but the buyers are responsible for the agent's fee if not paid by others. The concept of buyers' agency has been endorsed by many consumer groups such as the American Association of Retired Persons (AARP) and the Consumer Federation.

RELOCATION

The United States has become a nation of corporate nomads, a trend that has opened a new market for real estate brokers. The relocation field has become a viable force in the real estate industry, because corporations and brokers have become aware of the need to assist transferring families in a more professional and organized manner.

The involvement of the broker is best described as that of a liaison between the corporation and the transferred family. The corporation is concerned about time constraints, loss of manpower and image, while the family may feel discouraged, imposed upon and frustrated.

Regardless of the size firm you are affiliated with, the relocation aspect of the real estate industry can mean additional income. Many large firms in major cities have entire divisions devoted to the development of this particular market. At the other end of the spectrum, in areas that have a small corporate base to draw upon, individual sales associates are becoming specialists by gearing their talents to meet the needs of these families.

Referral Networks

Referral networks were established in the 1960s when brokers became aware of the potential market that could be developed by recommending a cooperating broker in another area to a family that needed assistance in either the purchase or sale of property.

In most cases, a referral fee is established and sent to the broker initiating the lead. Fees are normally established as a percentage of the earned commissions of the receiving broker.

Independent referral networks are available to brokers nationwide. Networks also are available to brokers affiliated with national franchises. In either case, a referral network is an added benefit to the real estate salesperson as an additional source of buyer and seller leads and as a way to provide a national image for any size firm.

Some firms limit their referrals to buyer agents because, in a referral, they feel that they have a special obligation to the buyer that can best be served by a buyer agent.

Relocation Firms

Relocation firms contract with corporations that are transferring employees. Employees are generally given the option of selling the property on their own or accepting an offer based on appraisals. The relocation firm then uses local brokers to market the property that it acquires.

100 PERCENT COMMISSION OFFICES

The 100 percent commission concept is basically that the broker maintains an office and provides salespeople with some support and services set forth in a broker-salesperson contract. The salesperson keeps all fees generated by his or her listings or sales and pays the broker a set monthly fee (and/or a fee per transaction) along with reimbursing the broker for specified costs.

The concept is best suited for experienced salespeople who are well motivated and are able to generate their own leads.

FRANCHISES

Franchises have become a major segment of the business community. From mufflers to donuts to hamburgers, people have seen the advantages of becoming affiliated with a national company. The benefits of being competitive combined with training and national identification have created a boom in the franchising business.

A real estate franchise offers the broker sales and management training programs, computer production reports and regional sales meetings. By being part of a national organization, a broker does not stand alone in the market but is allied with a network of real estate firms sharing the same identification. Thus, real estate franchises grew out of the desire of the independent real estate broker to be able to offer services competitive with those offered by the larger firms.

Century 21, RE/MAX, ERA, Realty World, Red Carpet and others entered the real estate franchising business and expanded rapidly. And the ranks grew as the benefits of a national affiliation have become apparent during recessionary times. A franchisor charges the franchisee a percentage of gross commission revenues as a service fee—typically 5 percent. There may be an additional contribution for a national advertising fund.

Joining a franchise is not a cure-all, however. You should thoroughly investigate the disadvantages as well as the advantages before making a decision to affiliate with a national firm.

PROPERTY MANAGEMENT

Some real estate offices deal exclusively in property management, while others have a separate property management department. Property management is an economically stable area of real estate in that regardless of economic conditions, property must be managed.

In property management, the property manager takes over the duties, responsibilities and problems of the owners. The property manager is involved in property problems, security and interpersonal problems.

Property management firms typically charge a percentage of the gross income as well as a minimum charge. Generally, property requiring more intensive work in relation to income would be charged a higher percentage. Depending upon the percentage charged, there could also be separate leasing fees. Many firms also charge a supervisory percentage on major repairs and/or remodeling work.

The property management contract between owners and broker would spell out all broker compensation as well as broker duties and any limitations on the broker's authority.

A growing area closely resembling property management is condominium and timeshare-type association management. While the manager is responsible for the physical aspects of the property as well as collecting and disbursing funds and providing an accounting function, management duties generally do not involve rentals. Typically, management charges are per unit and the management fees are collected from the owners' assessments. Some association management firms also handle rentals for individual owners.

LEASING

While property management involves leasing, many firms specialize in leasing without property management duties. Leasing agents may specialize in industrial, retail, office or residential property. These agents typically charge a percentage of the lease entered into. For multiyear leases, the percentage after the first year might be stepped down for subsequent years.

APPRAISAL

A separate license and/or certification is generally required for real estate appraisal. However, a great many appraisers started out as real estate salespeople and through training and experience were able to become appraisers. Some real estate firms have appraisal departments.

While real estate sales is a people-oriented profession, appraisal is more of a property-centered profession requiring keen analytical skills as well as an understanding of economic factors affecting value.

Like property management, appraisal tends to be relatively stable; however, there is greater activity in periods of active real estate sales as well as when interest rates drop and a great many owners are refinancing their properties.

EXCHANGE

There has been a renewed interest in real estate exchanging since the Tax Reform Act of 1986 did away with the favorable capital gains treatment for profit on sales.

A growing number of real estate professionals are devoting their efforts to exchanging property. They counsel owners on how they can dispose of property and obtain property that better meets their needs without paying any tax on their gains. These professionals have in-depth knowledge of tax-deferred exchanges.

AUCTIONS

Auctions have long been a common real estate marketing procedure in England and Australia. A growing number of U.S. firms are now realizing that auctions can play a significant role in marketing real estate in our country as well. There are now many firms that do nothing but handle auctions. Auctions have been held to dispose of large numbers of REOs (real estate owned) by lenders. They are also used by developers to dispose of their remaining parcels or units in order to generate the capital to proceed with other projects. In addition, successful auctions have been held for individual properties and even groups of unrelated properties.

Auction firms must publicize the auction. They generally receive advance advertising costs from the owner. They prequalify bidders and arrange financing prior to the auction as well as conducting the auction. Often, lender representatives are present at the auctions to complete loan applications.

Auctions might have minimum bids. Minimum bids are generally low enough to attract bidders. Some auctions offer some or all properties "without reserve," which means that the low bid, no matter what it is, will get the property.

FARM AND LAND BROKERAGE

Because of the specialized knowledge required for farm brokerage, farm brokers tend to devote all of their efforts to the sale of farms and land. These agents tend to work in larger areas, and many have their own airplanes to reduce travel time.

While farm brokers will generally also sell undeveloped land, many land brokers will not handle the sale of farms unless they are sold for land value and not for farming. Land brokers sell to investors, developers and to ultimate users as homesites, or for hunting, timber or mining purposes.

BUSINESS OPPORTUNITIES

In many areas, real estate agents can sell business opportunities with or without real estate. If real estate is involved, a real estate license is required. Business opportunities brokers require intensive business knowledge and must be able to understand balance sheets and profit and loss statements.

There are a great many business opportunity brokers who specialize in the sale of a particular type of business, such as bars, restaurants, mobile home parks, hotels, and so on.

FORECLOSURE SALES

A number of brokerage offices as well as salespeople specialize in selling foreclosure property. They might sell VA and HUD foreclosures; property owned by FDIC (Federal Deposit Insurance Corporation) or RTC (Resolution Trust Corporation); or REOs (real estate owned) that have been foreclosed by local lenders.

Salespeople active in foreclosure sales devote the majority of their time to locating buyers for this foreclosure inventory. To sell FHA property, the broker must qualify as a HUD broker, which is a relatively simple process. To sell VA property, the broker must qualify as a VA broker, which usually involves attending a free workshop. An advantage of these sales is that the selling broker generally gets the entire sales commission.

Fannie Mae (FNMA) uses independent brokers to market its property. These brokers are approved by FNMA and may receive an exclusive listing. The listing broker may also be expected to prepare the property for marketing.

Some lenders will give exclusive listings to real estate firms that can handle the protection and rehabilitation of their foreclosure inventory.

LOAN BROKERAGE

In many states, a real estate license allows a real estate broker to engage in the loan brokerage business. The broker acts as a middleman, finding borrowers who want to borrow on real property and lenders willing to make the loans. The loan broker allows individual investors to enter the mortgage market, obtaining greater yields than could be generated by other readily available investments. The broker's fees and costs are customarily paid by the borrower.

The interest charged is generally related to the investment risk. In some states, loans arranged by loan brokers are exempt from usury laws that limit interest charged by an individual.

BROKERAGE OF INVESTMENT OR INCOME-PRODUCING PROPERTIES

While the great majority of real estate brokers in the United States today are involved with the sale of single-family homes, an area of real estate brokerage that has grown tremendously in the past decade is the field of commercial and investment brokerage.

Although most homebuyers are concerned primarily with the amenities associated with the homes they live in, many have found that their residences are also one of the best investments they have made. Many homeowners have treated their home as just a first step in their real estate investment program.

Investment by individuals is the very foundation of the private enterprise economic system of the United States; a great majority of our population is involved in some form of investment. Since World War II, disposable personal income has risen, as has the number of individuals who are both able and willing to invest their excess funds in one of many investment alternatives available to them. Indeed, the number of investors has grown at a rate much higher than the population growth rate since 1940, and investment capital is available from the huge pool of middle-income families and individuals.

TREND TOWARD REAL ESTATE INVESTMENTS

Although there is a wide variety of alternative investments for the typical small investor, there has been a definite trend in recent years toward income-producing real estate. One of the most obvious reasons for this is the fluctuating purchasing power of the dollar because of periodic inflation. In addition, real estate offers some unique tax advantages not available in many other forms of investment. Finally, investment in real estate offers broad financing possibilities that are not present with most other forms of investment.

Inflation

The United States has experienced a number of inflationary cycles since World War II. Fixed-income investments have proven to be poor investments during inflationary periods, as the investor receives dollars back from an investment with decreasing purchasing power. When the principal is returned, it has far less value than it had when it was invested.

Real estate, on the other hand, historically has been one of the few investments that have significantly outpaced inflation in cash return and/or appreciation in value.

In periods of low interest rates, certificates of deposit offer returns barely equal to inflation rates. The only reasonable rates are for long-term investments that can be expected to decline in value during any future inflationary period.

During these slow-growth periods, current real estate investment returns can compare favorably with securities plus offer the likelihood of significant appreciation in value and income over subsequent years.

Tax Advantages

Although the Tax Reform Act of 1986 removed some of the tax advantages of real estate investments, real estate is the only major tax shelter still available for the average investor as well as the homeowner, and offers additional tax benefits.

Homeowners have the following tax advantages:

- Interest payments (with some limitations) and property taxes are deductible expenses for tax purposes.
- Homeowners who purchase another home costing the same or more within two years of the sale of their home can defer the gain.
- Homeowners age 55 or older who have lived in their residence three of the preceding five years may be eligible to exclude $125,000 of their gain from federal income taxation.

Investors have the following tax benefits:

- Depreciation is a noncash deductible expense for tax purposes. Residential income property is depreciated over 27 1/2 years and income property is depreciated over 39 years. Investors can show 1/27.5 or 1/39 of the value of the improvements as an expense each year. This depreciation thus reduces the investor's tax liability on his or her income. Depreciation can always shelter income from other real estate investments (passive income). Depreciation can even shelter active income, such as income from wages. Taxpayers with a gross adjusted income of $100,000 or less can shelter up to $25,000 of their active income. For taxpayers with between $100,000 and $150,000 of gross adjusted income, the $25,000 limit is reduced by $1 for each $2 of adjusted gross income over $100,000. The majority of investors thus are eligible to shelter some of their active income.
- Investors who qualify as real estate professionals can use passive losses to offset other income without limit provided they meet stated IRS criteria, including spending at least 750 hours per tax year in specified real estate–related activities.

Income

Of major importance to investors is present and future income.

When rents are increasing, investors will pay prices based on anticipated future earnings. Investors will accept significant negative cash flows if they have sufficient resources to make up the deficit and if they feel that the negative situation is short-lived.

For example, assume a building has a gross annual rent of $100,000, debt service of $90,000 and operating expenses of $30,000. This building would have an annual negative cash flow of $20,000. If rents increase 5 percent per year, in five years the rent would then be $130,627 (5 percent compounded on each prior year's rent). If the expenses also increased by 5 percent, at the end of five years they would be $38,284. This would provide an annual positive cash flow of $1,716. However, within a few more years there would be a significant positive cash flow. In addition, the investor's loss during the first few years would have been reduced by the tax benefits of the operational loss plus depreciation.

During periods when rent increases are not expected, investors are generally unwilling to accept a negative cash flow. They are interested in cash return on the total purchase price as well as cash return on cash invested.

Exchange

Investment real estate can be exchanged on a tax-deferred basis, an advantage not afforded many other investments. Briefly, Section 1031 of the Internal Revenue Code provides that no gain or loss is to be recognized for tax purposes if investment property is exchanged solely for property of a like kind that is also to be held as an investment, provided the replacement property is identified within 45 days of the transfer and title is obtained within 180 days.

If a person does not receive "boot" (cash, unlike property or debt relief), that person can have a tax-deferred exchange, keeping his or her old cost basis adjusted for any boot that he or she was given. Boot received in an exchange is taxed to the party receiving it.

If a person had sold a property rather than having a tax-deferred exchange, then the realized gain would be taxed and the seller would have less money to invest in another property.

Exchanging has become an important tool to the investment real estate broker. It requires clear understanding of the federal income tax code as well as an awareness of investor objectives. In the real market, exchanges may be a simple trade of one property for another, but more likely they involve complex multiple holdings involving many owners and lenders.

Leverage

Leverage is the use of borrowed funds with a fixed or limited borrowing cost to finance income properties. When an investor purchases a property, he or she acquires the rights to both the income generated by the property through its rent plus any appreciation that might occur. This usually provides a better rate of return on the dollar than most other types of investment can provide.

As the residential broker well knows, it is common to find 80 percent and above mortgage loans on owner-occupied homes. It is not as common to find such high loan-to-value ratios on commercial and investment property. During inflationary periods, borrowers want as large a loan-to-value ratio as possible to take advantage of inflation. During periods of slow economic growth, investors tend to be more conservative. A larger down payment reduces debt service costs and the likelihood of default should income fail to reach expectations. The loan-to-value ratio will vary considerably by type of property, but it is not uncommon to find commercial property financed so that the loan represents between 50 and 75 percent of value.

Installment Sale

When the proceeds of a sale are received over several years, the taxable gain is spread out as well. This could result in the gain being taxed at a lower rate. Installment sale benefits are not available to dealers engaged in buying and selling property.

ROLE OF THE REAL ESTATE INVESTMENT BROKER

When dealing with income-producing properties, real estate brokers play a number of highly specialized roles for which they may be paid a commission, a fee for services rendered or a combination of both. Increasingly, investment brokers are serving as real estate analysts and investment counselors to the ever-growing number of investors who seek out and rely upon their expertise.

For the smaller investors, investment brokers may provide assistance in first acquiring and then managing a portfolio of real estate holdings. During this process, they work closely with the investor's accountant and/or attorney to identify the tax consequences of the acquisition of the investment program. For larger investors or groups of investors, brokers may act as leasing agents, mortgage brokers and feasibility consultants. They often work closely with investors to identify feasible developments, present the loan package to potential mortgage lenders on the project, obtain tenants and even manage the property.

Clients

The clients and/or prospects of the investment property broker range from the owner of a very small duplex apartment property to the syndicated ownership of a larger shopping center or office building. At times the investment broker represents the seller, but often he or she represents someone who seeks to acquire an investment property by purchase, exchange or lease. Some investment brokers are paid an hourly fee for their advice.

TYPES OF INVESTMENT PROPERTIES

Investment property may be categorized into eight general types.

1. Single-Tenant Structure

Generally a freestanding building, it is often leased for a long period, such as five to ten years, with an option to renew. Longer leases generally provide for rent increases and may be tied to an economic index, such as the Consumer Price Index. This protects the owner against inflation eroding the value of the rent received.

When single-tenant buildings are built for a specific tenant, such as a large discount store or a major chain, the lease is likely to be for a period of from 15 to 30 years. The lease is likely to be a net lease, in which the tenant pays the owner a net amount. The tenant is responsible for taxes, insurance and all other expenses dealing with the structure. When the tenant is secure financially, this type of investment is desired by insurance companies, pension plans and other large investors desiring long-term secure income.

Generally, the rent and sale price would be related to the financial stability of the tenant. For example, investors would be willing to accept a lower rate of return for a structure leased to the U.S. Post Office than they would accept for a structure leased to a new fast-food franchise.

2. Multiple-Tenant Structure

This category is typically represented by the well-located, one-story multiple retail building, to be leased to national or local chains or to substantial independent operators. Assuming proper location, these parcels offer enhancement opportunities and are in great demand.

The lease terms under multiple-tenant structures would be tied to the desirability of the property as well as the market. Owners who believe rents will increase significantly in the future will want tenants to be on relatively short-term leases. When, however, an owner expects stable or declining rents and/or increased vacancies, owners will prefer longer-term leases.

Leases on multitenant properties are likely to be gross or flat leases (same rent each month), with the owner paying taxes, insurance and agreed maintenance and/or utilities. They may be tied to an index to protect the owner. Retail tenants in more desirable locations may have a percentage lease, which is rent based upon a percentage of the gross. There would also be a minimum rent.

Investors for these properties would be influenced by size, rent receipts, price and desirability of the property.

3. Shopping Centers

Shopping centers range from minicenters, with a fast-food or convenience store as the key tenant, to regional malls having a number of major department stores as key tenants and a great many smaller retail outlets.

Large malls are frequently owned by the developer corporation. Insurance companies, real estate investment trusts, syndicates and large real estate corporations like these investments, which could entail more than $1 billion.

Shopping center sales involve the ability to forecast future income and expenses considering population movement, competitive properties and other economic factors.

4. Mixed-Use Improvements

There are many structures that don't fit into a single-use category. For example, some large central-city structures have retail stores on the ground floor, offices on several floors and perhaps a health club, restaurant or even apartments or hotel rooms on the upper floors. There are also many older structures with retail stores and several floors of apartments. Buyers of mixed-use structures are investors who feel that the advantages of the property more than offset the negative features of managing a mixed-use structure.

5. Multifamily Housing

Most real estate investors invest in residential property. One reason is that there are so many more residential properties than any other property type.

Investors find apartment structures easy to relate to, and they like the fact that apartments have a far lower vacancy factor than commercial and industrial property. Other advantages include higher loan-to-value ratio loans and the fact that apartment rents tend to remain stable or actually increase even during slow economic periods.

Condominium conversion possibilities can provide added value to multifamily housing. Some brokers specialize in helping owners obtain the necessary approvals as well as help in marketing the property.

Actually, the condominium concept is not limited to residential properties. Agents have been involved in condominium conversions of factories, retail structures, garage space and even marinas.

6. Industrial

Industrial structures have undergone greater change in design than almost any other form of building. At one time, most industrial or manufacturing structures were multistory. The lack of operating efficiency in such buildings led to the modern plant, which is usually one story high except for the office portion.

The ground area in modern industrial buildings is much larger to provide adequate parking. If an industrial property can be turned into a substantial leaseback, it is salable at a fairly low return. Otherwise, the buyer is confronted with the possibility of single-purpose obsolescence and will show interest only if the return is high.

Vacant industrial property is a relatively high-risk investment, which is generally reflected in a price far less than would be asked for well-leased property.

7. Office Buildings

Because of the rapid expansion of office construction during the early 1980s and a general economic slowdown that began in the late 1980s, there is currently a glut of vacant office space in many market areas.

Prices of quality office buildings, which had been bid up based on increasing rent expectations, have fallen. Many owners were foreclosed when income failed to match debt service and operating expenses.

The depressed market has created an interest from bargain-hunting real estate investment trusts and syndicates that realize that real estate is cyclical and that it won't be many more years before demand catches up with the supply.

8. Transient Housing

Hotel and motel buildings have an appeal to many investors. New construction techniques make them adaptable to market conditions.

In many areas of the country, new hotel construction has resulted in a glut of rooms, and cash-rich investors are buying up properties at prices far below replacement costs.

Older hotel and motel properties in many major cities are being converted for SROs (single-room occupancy). In many markets, there is a great need for permanent low-cost housing for single people.

SPECIALIZED SALES TOOLS

Sale-Leaseback

Large corporations that operate numerous stores or agencies in cities across the nation sell and lease back their local buildings to increase their working funds. The common pattern is for the corporation to build, then sell the building, with the corporation as a tenant under a long-term lease. The selling price is related as much to the lease terms and financial strengths of the tenant as it actually is to property value. In fact, strong national tenants can get considerably more than their costs back if the lease terms justify the price. Other sale-leasebacks occur when a firm owning a property wishes to raise capital without incurring debt.

Frequently, a corporation furnishes exact specifications for a building in a new location and the owner has the structure built specifically for the corporation, which will move in as lessee (a build-to-suit transaction).

Sale-leaseback is, in truth, a single transaction. The property owner agrees to sell all or part of his or her holding with the stipulation that the buyer lease it back to him or her. On the other hand, the buyer agrees to buy only on the condition that the seller will lease the property over a given number of years. If this reciprocity is absent, the transaction, by definition, is not a sale-leaseback.

Motivations for pursuing a sale-leaseback may vary, but certain patterns are easily discerned: the need for long-term working capital, the fact that rent is a fully deductible business expense; and a sale-leaseback allows the corporate balance sheet to show less debt, because there is no longer a mortgage.

On the other side of the transaction, the buyer has negotiated for valuable real estate with a guaranteed net income computed to yield an equitable return on the investment.

Ground Leases

The ground lease has a history going back to ancient times. The use of another's unimproved land for a farm, a home or a business can often prove profitable for both landowner and tenant. The technique is most prevalent in Hawaii and is starting to see a lot of use in Florida and other areas, as well as on Indian-owned land. Most homes in Hawaii, for example, are sold on leasehold land, the most common application of the ground lease on residential property. In this case, a person buys a home but not the land under it. Instead, he or she signs a lease for the land, which is usually a long-term lease covering the expected life of the house.

Landowners are intrigued with ground leases, which give them a net rent each year and ownership of improved property at the end of the lease.

Downtown office building owners might well prefer a ground lease, because they then would not have the tremendous expense of buying land at rates that can exceed $100 per square foot. There are also some tax advantages for the commercial developer or firm. They can expense the rental while they could not depreciate the land, as it is a nonwasting asset. An owner who might want 7 percent return to rent a property might be willing to accept 4 percent or even less with the sweetener of getting the improvements for nothing in 30 years. A bargain rent can turn a property that would otherwise have a negative cash flow into one with a positive cash flow. Some sophisticated developers have found it advantageous to separate the land from the building and then place a master lease on the property. They sell the land subject to the ground lease to an investor looking toward the welfare of children or grandchildren, who will own the building when the lease expires. They sell the building to another investor subject to a master lease and either keep the master lease themselves as managers or sell the master lease. The holder of the master lease subleases the space and hopes to make a profit based on the difference between the master lease payments plus operating expenses and the actual rent received.

Increasing application of the ground lease theory is being seen in many areas. Among them is the procedure by which air rights over a piece of property are leased from the owner.

Other Specialties

Other areas of specialization include agents who handle the sale of mineral oil and gas properties and/or leases.

There are also brokers who counsel owners for a fee. These knowledgeable professionals might develop feasibility studies for a use, locate property and/or provide advice on marketing, and so on.

There are firms that will handle the paperwork for condominium conversions and/or subdivisions. You should realize by now that areas of specialization are limited only by the needs of others.

Chapter 13

Technology and Real Estate

The past two decades have seen a technological revolution in the way real estate business is conducted. Technology allows real estate professionals to maximize the value of their time.

CELLULAR TELEPHONES

Real estate salespeople can stay in ready contact with their office and clients through the use of cellular telephones. The cost of these phones has been decreasing, from original prices approaching $1,000 to current prices of less than $200. The salesperson pays a monthly fee to the cellular company of about $25 plus a charge for time. Hands-off dialing is now possible with voice-activated calling.

PAGERS

A low-cost alternative to cellular phones is a pager system. Originally, pagers simply told you to call a service or a number; sophisticated pagers now give you messages. You can put some pagers on a vibration mode so the audible signal does not interrupt a presentation. Today, many agents use a combination of cellular phone and pager.

800 NUMBERS

For agents who deal with people outside their local phone service, an 800 number is a valuable advantage. If your office does not have an 800 number, you might want to consider obtaining your own low-cost 800 service.

Your cards, letterheads and ads will indicate the 800 number and extension. When a caller dials the number and extension, a secretary answers with your name. Some service charges are as low as $10 per month plus $1 for each caller who leaves a name and/or number.

FAX MACHINES

By using fax machines, you can send contracts and information to buyers and sellers instantly. Some agents have fax machines for their car phones. Fax machines can also be connected to computers to give you laser printouts of faxes.

ELECTRONIC TAPE MEASURES

Small, hand-held electronic devices that sell for less than $50 can accurately measure the distance between two walls. This tool can be a tremendous timesaver in measuring rooms. In addition, it requires only one person to do the task.

TALKING SIGNS

Miniature radio transmitters are available (both AM and FM) that will broadcast a continuous message about a property within a 150-foot to 200-foot range. You can indicate on your For Sale signs that a property has a talking sign and at what radio frequency the message describing the home's features can be heard. Besides being an excellent sales tool, these transmitters are a great listing tool. Talking signs are now available for under $300 and are usually the property of the listing salesperson, not the broker.

ELECTRONIC TELEPHONE DIRECTORIES

Small battery-operated, electronic Rolodex-type telephone directories are available that can hold hundreds of names and telephone numbers. Many agents find these compact devices handy to have, especially for use with car phones.

VOICE MAIL

Sophisticated voice mail systems have replaced the old telephone answering machines. The new systems utilize computers. They can locate you and give you the message on your car or home phone, allowing immediate response.

LOAN QUALIFIERS

An electronic calculator is available that can quickly an accurately determine the income required to qualify for any given loan using various lender ratios. The device can calculate a buyer's actual debt and income ratio.

FINANCIAL CALCULATORS

Small electronic financial calculators will enable you to determine

- the original amount of a loan when you know the amount of the payment, interest rate and length of loan;
- what the balance will be on an amortized loan at any future date;
- payments on an amortized loan for any period at any interest rate;

. . . and a lot more.

The advantage of these calculators as well as the loan qualifier is size. These functions can generally be performed faster on computers.

ELECTRONIC LOCKBOXES

Electronic or computerized lockboxes are available for which the MLS agent employs a coded card. The listing agent can use the telephone to find out which agents showed a property and when. It allows the listing agent to get the reactions of other agents as well as report to the property owner on all showing activity. These lockboxes are usually the property of the listing agent.

COMPUTERS

A real estate professional without a computer will not be nearly as effective as one who owns and uses the computer to its capacity. There is a wide variety of software programs designed for the real estate professional. Generally, these specific programs will save time over more generic programs that can be adapted for your use. There are new programs available every month, and most of the software companies offer 800 numbers to assist users. Some companies conduct classes in major cities on the use of their software. You will be able to see many of these programs demonstrated at state and national REALTOR® conventions. Software programs are available to serve the general needs of real estate salespeople and brokers as well as particular specialties. The lists that follow describe just some of the functions presently possible with computer software.

Salesperson's Software

- Prepares competitive market analysis in minutes using MLS records or other database material. Includes cover letter, introduction, salesperson's resume and active, inactive, sales pending and sold listings with a summary.
- Can immediately locate property from calls by street name, area, features, property type or MLS number.
- Prepares a complete personalized listing presentation package.
- Contains service listing file.
- Contains listing data file (schools, zoning, etc.).
- Contains farming programs.
- Integrates tax assessor's data into farming data.
- Prepares newsletters.
- Prints professional-quality property briefs and agent open house announcements.
- Prints professional-quality floor plans of listings.
- Provides a history file on every contact.
- Prequalifies prospects quickly, showing qualification for available conventional fixed-rate and adjustable-rate loans as well as FHA and VA financing.
- Prepares income requirements by property.
- Prepares a prospect database.
- Prepares rent versus buy comparisons.
- Matches buyers from buyers' file with new listings based on buyers' needs parameters.
- Contains history file on every contact.
- Prepares call lists.
- Contains index of special contract clauses for listings and purchase contracts.
- Prepares seller estimated proceeds.
- Prepares buyer estimated costs.
- Registers client birthdate, anniversaries, etc.
- Graphs show salesperson's success in listing and sales by price range and type of property.
- Performs personal financial analysis.
- Performs financial analysis of investment property.

- Prepares pro forma statements (estimated projections) for income property.

Broker and Salesperson Software

- Calendar/Daily Planner
- "To Do" list
- Daily Reminder (from calendar)
- Word processor for preparing letters, brochures, flyers, etc.
- Phone directory
- Floor-time register and display
- Listing files
- Listing expiration reports
- Listing history (includes advertising, open houses, showings)
- Listings by areas
- Listings by sources (FSBO, referrals, etc.)
- Letters (software for commonly used letters)
- Print shop capability
- Marketing plan preparation
- Pinpoints "hot" areas of activity by geographical area, price and buyer category, as well as changes in activity.
- Personal financial analysis
- Escrow/settlement tracking

Broker Software

- Recruiting software—provides data on successful salespeople in other offices with breakdowns for area, price range and type of property.
- Market penetration analysis shows percentage of sales and dollar amounts by area and/or type of property for firm as well as competition.
- Analysis of areas of company strength and company weaknesses
- Visual graphs showing activity of firm by month, quarter and year as well as comparison graphs showing market share by time period
- Comparison of office production (multioffice brokers)
- Expense projections
- Cash projections based on pending closing (cash flow)
- Profit and loss statements
- Balance sheets
- Trust account journal
- Checkbook reconciliation
- Warnings when ledgers do not balance
- Printing commission checks
- Income statements for salespeople

- Analyzes producers by month and type of production.
- Identifies agents who need help or appear to have problems.
- Income and expenses by agent
- Determines monthly desk costs.
- Evaluates changes in desk costs.
- Agent billings for desk costs/fees, etc.
- Analyzes advertising effectiveness.
- Visual graphs showing monthly advertising by type
- Advertising costs by listing
- Insurance register for company coverage
- Franchise reports
- Employee checks, withholding and reports
- Employees'/salespeople's birthdates, anniversaries, etc.
- Employee benefits accounting
- Compares budgeted expense to actuals.
- Analyzes co-broker activity.
- Market change analysis
- Referral tracking

Property Management Software

- Lease files, including terms and clauses
- Lease expiration register
- Comparative lease analysis
- Inactive property files
- Trust journals with balances by property and owners
- Security deposit register
- Audit of security deposit
- Monthly, quarterly and annual owner financial statements and checks
- Owner 1099s
- Owner billing
- Check register
- Matching of owners with addresses, property numbers or tenant names
- Work orders
- Work order warnings (if exceeds limitation)
- Work order tracing (includes vendor, cost and check payment)
- Preventive maintenance program
- Maintenance cost history by property and/or major system
- Vendor lists
- Vendor history (by vendor)
- Tickler files for scheduling, payments, etc.
- Utility payments
- Significant changes in utility costs

- Mortgage payments
- Insurance register and insurance payments
- Accounts payable ledger
- Accounts receivable ledger
- Operational account ledger
- Rent ledger
- Rent increase billing
- Tenant rent-paying history
- Tenant delinquency register
- Late charges
- Bad-check register
- Tenant notices and unlawful detainers
- Occupancy reports
- Change in occupancy graphs
- Vacancy reports and graphs
- Vacancy changes
- Analysis of the effect of rent increase or decrease
- Inventory of furnishings
- Appliance inventory
- Tenant parking
- Budget preparation
- Association fees
- Free rent or incentive register
- Employee payroll including withholding
- Repetitive correspondence

Additional Software

A wide variety of software packages are available for special purposes, such as syndication, subdividing, appraisal, and property association or timeshare management. Many of these packages will handle a number of functions. By witnessing actual demonstrations and talking with software users, you can determine which programs are appropriate for your specific needs.

NOTEBOOK COMPUTERS

Many salespeople keep powerful small portable computers in their automobiles. By using a cellular telephone and a modem, they can access board and/or office computers.

Wallet-size personal notebooks are also available. These small 64K-memory computers are not toys by any means. They can organize your calendar. Many agents input prospect files so that when they look at a new listing, they can enter the data on the property for likely buyers. This allows them to arrange showings before other agents have returned to their offices. Wallet-size computers are limited only by your imagination and the capacity of the memory chip.

MODEMS

Computer modems will allow you to send data in computer language from one computer to another. Advantages over a fax machine are speed and that data does not need to be printed out. When received, it can be viewed on the receiving computer screen or printed out.

Glossary

The Glossary is one of the most important features in the Handbook. It contains essential information, not only for everyone in the real estate field but also for those in allied professions. Therefore, readers would do well to master the definitions so that they can make accurate descriptions, analyze transactions succinctly and communicate with REALTORS® and other sales associates by using exact terminology. They must also be able to clarify clients' problems by explaining precisely the terms that may be confusing to them.

Definitions included in this Glossary are original or are from standard textbooks: *Houses: The Illustrated Guide to Construction, Design and Systems* by Henry Harrison (REALTORS NATIONAL MARKETING INSTITUTÊ); *Appraisal Terminology* (AMERICAN INSTITUTE OF REAL ESTATE APPRAISERS); *Advanced Principles of Real Estate Practice* by Ernest M. Fisher (Macmillan); *Real Estate, Fifth Edition,* by Arthur M. Weimer and Homer Hoyt (John Wiley).

abandonment The voluntary relinquishment or surrender of possession of property.

abatement Reduction in degree, worth, amount or intention. It is also an action to end a nuisance.

abstract of title A summary of all conveyances, such as deeds or wills and legal proceedings, giving the names of the parties, the description of the land and the agreements, arranged to show the continuity of ownership. (See also *title.*)

abutment Touching or joining.

acceleration clause A clause in a mortgage, lease or land purchase contract providing for the balance of the obligation to become due and payable at once when a payment due is in default.

acceptance Offeree notifying offeror of his or her concurrence as to the agreement.

access The right to enter and leave a tract of land from a public way.

accession Addition to property by such methods as accretion or annexation.

ACCREDITED LAND CONSULTANT (ALC) Professional designation earned by members of the REALTORS'® Land Institute.

ACCREDITED MANAGEMENT ORGANIZATION® (AMO®) Designation earned by members of the INSTITUTE OF REAL ESTATE MANAGEMENT.

ACCREDITED RESIDENT MANAGER® (ARM®) Designation awarded by the INSTITUTE OF REAL ESTATE MANAGEMENT to on-site managers meeting specified requirements.

accretion An addition to land through natural causes (opposite of erosion). Generally the mineral deposits left on riparian lands by movement of waters.

accrued depreciation See *depreciation, accrued.*

acknowledgment The act by which a party executing a legal document goes before an authorized officer or notary public and declares the same to be his or her voluntary act and deed.

acre A measure of land consisting of 43,560 square feet.

adjacent Close or contiguous.

adjustable-rate mortgage A loan written for a fixed period of time with an interest rate that is adjusted at specified intervals based on the monetary index to which it is keyed.

administrator A person appointed by a probate court to settle the affairs of an individual dying without a will.

administrator's deed Type of deed used in conveying the real property of an intestate when authorized by the court. It is executed by an administrator and should recite the proceeding under which he or she is directed to sell.

ad valorem Designates an assessment of taxes against property. Literally, according to value; based on the "ability to pay" theory.

advance fee Fee paid in advance for services rendered.

adverse possession The actual, exclusive, open, notorious, hostile and continuous possession and occupation of real property under an evident claim of right or title. The time required legally to obtain title by adverse possession varies from state to state.

affidavit A sworn statement in writing.

affirm To make a formal judicial statement but not under oath.

after-acquired property Property acquired after a certain event takes place, such as a person acquiring title after he or she has conveyed the property.

agency A contract by which the agent undertakes to represent the principal in business transactions, using some degree of discretion.

agent One who represents another who has given authority to do so.

agency coupled with an interest An agency relationship in which the agent has an estate or interest in property handled by the agency.

air rights The rights vested by a grant (fee simple, lease agreement or other conveyance) of an estate in real property to build upon, occupy or use, in the manner and degree permitted, all or any portion of space above the ground or any other stated elevation within vertical planes, the basis of which corresponds with the boundaries of the real estate described in the grant.

alienation Transfer of property from one owner to another.

alienation clause Provides that the balance of the debt be paid upon transfer of title.

alloidal system Absolute ownership of land, free from rent or service.

alluvion Increase of land by water flowing by and depositing soil on a shore or river bank.

amenities The qualities and state of being pleasant and agreeable. In appraising, those qualities that attach to property in the benefits derived from other than monetary. Satisfactions of possession and use arising from architectural excellence, scenic beauty and social environment.

AMERICAN INSTITUTE OF REAL ESTATE APPRAISERS (AIREA) (See Chapter 2)

American Land Title Association Association of land title companies, created to aid in safe transfer of title and property and educate consumers.

AMERICAN SOCIETY OF REAL ESTATE COUNSELORS (ASREC) (See Chapter 2)

Americans with Disabilities Act Legislation that prohibits discrimination against the disabled as concerns access to public accommodations and employment.

amortization The act or process of extinguishing a debt, with equal payments at regular intervals over a specific period of time.

Annual Percentage Rate (APR) The effective rate of interest based upon the rate stated plus specified loan costs.

annuity A sum of money or its equivalent that constitutes one of a series of periodic payments. Any advantage that may be interpreted in terms of money and answers the requirements of regularity may be considered an annuity.

appraisal An estimate of quantity, quality or value. The process through which conclusions of property value or property facts are obtained; also, commonly, the report setting forth such estimate and conclusion. (See also *valuation.*)

appraiser One who is authorized to appraise property.

appreciation An increased conversion value of property or mediums of exchange, either temporary or permanent, that is due to economic or related causes. Appreciation is the antonym of depreciation, which denotes shrinkage in conversion value. Also, the excess of appraisal value over book value of property. Also, the process of developing appraised value by the application of price indices to actual costs or estimated cost of another date and of lower price levels. (See also *depreciation.*)

appreciation rate The index figure used against the actual or estimated cost of a property in computing its cost of reproduction new as of a different date or under different conditions of a higher price level.

appurtenance Something that has been added to another thing; something that, when added or appended to a property, becomes an inherent part of the property and passes with it when it is sold, leased or devised.

arbitration A method of nonjudicial dispute resolution by which the parties designate a neutral arbitrator to decide the conflict.

assemblage The act of bringing two or more individuals or things together to form an aggregate whole; specifically, the cost or estimated cost of assembling two or more parcels of land under a single ownership and unit of utility over the normal cost or current market price of the parcels held individually.

assessed value A value assigned to real estate by governmental assessors for the purpose of assessing taxes.

assessment A nonrecurring charge levied against property to meet some specific purpose portioned either by benefit derived to property or based on value of property. The valuation of property for taxation; also, the value so assigned. (See also *taxable value.*)

assessor A public official who evaluates property for the purpose of taxation.

assets Property of all kinds under a single ownership. (See also *current assets.*)

assignee One to whom a transfer of interest is made.

assignment The transfer of an interest in a bond, mortgage, lease or other instrument, in writing.

assignor One who makes an assignment.

assumption of mortgage When a buyer takes ownership to real estate encumbered with a mortgage, he or she may assume the responsibility as the guarantor for the unpaid balance of the mortgage. Such a buyer is liable for the mortgage repayment.

attachment Legal seizure of property to force payment of a debt.

attorney-in-fact One who is authorized to perform certain acts under a power of attorney.

auction A public sale of property to the highest bidder after successive increased bids are made.

avulsion Loss of land by sudden action of nature, as a flood.

balance sheet Financial statement showing assets and liabilities of a business. It indicates net worth.

balloon mortgage payment Payment that is a great deal larger than earlier payments; frequently the last payment, which pays the mortgage in full.

bankrupt A person who, through a court proceeding, is relieved from the payment of all debts after surrender of all assets to a court-appointed trustee is bankrupt.

bargain and sale deed Conveys title; does not include warranties of title.

base line East-west line used by surveyors to locate and describe land.

basis Original cost of property plus value of any improvements put on by the seller and minus the depreciation taken by seller.

benchmark A permanent surveying point set by the U.S. Geological Survey.

beneficiary One entitled to the proceeds of property held in trust or to proceeds of wills, insurance policies or trusts.

bequeath To give personal property to another by will.

bilateral contract Parties exchange reciprocal contracts; that is, each party agrees to perform an act for the other.

bill of sale Written agreement transferring personal property from one person to another.

binder An agreement to cover a down payment as evidence of good faith on the part of the purchaser of real estate.

blanket mortgage A mortgage that has two or more properties pledged or conveyed as security for a debt, usually for subdividing and improvement purposes.

blight A reduction in the productivity of real estate from a wide variety of causes and having a multitude of visible effects on the physical appearance and condition of the property or area affected.

blockbusting Illegal practice by which owners in a specific neighborhood are persuaded to sell because certain racial, ethnic or social groups moving in will reduce neighborhood housing values.

bona fide In good faith.

book depreciation The amount reserved upon books or records to provide for the retirement or replacement of an asset.

boot That with which the exchangor "sweetens the pot": cash, note, mortgage, car, a boat—anything other than the prime article that is being exchanged that is needed to balance equities.

broker   An agent who buys or sells for a principal for a fee without having title to property.

brokerage   The buying and selling business of a broker.

building code   Government regulations specifying minimum construction standards.

building restrictions   Limitations on the use of property or the size and location of structures, established by legislation or by covenants in deeds.

bulk sale   A sale of inventory not in the normal course of business, such as in a sale of the business.

bulk zoning   Zoning for density by restrictions as to height, setback, unit size, parking, etc.

bundle of rights theory   An undivided ownership of a parcel of real estate embraces a great many rights, such as the right to its occupancy and use, the right to sell in whole or in part, the right to bequeath, the right to transfer by contract for specified periods of time, and the benefits to be derived by occupancy and use of the real estate. These rights of occupancy and use are called beneficial interests. An owner who leases real estate to a tenant transfers one of the rights in this bundle—namely, the beneficial interest or the right to use or occupancy—to the tenant in accordance with the provision of the lease contract. He or she retains all the other rights in the bundle. As compensation for temporarily relinquishing the beneficial interest in the real estate, the owner receives rent.

business opportunity   A business for sale (may include real property or be entirely personal property).

buydown   A prepayment of interest to a lender to obtain a lower interest rate on a loan.

buyer's agent   An agent representing the buyer only.

cap   A limit on the adjustments in interest and payments possible for an adjustable-rate mortgage.

capital   Accumulated wealth. A portion of wealth that is set aside for the production of additional wealth; specifically, the funds belonging to the partners or shareholders of a business, invested with the expressed intention of their remaining permanently in the business.

capital asset   All property except that which is for sale in the ordinary course of business, such as stock, place of residence and equipment used in conducting business.

capital charges   Sums required to satisfy interest upon and amortization of monies invested in an enterprise.

capital expenditures   Investments of cash or other property or the creation of liability in exchange for property to remain permanently in the business; usually land, buildings, machinery and equipment.

capital gain A profit from sale of a capital asset.

capital loss A loss from the sale of a capital asset.

capital requirements The total monetary investment essential to the establishment and operation of an enterprise; usually the appraised investment in plant facilities and normal working capital. May or may not (for certain purposes) include appraised cost of business "rights," such as patents, contracts, etc.

capitalization The act or process of converting (obtaining the present worth of) future incomes into current equivalent capital values; also, the amount so determined. Commonly refers to the capital structure of a corporation.

capitalization rate The rate of interest or return adopted in the process of capitalization; ordinarily assumed to reflect factor of risk to capital so invested.

carrying charges Expenses necessary for holding property, such as taxes on idle property or property under construction.

cash flow The actual spendable income from a property.

cash-on-cash Investment return based on actual cash invested.

certificate of eligibility A certificate issued to a veteran by the Department of Veterans Affairs showing eligibility for a guaranteed loan.

certificate of reasonable value (CRV) Certificate issued by the Department of Veterans Affairs showing the property's current market value estimate.

certificate of title A document usually given to the homebuyer with the deed stating that title of the property is clear; it is prepared by a title company or an attorney and is based on the abstract of title; sometimes an opinion of title serves the same purpose.

CERTIFIED COMMERCIAL-INVESTMENT MEMBER (CCIM) The CCIM designation is awarded by the Commercial-Investment Real Estate Institute to the REALTOR® or REALTOR-ASSO-CIATE® who is active in providing services to the public primarily in selling, exchanging, leasing, managing, developing and syndicating commercial and investment real estate and, further, who has (1) achieved a superior level of knowledge through the successful completion of certain prescribed courses; (2) proved his or her competence in the application of that knowledge through documented practical experience as approved by the Admissions Committee; and (3) demonstrated and maintained a high standing of character, ethical practice and financial responsibility in his or her community and marketplace.

CERTIFIED PROPERTY MANAGER® (CPM®) Designation awarded by the INSTITUTE OF REAL ESTATE MANAGEMENT.

CERTIFIED REAL ESTATE BROKERAGE MANAGER (CRB) The CRB designation is awarded by the Real Estate Brokerage Council of the REALTORS NATIONAL MARKETING INSTITUTE® to the REALTOR® or REALTOR-ASSOCIATE® who has proven competence in the management of a real estate brokerage firm and who has (1) achieved a superior level of knowledge through the successful completion of certain prescribed courses; (2) proved his or her competence in the application of that knowledge through documented practical experience as approved by the Admissions Committee; and (3) demonstrated and maintained a high standing of character, ethical practice and financial responsibility in his or her community and marketplace.

CERTIFIED RESIDENTIAL SPECIALIST (CRS) The CRS designation is awarded by the Residential Sales Council of the REALTORS NATIONAL MARKETING INSTITUTE® to the REALTOR® or REALTOR-ASSOCIATE® who has demonstrated expertise in the field of residential marketing and who has (1) achieved a superior level of knowledge through the successful completion of certain prescribed courses; (2) proved his or her competence in the application of that knowledge through documented practical experience as approved by the Admissions Committee; and (3) demonstrated and maintained a high standing of character, ethical practice and financial responsibility in his or her community and marketplace.

chain A surveyor's measurement; four rods, or 66 feet.

chain of title The succession of conveyances from some accepted starting point whereby the present holder of real property derives his or her title.

chattel Any item of movable or immovable property other than real estate.

chattel mortgage A mortgage on personal property; now known as a security agreement, under the Uniform Commercial Code.

chattel, personal An item of movable property.

chattel, real An estate annexed to or concerned with real estate.

circuit breaker A device in the electrical system to interrupt the circuit when an overload occurs; an automatic switch that can be reset is used to protect each circuit instead of a fuse.

Civil Rights Act of 1968 Title VIII of the act is the Fair Housing Act.

clear title A title that is not encumbered or burdened with defects.

client Person who employs the agent. Typically, the client is the seller and the buyer is the customer.

closing Point in a real estate transaction when the seller transfers title to the buyer in exchange for the purchase price.

closing statement A listing of the debits and credits of the buyer and seller to a real estate transaction for the financial settlement of the transaction.

cloud on the title An outstanding claim or encumbrance that, if valid, would affect or impair the owner's title.

code of ethics Standards subscribed to by members of the NATIONAL ASSOCIATION OF REALTORS®. (See page 27).

codicil Addition to a will.

color of title Condition in which the title appears to be valid and actually is not because of some defect.

commercial acre What is left of an acre after areas for streets, sidewalks and alleys are deducted.

Commercial-Investment Real Estate Institute (CIREI) (See Chapter 2.)

commercial property Property intended for use by all types of retail and wholesale stores, office buildings, hotels and service establishments.

commingling The illegal mixing of trust funds with personal funds.

commission Payment for the performance of specific duties; in real estate, usually payment measured by a percentage of another sum—such as a percentage of the sales price paid for selling a property.

common law Rules based on usage as demonstrated by decrees and judgments from the courts.

common wall Wall separating two housing units.

community property Property owned jointly by husband and wife.

compaction Compression of soil. Compaction tests determine if property will support a planned structure.

comparables Properties that are similar in value to a particular property and are used to indicate fair market value for that property.

compound interest Interest paid both on the original principal and on interest that accrued from the time it fell due.

condemnation The taking of private property for public use through the exercising of due process of law. (See also *eminent domain* and *expropriation*.)

conditional sales contract A contract in which the seller retains title of the property until paid in full, while allowing buyer use of that property, as long as buyer obeys all conditions of the contract.

condominium A form of property ownership providing for individual ownership of a specific apartment or other space not necessarily on the ground level together with an undivided interest in the land or other parts of the structure in common with other owners.

conforming loan A loan that meets the purchase standards of the Federal National Mortgage Association (FNMA).

conformity, principle of Holds that the maximum of value is realized when a reasonable degree of homogeneity, sociological as well as economic, is present. Thus conformity in use is usually a highly desirable adjunct of real property, because it creates and/or maintains maximum value, and it is maximum value that affords the owner the maximum returns.

consideration The price or subject matter that induces a contract; may be in money, commodity exchange or a transfer of personal effort. In appraising, usually the actual price at which property is transferred.

construction loan A loan to finance the improvement of real estate.

contiguous Adjacent; in actual contact; touching; near.

contingencies Possible happenings that are conditioned upon the occurrence of some future event that is itself uncertain or questionable; for example, an offer to purchase conditioned upon a termite inspection or the commitment of a mortgage loan.

contingent fees Remuneration based or conditioned upon future occurrences, conclusions or results of services to be performed.

contract An agreement entered into by two or more parties by which one or more of the parties, for a consideration, undertakes to do or to refrain from doing some act or acts in accordance with the wishes of the other party or parties. To be valid and binding, a contract must (1) be entered into by competent parties, (2) be bound by a consideration, (3) possess mutuality, (4) represent an actual meeting of minds and (5) cover a legal and moral act.

contract for deed Similar to a mortgage but different in its use as evidence of equity of the seller of a piece of property when he or she does not receive the entire purchase price either in cash or a purchase-money mortgage. (See *Land contract, installment contract.*)

conventional loan A loan made without government insurance guarantees.

conversion The misappropriation of trust funds for personal use.

convey The act of deeding or transferring title to another.

conveyance A written instrument that passes an interest in real estate from one person to another, including land contracts, leases, mortgages, etc.

cooperative apartment An apartment owned by corporations, either for or not for profit, or by trusts, in which each owner purchases stock to the extent of the value of his or her apartment, title being evidenced by a proprietary lease.

corner influence The effect of street intersections upon adjacent property—the cause of a different value for real estate adjacent to a corner, as compared with property away from a corner.

corporeal Pertaining to a right or group of rights of a visible and tangible nature.

correction deed A deed that corrects a previous erroneous deed.

cost approach to value Valuation set by estimating cost of reproduction of the building plus the value of the property on which it stands less the accrued depreciation.

cost of reproduction The normal cost of exact duplication of a property.

counteroffer A new offer made as a result of another offer, which cancels the original offer.

COUNSELOR OF REAL ESTATE (CRE) Designation awarded by the AMERICAN SOCIETY OF REAL ESTATE COUNSELORS.

covenant An agreement written into deeds and other instruments promising performance or nonperformance of certain acts or stipulating certain uses or nonuses of a property.

covenants, conditions and restrictions (CC&Rs) Private restrictions on land use that transfer with the real property.

cubical content The actual space within the outer surfaces of the outside or enclosing walls and between the outer surfaces of the roof and the finished surface of the lowest basement or cellar.

cul de sac The terminus of a street or alley. Usually laid out by modern engineers to provide a circular turnaround for vehicles.

current assets Assets that are readily convertible into cash, usually within one year, without loss of value.

curable depreciation Depreciation that can be economically cured.

current liability Indcbtcdness maturing within one year.

curtesy The estate to which, by common law, the husband is entitled in the land of his deceased wife. The extent varies with statutory provision.

custodian One who has care or custody, as of some public buildings; a keeper.

damages The estimated reparation in money for injury sustained; for example, by the taking of a portion of property (in condemnation) for street widening. (See also *consequential damage* and *severance damage.*)

datum plane The horizontal plane from which heights and depths are measured.

d/b/a Abbreviation for "doing business as"; used as an assumed name, usually a corporation name other than the owner's name.

dealer A person considered by the IRS to be in the business of buying and selling real estate.

debentures Certificates of obligation and promise to pay; commonly, loans to limited companies issued on the general credit of the company without any specific pledged security and bearing a fixed rate of interest, the principal being either repayable after a certain number of years or unredeemable during the existence of the company. Unredeemable debentures are generally issued by railway and like companies.

debt service Sum of money needed to pay mortgage obligations.

declaration of restrictions The covenants, conditions and restrictions that are declared and recorded by a developer.

dedication The voluntary giving of private property by the owner to some public use, such as the dedication of land for streets, schools, etc., in a development.

deed An instrument in writing that, when executed and delivered, conveys an estate in real property.

deed in lieu of foreclosure A deed from a borrower in default to the mortgage lender.

deed of reconveyance A deed from the trustee under a trust deed to the trustor satisfying the trust deed (release deed).

deed of trust (See *trust deed.*)

deed restrictions Limitations placed on use of real property by written deed.

deed, quit claim (See *quit claim deed.*)

deed, warranty (See *warranty deed.*)

default Failure to meet an obligation when due; mortgagors are in default when they fail to pay interest or principal on their mortgage when due.

defeasance A provision or condition in a deed or in a separate instrument that, being performed, renders the instrument void.

defects in title Title impaired by outstanding claim.

defendant Person being sued in a lawsuit.

deferred maintenance Existing but unfulfilled requirements for repairs and rehabilitation.

deferred payments Money payments to be made at some future date.

deficiency judgment A judgment rendered for the difference between the amount owed on a mortgage and the amount realized at the foreclosure sale.

degree 1/360th of a circle (used in surveying).

delayed exchange (Starker Exchange) A tax-deferred exchange in which exchange property must be identified within 45 days of closing and purchased within 180 days of the closing.

delivery The final and absolute transfer of a deed from seller to buyer in such a manner that it cannot be recalled by the seller. A necessary requisite to the transfer of title.

demise A transfer of an estate to another for years, for life or at will.

deposit, earnest money A sum of money or other consideration tendered in conjunction with an offer to purchase rights in real property.

depreciation A loss from the upper limit of value caused by deterioration and/or obsolescence. Deterioration is evidenced by wear and tear, decay, dry rot, cracks, encrustations or structural defects. Obsolescence is divisible into parts. Functional obsolescence may be due to poor plan or functional inadequacy or overadequacy of size, style, age or otherwise. It is evidenced by conditions within the property. Economic obsolescence is caused by changes external to the property, such as neighborhood infiltrations of inharmonious property uses, legislation and the like. (See also *appreciation.*)

depreciation, accrued The actual depreciation existing in a property at a given date.

depreciation methods Methods used to measure loss in value of an improvement through depreciation. In appraising, the methods generally used are annuity, sinking fund and straight-line. In accounting, the term relates to various methods by which capital impairment is computed.

depreciation rate The periodic amount of percentage at which the usefulness of a property is exhausted, especially the percentage at which amounts are computed to be set aside as accrual for anticipated depreciation.

depreciation reserve The capital amount that summarizes the annual charges to operations by reason of depreciation. In accounting, the account on the books of a concern wherein the accruals for depreciation are recorded.

depreciation, straight-line An accounting term designating the deduction of the cost or other basis of property, less estimated salvage value, in equal amounts over the estimated useful life of the property.

depth tables Tabulations of factors or coefficients representing the rating of value per front foot between a lot of a selected "standard" depth and other lots of greater or lesser depth.

dereliction (reliction) The gaining of land when water recedes.

descent Acquisition of an estate by inheritance.

devise A gift of real property by last will and testament.

disposal field A drainage area, not close to the water supply, where waste from a septic tank is dispersed, being drained into the ground through tile and gravel.

documentary stamp A revenue stamp issued for the payment of a tax on documents, such as deeds, checks or wills.

domicile Permanent home.

dominant tenement An easement holder who benefits from the land of another.

donor One who gives a gift.

dower That portion of, or interest in, the real estate of a deceased husband that the law gives for life to his widow. The extent varies with statutory provisions. Cannot be cut off without wife's consent.

downzoning Change in existing zoning to a lower classification.

dragnet clause A clause in a mortgage that allows the mortgage to cover future advances.

dual agency An agency in which the broker represents both buyer and seller.

due-on-sale clause A clause in a mortgage requiring it to be paid off at time of sale. The loan cannot be assumed.

duress Unlawful pressure to force a person to do something against his or her will.

earnest money Advance payment of part of the purchase price to bind a contract for property.

easement The right to use or enjoy certain privileges that appertain to the land of another, such as the right of way, or the right to receive air and light by reason of an agreement of record with the owner of adjacent property.

easement appurtenant An easement that goes with property being sold.

easement by prescription An easement acquired by adverse use.

economic life The period over which a property may be profitably utilized. The period during which a building is valuable.

economic obsolescence Impairment of desirability or useful life arising from economic forces, such as changes in optimum land use, legislative enactments that restrict or impair property rights and changes in supply-demand relationships. Loss in the use and value of property arising from the factors of economic obsolescence is to be distinguished from loss in value from physical deterioration and functional obsolescence. (See also *obsolescence.*)

economic rent The base rental justifiably payable for the right of occupancy.

effective age Statement of amount of depreciation suffered by property in terms of the property's condition as opposed to its actual age.

effective gross revenue Total income less allowance for vacancies, contingencies and sometimes collection losses but before deductions for operating expenses.

ejectment An action to dispossess a party who has no possessory right.

emblements That which grows on the land and can be harvested— for example, crops.

eminent domain The power to appropriate private property for public use. If public welfare is served, the right of eminent domain may be granted by the state to quasi-public or even private bodies, such as railroad, water, light and power companies. (See also *condemnation* and *expropriation.*)

enabling act State statute to provide a legal base for zoning codes.

encroachment The act of trespassing upon the domain of another. Partial or gradual invasion or intrusion.

encumbrance An interest or right in real property that diminishes the value of the fee but does not prevent conveyance of the fee by the owner thereof. Mortgages, taxes and judgments are encumbrances known as liens. Restrictions, easements and reservations are encumbrances but not liens.

Equal Credit Opportunity Act An antidiscrimination act applicable to lenders.

equitable title The right to obtain ownership to property when legal title is in someone else's name.

equity In finance, the value of the interest of an owner of property exclusive of the encumbrances on that property; also, justice.

equity of redemption The right of a mortgagor to redeem property forfeited by default.

erosion The wearing away of land through natural causes, such as running water, glaciers and winds.

escalator clause Clause permitting adjustment of payments either up or down.

escheat Reversion of property to the state when an owner dies without a will and there are no known heirs.

escrow A deed or other instrument placed in the hands of a disinterested person (sometimes called the escrowee) for delivery upon performance of certain conditions or the happening of certain contingencies.

escrow holder One who receives a deed or item from a grantor to be delivered to his or her grantee upon the performance of a condition or the occurrence of a contingency.

estate A right in property. An estate in land is the degree, nature or extent of interest a person has in it.

estate at will Possession of property at the discretion of the owner.

estate for years Tenant has rights in real property for a designated number of years.

estate in reversion The residue of an estate left in the grantor, to commence possession after the termination of some particular estate granted by him or her. Not to be confused with *remainder estate.*

estoppel An impediment to a law of action whereby one is forbidden to contradict or deny one's own previous statement or act.

estoppel certificate Certificate that shows the unpaid principal sum of a mortgage and the interest thereon, if the principal or interest notes are not produced or if the seller claims that the amount due under the mortgage that the purchase is to assume is less than that shown on record.

et al. And others.

ethics Moral values as to what is right measured by the application of the Golden Rule.

et ux. And wife.

et vir And husband.

eviction Physical removal of tenant from property.

exception Withholding of an interest from a grant.

exchange The trading of an equity in a piece of property for the equity in another piece of property.

exchangor The broker or salesperson who performs the exchange.

exclusionary zoning Zoning that forbids specified uses.

exclusive agency A contract that gives the agent the exclusive right to sell the property. However, the owner reserves the right to sell the property and not pay the commission. The term is also applied to the property so listed.

exclusive right to sell Contract, for a specific time period, between owner and broker that gives the broker sole and exclusive right to sell the property. The broker is thus entitled to the commission regardless of who sells the property.

exculpatory clause A hold-harmless clause in a contract.

execute Making a document legally valid, as by signing a contract.

executed contract One that has been fully performed.

executor Person appointed in a will to carry out requests in that will.

executor's deed A deed given by an executor.

executory contract One that has yet to be performed.

existing mortgage Mortgage contract to be assumed by the purchaser from the seller of the house, who is the mortgagor.

facade The principal face of a structure.

facilitator A person acting as a middleman between a buyer and seller rather than as an agent.

fair value Value that is reasonable and consistent with all known facts.

familial Children under the age of 18 living with a parent or guardian as well as a pregnant person.

Farmers Home Administration (FmHA) Federal agency handling guaranteed loans in rural areas.

feasibility survey An analysis of the cost-benefit ratio of an economic endeavor.

Federal Deposit Insurance Corporation Agency of the federal government that insures deposits at banks and savings and loans.

Federal Home Loan Bank A district bank of the Federal Home Loan Bank System that lends only to member financial institutions.

Federal Home Loan Mortgage Corporation (Freddie Mac) Owned by the 12 Federal Home Loan Banks, it buys residential mortgages, and sells mortgage-backed securities.

Federal Housing Administration (FHA) An agency of the federal government that insures mortgage loans.

Federal National Mortgage Association (Fannie Mae) A private corporation regulated by HUD that buys and sells FHA-insured and VA-guaranteed mortgage loans as well as conventional mortgages. It provides the primary market, banks and savings and loan associations with a ready market for mortgages to permit a greater turnover of money for loans.

Federal Savings and Loan Association A savings and loan association with a federal charter issued by the Federal Home Loan Bank Board. A federally chartered savings and loan association as opposed to a state-chartered savings and loan association.

Federal Savings and Loan Insurance Corporation An agency of the federal government that insured savers' accounts at savings and loan associations (no longer in existence).

fee Remuneration for services. When applied to property, an inheritable estate in land.

fee simple absolute Highest and most complete ownership or enjoyment of real estate: (1) Ownership of unlimited duration; (2) Do as one pleases with land as long as one obeys the law; (3) Upon owner's death, real estate will go to heirs.

fictitious name A business (or assumed) name that does not include the surname of every principal.

fiduciary The relationships of trust between a person charged with the duty of acting for the benefit of another, as between guardian and ward. The person so charged.

filtering down The process housing undergoes when it passes to lower economic groups as it ages.

financing statement A document prepared for filing with the registrar of deeds or secretary of state, indicating that personal property or fixtures are encumbered with a debt.

finder's fee A fee or commission paid to a broker to obtain a mortgage or to refer a loan to a mortgage broker; also refers to a commission paid for locating a property or a buyer.

firm commitment An agreement by FHA to insure a specific property and borrower.

first mortgage A mortgage that has priority as a lien over all other mortgages.

fixed charges The regular, recurring costs or charges required in the holding of a property or for the guarantee of the unimpairment of capital invested therein, as distinguished from the maintenance of the condition or utility of the property and other direct expenses of operation.

fixed-rate mortgage A loan that bears the same interest rate to maturity.

fixer-upper A property needing work that is generally offered at a discount.

fixtures Appurtenances affixed to structures or land, usually in such manner that they cannot be independently moved without damage to themselves or the property housing, supporting or pertinent to them. Variable under state laws.

flag lot A lot that resembles a flag and pole, with the pole being the access.

flashing Metal used in waterproofing the joint between chimney and roof or in roof valleys and hips.

floor load As commonly used, the live weight-supporting capabilities of a floor, measured in pounds per square foot; the weight, stated in pounds per square foot, that may be safely placed upon the floor of a building if uniformly distributed.

footing A concrete support under a foundation, chimney or column that usually rests on solid ground and is wider than the structure being supported.

forced sale The act of selling property under compulsion as to time and place. Usually a sale made by virtue of a court order, ordinarily at public auction.

forced sale value Amount that may be realized at a forced sale. The price that could be obtained at immediate disposal. (Actually an improper use of the word "value." The term "forced sale value" is used erroneously to designate "forced sale price.")

foreclosure The legal process by which a mortgagee, in case of default by the mortgagor, forces sale of the property mortgaged in order to recover his or her loan.

Foreign Investment in Real Property Tax Act An act requiring buyer withholding of 10 percent of the price when there is a foreign seller and the sale is not exempt from withholding.

forfeiture The means by which the property of the citizen inures to the benefit of the state through the violation of law and occurring in the United States in case of seizure for taxes.

franchise A privilege or right conferred by governmental grant or contractually by a business enterprise upon an individual or group of individuals. Usually, an exclusive privilege or right to furnish public services or sell a particular product in a certain community.

fraud Intentional deceit that influences another to act to his or her detriment.

freehold   A tenure of land held in fee simple absolute, fee simple limited or fee tail unencumbered by lease.

front foot   A measure (one foot in length) of the width of lots applied at their frontage upon a street.

front foot cost   Cost of a parcel of real estate expressed in terms of front foot units.

functional obsolescence   Built-in impairment of functional capacity or efficiency. (See also *obsolescence.*)

funding fee   A fee paid to the Department of Veterans Affairs for a VA loan.

general mortgage bond   A written instrument representing an obligation secured by a mortgage but preceded by senior issues.

general partner   An active partner in a partnership, who has unlimited liability.

gift deed   Deed with no consideration.

GI loan   A mortgage loan for which veterans are eligible and that is guaranteed by the Department of Veterans Affairs, subject to VA regulations similar to an FHA loan.

girder   A heavy wood or steel structural member supporting beams, joists and partitions.

good faith   Bona fide.

goodwill   Intangible asset derived from good public business reputation and expectation of continued good business.

Government National Mortgage Association (Ginnie Mae)   A division of the U.S. Department of Housing and Urban Development (HUD) that operates the special assistance section of federally aided housing programs. GNMA guarantees payment on securities issued and sold by FNMA and on securities issued and sold by private offerers (such as banks) if these securities are backed by pools of VA, FHA or FmHA mortgages.

government survey   System of land description used in the United States.

grade   The ground level at the foundation.

grading   The process of plowing and raking to effect desired contour and drainage.

graduated lease   A lease that provides for a certain rent for an initial period, followed by an increase or decrease in rent over stated periods.

GRADUATE, REALTORS® INSTITUTE (GRI)   Designation awarded by the individual state board of REALTORS®.

grant   To transfer title to real property.

grant deed   A deed used in several states warranting only that the seller has not previously conveyed the property or encumbered the property with any undisclosed liens.

grantee One who receives a transfer of real property by deed.

grantor One who transfers real property by deed.

grantor-grantee index A county recorder index of grantor and grantee names listed alphabetically.

gross earnings Revenue from operating sources before deduction of the expenses incurred in gaining such revenues.

gross income Total receipts during a given period.

gross income multiplier A figure that, times the gross income of a property, produces an estimate of value of that property. It is obtained by dividing the selling price by the monthly gross rent (gross income).

gross lease A lease of property under the terms of which the lessor is to meet all property charges regularly incurred through ownership.

gross profits Profits computed before the deduction of general expenses.

gross revenue Total revenue from all sources before deduction of expenses incurred in gaining such revenue.

gross sales The total sales as shown by invoices, before deducting returns, allowances, etc.

ground rent The net rent paid for the right of use and occupancy of a parcel of unimproved land; or that portion of the total rental paid that is considered to represent return upon the land only.

guarantee (of sale) The written commitment by a broker that within a certain period of time he or she will, in absence of a sale, purchase a given piece of property at a specified sum.

guaranteed mortgage A mortgage from a mortgage company that buys the mortgages with its own funds and, in turn, sells them to its clients, who receive all of the papers in connection with the mortgage, including the bond, the mortgage and the assignment, together with the company's policy of guarantee. The company guarantees the payment of both principal and interest and assumes the responsibility of complete supervision of the mortgage, for which it receives a fee out of the interest as it is collected.

habendum clause A clause in a real estate document that specifies the extent of the interest (as life or fee) to be conveyed.

hard money mortgage A mortgage loan given in exchange for cash, instead of to finance a real estate purchase.

heir One who might inherit or succeed to an interest in lands under the rules of law, applicable where an individual dies without leaving a will.

hereditaments Every sort of inheritable property, including real, personal, corporeal and incorporeal.

highest and best use   The use of, or program of utilization of, a site that will produce the maximum net land returns in the future. The optimum use for a site.

holdover tenant   A tenant remaining in possession after the expiration of the tenancy.

holographic will   Will written in testator's handwriting and not witnessed.

homestead   Tract of land occupied as a family home.

Housing and Urban Development (HUD)   A federal cabinet department that administers federal funds for public housing programs, including rehabilitation loans, urban renewal, public housing, model cities, new FHA-subsidy programs and water and sewer grants.

hundred percent location   The location or site in a city that is best adapted to carrying on a given type of business.

hypothecate   To pledge property as security while retaining possession; to mortgage.

implied agency   An agency that arises because of the conduct of the parties. It is understood but not actually expressed.

impound account   A lender account for taxes and insurance that are included in the mortgage payments.

improvements   Valuable additions to property that raise the value of the property.

improvements on land   Structures, of whatever nature, usually privately rather than publicly owned, erected on a site to enable its utilization; e.g., buildings, fences, driveways, retaining walls, etc.

income   A stream of benefits generally measured in terms of money over a certain time; a flow of service. It is the source of value.

income approach   Method of valuation of property determined by its future income.

income-price ratio   Obtained by dividing the net income of a property by the selling price.

inclusionary zoning   Zoning that requires the inclusion of some element (often a percentage of low-income housing).

income property   A property whose income is derived from commercial rentals or whose returns attributable to the real estate can be so segregated as to permit direct estimation. The income production may be in several forms: commercial rents, business profits attributable to real estate other than rents, etc.

incompetent   Incapable of managing one's affairs because one is mentally deficient or underdeveloped; as, children are incompetent in the eyes of the law.

incorporeal rights   Nonpossessory rights in real property, such as easements.

increment An increase; most frequently used to refer to the increase in the value of land that accompanies population growth and increasing wealth in the community. The term "unearned increment" is used in this connection, because values are supposed to increase without effort on the part of the owner.

incurable depreciation Depreciation to the extent that it is not practical to restore or replace that which is depreciating.

independent contractor One who is hired to perform an act but is subject to control only as to the end result, not how it was reached.

index lease A lease tied to an index rate, such as the Consumer Price Index.

industrial property Land zoned and suited for the use of factories, warehouses and other similar purposes.

in-house sale A property that is sold by the listing office.

injunction Judicial order requiring the party enjoined to take or not take a specific action.

installment contracts A contract between the buyer and the seller whereby the purchase price is paid in installments. The buyer has possession of the property and equitable title to it, while the seller has legal title. (Also called *contract for deed.*)

INSTITUTE OF REAL ESTATE MANAGEMENT (IREM) (See Chapter 2.)

institutional lender Banks, insurance companies, savings and loans and any lending institution whose loans are regulated by law.

instrument Any formal legal document.

insurance rate The ratio of the insurance premium to the total amount of insurance carried; usually expressed in dollars per $100 or per $1,000, or sometimes in percent.

intangible property Property that has no physical value itself but is valued by what it represents, such as a promissory note or the goodwill value of a business.

interest rate The percentage of the principal sum charged for its use.

interpleader A legal action commenced by a broker or escrow holder to have the court make the decision when both buyer and seller make demands on the buyer's deposit.

Interstate Land Sales Full Disclosure Act Federal law requiring disclosure for specified sales of undeveloped parcels sold in interstate commerce.

intestate Having died without leaving a valid will.

inventory A tabulation of the separate items constituting an assembled property.

inverse condemnation An action brought by an owner to force a government unit to buy the owner's property when the government's action has materially restricted its use.

investment Monies placed in a property with the expectation of producing a profit, assuming a reasonable degree of safety and ultimate recovery of principal; especially for permanent use, as opposed to speculation.

investment property Property in which a person would invest to earn a return on his or her money.

joint and several liability More than one signer of a note of contract is liable for a debt, and a creditor can obtain payment either individually or jointly from the parties.

joint tenancy A tenancy shared equally by two or more parties with the right of survivorship.

joint venture An arrangement under which two or more people or businesses go into a single venture as partners.

joist A horizontal board supporting a floor or ceiling.

judgment Formal decision of a court as to the rights and claims of parties to a suit.

junior lien A lien placed on property after a previous lien has been made and recorded.

key money Money paid in addition to rent to secure possession.

laches Unreasonable and inexcusable delay in asserting a right, so that the court is justified in refusing to honor that right.

land contract Sometimes called "contract for deed"; a contract given to a purchaser of real estate who pays a small portion of the purchase price when the contract is signed but agrees to pay additional sums at intervals and in amounts specified in the contract until the total purchase price is paid and the seller gives a deed.

land economics The study of land from the standpoint of its ability to meet the needs or desires of man.

land improvements Physical changes in or construction of a more or less permanent nature attached to or appurtenant to land, of such character as to increase its utility and/or value.

landlocked A property having no access route for ingress or egress except over the land of another.

land trust certificate A certificate of beneficial ownership in real estate, title to which is held in trust by the trustee who issues the certificate.

late charge A charge made to tenants and mortgagors for late payments.

lateral support The right of landowners to have their property supported by adjacent property.

latent defect Hidden structural defect.

lease A transfer of possession and the right to use property to a tenant for a stipulated period during which the tenant pays rent to the owner; the contract containing the terms and conditions of such an agreement.

lease option A lease in which the lessee has the right to purchase the real property for a stipulated price at or within a stipulated time.

leasehold, leasehold estate An estate held under a lease.

legal description A statement containing a designation by which land is identified according to a system set up or approved by law.

less than freehold estate Land held by person who rents or leases property.

lessee One who possesses the right to use or occupy a property under lease agreement.

lessor One who holds title to and conveys the right to use and occupy a property under lease agreement.

leverage The use of borrowed funds in financing with the anticipation that the property acquired will increase in return so that the investor will realize a profit not only on his or her own investment but also on the borrowed funds.

levy To impose or collect by authority or force.

license Permission or authority to engage in a specified activity or perform a specified act.

lien A charge against property whereby the property is made security for the payment of a debt.

life estate A freehold interest in land, the duration of which is confined to the life of one or more persons or contingent upon certain happenings.

limited partnership An arrangement in which some partners have no say in the management of the business and are liable only for the sum of their investment.

line fence A common expression for a fence placed on a boundary line.

liquidity The ability to convert assets to cash. Real estate is considered an illiquid asset.

liquidated damages A predetermined amount to be the compensation in case of breach of contract by one of the parties.

lis pendens Legal document indicating that action is pending on a specific property.

listing A record of property for sale by a broker who has been authorized by the owner to sell. Also used to denote the property so listed.

littoral A shore and the area contiguous to it. The zone between high and low water marks.

load-bearing wall An integral part of a building that helps to support the floors or roof and cannot be moved readily, if at all, as distinguished from a partition which carries no load and can be removed.

loan discount fee (See *points.*)

loan relief When the principal walks away via a cash or an exchange deal from an encumbrance that he or she had on a particular piece of property.

loan-to-value ratio (LTV) The ratio of a loan to the appraised value of a property.

lockbox A large lock, usually attached to a door, gate or gas meter, that contains a compartment where a key is kept for showing property.

lock-in clause A clause in a loan that, while allowing prepayment, requires interest to be paid to maturity.

louver Slats set at an angle to provide ventilation without admitting rain or direct light.

margin The amount over the index that the rate is set at for an adjustable-rate mortgage.

marginal land Land that barely pays the cost of working or using. Land whereon the costs of operating approximately equal the gross income.

marketable title Clear title with no undisclosed encumbrances, has no serious defects and will not expose the buyer to litigation.

marketing The management process through which efforts to conceive, develop and deliver goods and services are integrated to satisfy the needs and wants of selected customers as a means of achieving company objectives.

market price The price paid for a property; the amount of money that must be given or that can be obtained at the market in exchange under the immediate conditions existing at a certain date. To be distinguished from market value.

market value The quantity of other commodities a property would command in exchange; specifically, the highest price estimated in terms of money that a buyer would be warranted in paying and a seller justified in accepting, provided both parties were fully informed and acted intelligently and voluntarily, and, further, that all the rights and benefits inherent in or attributable to the property were included in the transfer. At any given moment in time, market value connotes what a property is actually worth and market price that it can be sold for. The amounts may or may not coincide, because current supply and demand factors enter strongly into market price. (See also *market price* and *value.*)

master lease A lease on a property that the lessee will sublease to user tenants.

master's deed (See *sheriff's deed.*)

maturity Date when an indebtedness comes due.

maximum rent Rent established by any maximum rent regulation or order for the use of housing accommodations within any defense-rental area. Regulations from rent control administrator.

mechanic's lien A statutory lien given to those who perform labor or furnish materials in the improvements of real property.

mediation Dispute resolution by use of a middleman.

megalopolis Urban complex encompassing several major cities.

Member, Appraisal Institute (MAI) Designation awarded by the Appraisal Institute.

merger Loss of a lesser interest when joined with a greater interest (lease rights are lost when tenant becomes the owner).

metes and bounds The lengths and direction of the boundaries of a tract of land, usually irregular in shape.

mill One-tenth of a cent (.001); used in property taxation.

mineral rights Right to mine property. Mineral rights can be separated from the land.

Minimum Property Requirements FHA housing requirements for insured loans.

misplaced improvements Improvements (on land) that do not conform to the best utilization of the site.

misrepresentation False statement made to or concealment of knowledge from another party with the intent to provoke action from that party.

month-to-month tenancy Tenant rents for a month at a time.

monument A stone or other fixed object used to establish real estate boundaries.

mortgage A conditional conveyance of property contingent upon failure of specific performance, such as the payment of a debt; the instrument making such conveyance.

mortgage banker A person or mortgage company that uses its own funds to make loans that are generally sold in the secondary mortgage market.

mortgage broker A person who brings lenders and borrowers together, charging the borrower costs and fees.

mortgage guarantee policy A policy issued on a guaranteed mortgage.

Mortgage Guaranty Insurance Corp. (MGIC) Independent insurance company that will insure a percentage of the principal of a loan made by approved lenders to qualified buyers.

mortgagee The source of the funds for a mortgage loan and in whose favor the property serving as security is mortgaged.

mortgagor The owner of property who borrows money and mortgages the property as security for the loan.

multiple listing service A computerized system that makes possible the orderly dissemination and correlation of listing information to its members so that REALTORS®— may better serve the buying and selling public.

Mutual Mortgage Insurance FHA mortgage insurance.

narrative report A complete written appraisal report, including supporting data.

National Association of Real Estate Brokers An organization primarily of African-American real estate professionals using the designation "Realtist."

NATIONAL ASSOCIATION OF REALTORS® (See Chapter 2.)

negative amortization When the balance owed on a loan increases because the payments are insufficient to cover the interest.

negative cash flow When actual cash expenditures exceed the gross cash income on a property.

negative easement An easement that prohibits the property owner from doing something he or she otherwise could do, such as blocking a view.

net earnings Revenue from operating sources, after deduction of the operating expenses, maintenance, uncollectable revenues and taxes applicable to operating properties or revenues but before deduction of financial charges, and generally before deduction of provision for depreciation and retirements.

net income In general, synonymous with net earnings but considered a broader and better term; the balance remaining after deducting from the gross income all operating expense, maintenance, taxes and losses pertaining to operating properties, except interest or other financial charges on borrowed or other capital.

net income multiplier A figure that, times the net income of a property, produces an estimate of value of that property. It is obtained by dividing the selling price by the monthly net rent (net income).

net lease Lessee pays rent plus maintenance and operating expenses.

net listing Broker receives as commission all monies received above minimum sales price agreed to by owners and broker.

net-net-net (triple-net lease) A lease that requires the tenant to pay all maintenance and operating expenses as well as taxes and insurance.

net profits Used without qualifying expression to describe the profits remaining after including all earnings and other income or profit and after deducting all expenses and charges of every character including interest, depreciation and taxes.

net worth Assets left after subtracting liabilities.

nonconforming use A use that was lawfully established and maintained but, because of the application of a zoning ordinance to it, no longer conforms to the use regulations of the zone in which it is located. A nonconforming building or nonconforming portion of a building is a nonconforming use of the land upon which it is located. Such uses preclude additions or changes without municipal approval.

note An instrument of credit given to attest a debt.

novation Substitution of a new obligation for an old one or a new party to a contract.

nuisance A use that interferes with the quiet enjoyment of property by others.

obligee One to whom debt is owed.

obligor One who owes a debt.

obsolescence Impairment of desirability and usefulness brought about by changes in the art, design or process or from external influencing circumstances that make a property less desirable and valuable for a continuity or use. (See also *depreciation, functional obsolescence* and *economic obsolescence.*)

offer A promise by one party to do a specified deed as the other party in turn performs a specific deed.

open-end mortgage A mortgage with a clause giving the mortgagor the privilege of borrowing additional money after the loan has been reduced without rewriting the mortgage.

open listing A listing available for sale from more than one broker.

operating expenses Generally, all expenses occurring periodically that are necessary to produce net income before depreciation.

operating income Income derived from the general operation of a business. It is not synonymous with net profit, but rather indicates a stage in the profit and loss account where all direct costs of operation and all direct income from operation have been taken into account and nothing else.

operating profit Profit arising from the regular operation of an enterprise engaged in performing physical services (public utilities, etc.) excluding income from other sources and excluding expenses other than those of direct operation.

opinion of title Legal opinion stating that title to a property is clear and marketable; serves the same purpose as a certificate of title.

option An agreement granting the exclusive right during a stated period of time, without creating any obligation, to purchase, sell or otherwise direct or contract the use of a property.

orientation Siting, or the positioning of a structure on its lot, with regard to the points of the compass, prevailing winds, privacy from the street and protection from outside noises.

original cost The actual cost of a property to its present owner; not necessarily the first cost at the time it was originally constructed and placed in service.

"or more" clause A clause in a loan allowing prepayment without penalty.

over-improvement An improvement that is not the highest and best use for the site on which it is placed by reason of excess in size or cost.

ownership The right to possess and use property to the exclusion of others.

package mortgage A mortgage that finances the purchase of real estate and specific household appliances.

panic peddling Illegally inducing listings or sales based on the fear that certain racial, ethnic or social groups are entering or will be entering the area and values will drop. (See also *blockbusting.*)

parol evidence Legal rule that prevents previous oral or written negotiations to a signed contract from changing the contract.

participation mortgage A loan in which the lender takes an equity position, usually in exchange for favorable loan terms.

partition action A legal procedure by which an estate held by tenants in common is divided and title in severalty to a designated portion is passed to each of the previous tenants in common, or the property is sold and the proceeds divided.

partnership "An association of two or more persons who carry on a business for profit as co-owners." (from Uniform Partnership Act)

party wall A dividing wall erected upon and over a line separating two adjoining properties; the owners of the respective parcels have common rights to its use.

passive loss A loss from a passive investment (in which the investor has no active control—such as a limited partnership).

patent Government grant or franchise of land.

percentage lease Lease whose rental is based on a percentage of the gross income of the tenant.

percolation test A soil test to determine if it will handle water seepage from a septic tank.

performance bond A bond to guarantee specific completion of an undertaking in accordance with an agreement, such as that supplied by a contractor guaranteeing the completion of a building or a road.

perimeter heating Baseboard heating, or any system in which registers or radiators are located along the outside walls of a room, particularly under the windows.

periodic tenancy A period-to-period tenancy that automatically renews itself unless notice is given. (See also *month-to-month tenancy.*)

perpetual easement An easement constantly maintained. (See also *easement.*)

perpetuity Going on for an unlimited time.

personal property Property that is movable. All property is either personal property, real property or mixed.

physical depreciation A term that is frequently used when physical deterioration is intended. In a broad concept, it may relate to those elements contributing to depreciation that are existent or inherent in the physical property itself, as distinguished from other and external circumstances that may influence its utilization. Not a clear or proper term without qualification and explanation.

plat A plan or map of a certain piece or pieces of land.

plat book A record showing the location, size and name of owner of each plot of land in a stated area.

plenum A chamber in a furnace in which the air is heated and from which the ducts carry the warm air to the registers.

plottage increment The appreciation in unit value created by joining smaller ownerships into one large single ownership (assemblage process).

points One point is 1 percent of the amount of the loan. A charge of the lender to make the loan competitive.

police power Authority of a state to adopt and enforce laws to promote public health and safety.

potable Suitable for drinking; said of water.

power of attorney Written instrument authorizing a person to act for another as an attorney in fact.

power of sale A clause inserted in a will or deed of trust agreement authorizing the sale or transfer of land in accordance with the terms of the clause.

prefabricated house, prefab A house manufactured, and sometimes partly assembled, before delivery to the site.

preliminary title report Title report that reports only on documents having an effect on the title.

prepayment penalty Penalty for paying off a loan prior to maturity.

prepayment privilege Right of a debtor to pay off a loan before maturity.

presumption Inference of a fact from circumstances that usually attend such a fact.

primary mortgage market The direct lending to borrowers by lenders.

principal (1) A sum lent or employed as a fund or investment, as distinguished from its income or profits; (2) the original amount (as of a loan) of the total due and payable at a certain date; (3) a party to a transaction, as distinguished from an agent; (4) head of a real estate firm.

principal meridian Line used in surveying.

private mortgage insurance (PMI) A private insurance policy issued to protect lender against loss by borrower default.

probate Judicial proceeding to prove validity of a will.

procuring cause The party who started an uninterrupted course of action that resulted in a sale or lease.

profit and loss statement Statement that shows total financial condition of a business.

pro forma statement An estimated future operating statement.

progression The increase in value caused by the presence of homes of greater value in the neighborhood.

property The exclusive right to control an economic good. The recognized attribute that human beings may have in their relation with wealth. A "property" refers to units capable of being used independently in a single ownership. A "property" may consist of the rights to a single parcel of land, a house and lot, a complete manufacturing plant or any one of the items assembled together to constitute such a plant. It may also consist of the rights developed and inherent in the attached business of an enterprise or any one of the elements reflected therein, such as the rights to a patent, a trademark, a contract or the proven goodwill of the public.

property brief A description of a property for sale with complete details and pictures in a form suitable for presentation to a prospect.

property management The operation of real property, including the leasing of space, collection of rents, selection of tenants, and the repair and renovation of the buildings and grounds.

prorate To allocate between seller and buyer their proportionate share of an obligation paid or due. For example, to prorate real property taxes or fire insurance.

punitive damages Damages assessed against someone because of malicious acts that person has committed.

public property A property the ownership of which is vested in the community.

puffing Exaggerated sales talk—usually statements of opinion—that falls short of being misrepresentation.

purchase money mortgage A mortgage that is executed by the purchaser at closing as a part or all of the purchase price. The same as a second mortgage held by the seller.

quantity survey Method of estimating building costs by estimating all raw materials, labor and installation costs.

quiet enjoyment Right of the owner to enjoy his or her property with no interference.

quiet title action Court action to settle the title of a property when there is a cloud on the title.

quit claim deed   A deed of conveyance whereby whatever interest the grantor possesses in the property described in the deed is conveyed to the grantee without warranty.

real estate   Land and hereditaments or rights therein and whatever is made part of or is attached to it by nature or man.

real estate broker   Any person, firm, partnership, co-partnership, association or corporation that, for a compensation, sells or offers for sale, buys or offers to buy, negotiates the purchase or sale or exchange of real estate, leases or offers to lease or rents or offers for rent any real estate or the improvements on real estate for others as a whole or partial vocation.

real estate investment trust   An unincorporated trust or association set up to invest in real property and that has centralized management, issues beneficial interest to 100 or fewer persons and meets other strict requirements of the income tax laws; 90 percent of income must come from real property rentals, dividends, interests or gains from sale of securities or real estate.

real estate salesperson   A salesperson who is responsible to a real estate broker and who assists the broker in the business of buying, selling, exchanging, appraising and managing property.

Real Estate Settlement Procedures Act (RESPA)   Federal law that ensures that both buyer and seller know all aspects of settlement costs when a residence is financed by a federal mortgage loan.

real estate syndicate   Partnership of members who join in order to participate in real estate ventures.

real estate tax   A pecuniary charge laid upon real property for public purposes.

real property   Property and what is on it (immovable).

Realtist   A member of the National Association of Real Estate Brokers.

REALTOR®   A professional in real estate who subscribes to a strict code of ethics as a member of the local and state boards and of the NATIONAL ASSOCIATION OF REALTORS®.

REALTOR-ASSOCIATE®   An individual engaged in the real estate profession other than as a principal, partner, corporate officer or trustee, who is associated with an active member of a board and who holds associate membership in a board, its respective state association and the NATIONAL ASSOCIATION OF REALTORS®.

REALTORS® LAND INSTITUTE   A professional organization for land brokerage.

REALTORS NATIONAL MARKETING INSTITUTE® (RNMI®)   (See Chapter 2.)

realty   A synonym for real estate.

recapture clause A clause in an agreement providing for retaking or recovering possession. As used in percentage leases, to take a portion of earnings or profits above a fixed amount of rent.

reciprocity Mutual agreement between states for recognizing licenses of salespeople.

reconciliation Appraiser brings all information together to arrive at the estimate of market value for the property.

recording The entering or placing of a copy of certain legal instruments or documents, such as a deed, in a government office provided for this purpose, thus making a public record of the document for the protection of all concerned and giving constructive notice to the public at large.

rectangular survey Government survey method using principal meridians and base lines to form quadrangles, townships and ranges.

redemption The recovery, by payment of all proper charges, of property that has been lost through foreclosure of a mortgage or other legal process.

red flag Anything that should put a real estate agent on notice of a likely problem.

redlining The illegal practice of refusing or limiting loans within an area.

reformation Legal action to have an agreement rewritten to reflect how the parties intended it to read.

regression Loss in value because of lower-priced homes in the area.

Regulation Z Regulation developed by the Federal Reserve System for aiding in reinforcement of the Truth-in-Lending Act.

release clause A clause relinquishing a right or claim by the person in whom it exists to the person against whom it could be enforced, such as a clause in a mortgage deed reconveying the legal title to the mortgagor upon payment of the mortgage debt.

reliction (See *dereliction*.)

remainder A future interest in an estate that matures at the end of another estate.

remainder estate An estate in property created simultaneously with other estates by a single grant and consisting of the rights and interest contingent upon and remaining after the termination of the other estates.

renegotiable-rate mortgage A short-term loan amortized over a long period, with an interest rate that is to be readjusted at set periods to reflect the market interest.

rent Payment made to the owner of property in return for use of that property.

rent control Control by a government agency of the amount to be charged as rent.

rental value   A term of specifically limited significance and application; the worth for a stated period of the right to use and occupy property; the rent that a prospective tenant is warranted in paying for a stated period of time—a month, a year, etc.—for the right to use and occupy certain described property under certain prescribed or assumed conditions.

REO (real estate owned)   Foreclosed inventory of lender.

replacement cost   (1) The cost that would be incurred in acquiring an equally desirable substitute property; (2) the cost of reproducing new, on the basis of current prices, a property having a utility equivalent to the one being appraised; it may or may not be the cost of a replica property; (3) the cost of replacing unit parts of a structure to maintain it in its highest economic operating condition.

reproduction cost   (See *cost of reproduction.*)

rescission   Cancelling or repealing a contract by mutual consent of the parties and the returning of parties to their original positions.

reservation   A right reserved by an owner in the grant (sale or lease) of a property.

reserves   Capital set aside for payment of future taxes or maintenance.

Residential Member (RM)   Designation awarded by the Appraisal Institute.

restrictions   A limitation upon the use or occupancy of real estate placed by covenant in deeds or by public legislative action.

reversion   The right of a lessor to recover possession of leased property upon the termination of the lease, with all the subsequent rights to use and enjoyment of the property.

reversionary right   The right to receive possession and use of property upon the termination or defeat of an estate carrying the rights of possession and use and vested in another.

revocation   Termination of an offer or agreement.

R-factor   Insulation rating.

right of first refusal   The right to buy or lease by meeting the price and terms an owner is willing to accept from another.

right of occupancy   A privilege to use and occupy a property for a certain period under some contractual guarantee, such as a lease or other formal agreement.

right-of-way   The term has two significances: As a privilege to pass or cross, it is an easement over another's land; it is also used to describe the strip of land that railroad companies use for a roadbed or as dedicated to public use for roadway, walk or other way. However, the best thought appears to be toward a fine distinction in usage as follows: (1) a single right or easement for several independent or combined uses—for example, in a right for a pipeline for the combined use of pipes, poles, sewers, etc.; (2) two or more rights or easements from different parties and over different parcels but for a single use (rights-of-way); (3) two or more rights or easements from different parties or for different parties and over different parcels for several independent or combined uses (rights-of-ways).

riparian Pertaining to the banks of a river, stream, waterway, etc.

riparian grant The conveyance of riparian rights.

riparian lease The written instrument setting forth the terms, conditions and date of expiration of the rights to use lands lying between the high water mark and the low water mark.

riparian rights All phases of right and title of the upland owner in and to the water and land below the high water mark; the owner is entitled to have water wash his or her land and rights to construct on or over it to the extent it does not interfere or injure another's riparian rights.

rod A measure of length containing 5½ yards or 16½ feet; also, the corresponding square measure.

row houses A series of individual houses having architectural unity and a common wall between each unit.

safety clause Clause in a listing providing that the agent earns a commission if the owner sells or leases, within a stated period of time, to a prospect registered by the agent prior to the expiration of the listing.

sale-leaseback A financing technique in which the owner sells property to an investor and then leases it back.

sales contract A contract embodying the terms of agreement of a sale.

salvage value Value of a property after full depreciation.

sandwich lease A leasehold in which the interest of the sublessor is inserted between the fee owner and the user of the property. For example, the owner of a fee simple ("A") leases to "B" who in turn leases to "C." The interest of "A" may be called the leased fee, that of "B" the sandwich lease and that of "C" the leasehold.

satisfaction of mortgage Document issued by mortgagee when mortgage is paid off.

seasoned loan Loan having a payment history.

secondary financing Junior liens (second mortgages).

secondary mortgage market The buying and selling of existing loans.

second mortgage Mortgage made on top of another and subordinate to the first. (Also called a *junior mortgage.*)

section (of land) One of the portions, of one square mile each (640 acres), into which the public lands of the United States are divided; one thirty-sixth part of a township.

seisin A feudal term defining possession of property by one who claims rightful ownership. Generally accepted today as synonymous with ownership.

seller financing Seller carrying back a loan as part or all of the purchase price or seller financing by land contract.

septic tank An underground tank in which sewage from the house is reduced to liquid by bacterial action and drained off.

service property A property devoted to or available for utilization for a special purpose but that has no independent marketability in the generally recognized acceptance of the term, such as a church property, a public museum or a school.

servient tenement The property encumbered by the easement.

setback The distance a structure must be set back from the street in accordance with local zoning rules.

settlement (See *closing*.)

severalty A holding by individual right; separate state or character.

severance damage The impairment in value caused by separation. Commonly, the damage resulting from the taking of a fraction of the whole property, reflected in a lowered utility and value in the land remaining and brought about by reason of the fractional taking.

shared-appreciation mortgage (SAM) Loan in which the lender shares in future appreciation at a future date.

sheriff's deed An instrument drawn under court order to convey title to property sold to satisfy a judgment at law.

simple interest Interest computed only on the principal balance.

sill The board or stone at the foot of a door or the woodwork or masonry on which a window frame stands.

SOCIETY OF INDUSTRIAL AND OFFICE REALTORS® (SIOR) (See Chapter 2.)

soft money loan Seller carryback financing (no cash involved).

special assessment (improvements) A charge laid against real estate by public authority to defray the cost of making public improvements from which the real estate benefits.

special warranty deed A warranty only against the acts of the grantor and all persons claiming by, through or under him or her. (See also *warranty deed*.)

specific performance, specifically enforceable The requirement that a party must perform as agreed under a contract in contrast to compensation or damages in lieu of performance; the arrangement whereby courts may force either party to a real estate contract to carry out an agreement exactly.

spot zoning Change in zoning that allows a nonconforming use in an area zoned for another purpose.

square foot method One of the methods of estimating construction, reproduction or replacement costs of a building by multiplying the square foot floor area by an appropriate square foot construction cost figure.

squatter's rights The rights to occupancy of land created by virtue of long and undisturbed use but without legal title or arrangement; in the nature of right at common law.

standard metropolitan statistical area (SMSA) City or cities and their suburbs with a minimum population of 50,000 that constitute a metropolitan area by Bureau of Census standards.

statute of frauds Law that requires certain contracts, such as agreements of sale, to be in writing in order to be enforceable.

statutory warranty deed A warranty deed form prescribed by state statutes.

straight-line depreciation (See *depreciation, straight-line.*)

statute of limitations The statutory periods in which to bring various legal actions.

steering Illegal practice of directing prospective buyers toward or away from areas based on race.

step-up lease Lease that allows for increases and decreases in rent on a predetermined basis.

subagent An agent of a person acting as an agent (subagent of principal).

subdivision Area of land that is subdivided and suitable for building.

subject-to loan A purchase in which the buyer takes the property with a loan but does not agree to be personally liable to pay it.

sublease An agreement conveying the right of use and occupancy of a property in which the lessor is the lessee in a prior lease.

subordination The regulation to a lesser position, usually in respect to a right or security.

supply and demand, law of Holds that price or value varies directly, but not necessarily proportionately, with supply.

surrender To give up possession to the landlord and be released from future obligations under the lease.

survey The process of ascertaining the quantity and/or location and boundaries of a piece of land; it may include physical features affecting it, such as grades, contours, structures, etc. A statement of the courses, distance and quantity of land.

survivorship All rights of a joint tenant pass to the surviving joint tenant.

sweat equity Equity created by labor of purchaser or borrower that increases the value of the property.

swing loan A short-term gap or bridge loan; generally, a term loan.

syndication A combining of persons or firms to accomplish a joint venture that is of mutual interest.

tacking Combining successive periods of occupation of property so one can establish a claim of adverse possession or prescriptive easement.

tangible property Property that by its nature is susceptible to the senses. Generally the land, fixed improvement, furnishings, merchandise, cash and other items of working capital used in carrying on an enterprise.

tax A charge or burden, usually pecuniary, laid upon persons or property for public purposes; a forced contribution of wealth to meet the public needs of a government.

tax abatement Reduction in taxes assessed.

tax deed A deed given to purchaser upon a tax sale.

tax penalty Forfeiture of a sum because of nonpayment of taxes.

tax sale A sale of property for delinquent payment of taxes assessed upon its owner.

tax shelter Taxable loss to apply against taxable income.

taxable value The total amount or base upon which taxes are computed under predetermined tax rates. May cover all or any part of the assets represented in tangible and/or intangible property and may be for ad valorem or other forms of taxation. (See also *assessment.*)

taxpayer (1) One who pays a tax; (2) a building erected for the primary purpose of producing revenues to meet the taxes on the land.

tenancy A holding, as of land, by any kind of title, occupancy of land, a house or the like under a lease or on payment of rent or tenure.

tenancy at sufferance A tenancy that arises when a tenant holds over after expiration of his lease.

tenancy at will A tenancy that may be terminated at the will of either the lessor or lessee.

tenancy by the entirety A joint estate equally owned by husband and wife, with the survivor receiving the entire estate. Each party must consent to its termination.

tenancy for years A lease with a definite termination date.

tenancy in common A tenancy shared by two or more parties.

tenancy in severalty Ownership by a single person or entity.

tenant Any person in possession of real property with the permission of the owner.

tender An offer of performance.

tenement Term describing buildings and structures on property.

term loan (straight loan) A loan in which payments are made on interest only; the principal is paid upon maturity.

testate Having made a will before death.

"time is of the essence" clause A clause in a contract that makes performance dates firm; failure to meet the dates would constitute a breach of contract.

time-sharing (interval ownership) Exclusive right of occupancy during set time periods. Can be a leasehold or fee interest.

title The union of all the elements that constitute proof of ownership. (See also *abstract of title.*)

title company A corporation organized for the purpose of issuing or insuring title to real property.

title guarantee (See *title insurance.*)

title guarantee policy Title insurance furnished by the owner, provided as an alternative for an abstract of title. Also called Torrens certificate.

title insurance An agreement binding the insurer to indemnify the insured for losses sustained by reason of defects in title to the real estate.

title theory System in which mortgagee has legal title to the mortgaged property and mortgagor has equitable title.

topography The contour of land, its elevation, surface variations and location of physical features.

Torrens system A system of land registration used in some jurisdictions in which the sovereign issues title certificates covering the ownership of land that tend to serve as title insurance.

tract book (See *plat book.*)

trade (See *exchange.*)

trade fixtures Articles of personal property attached to property that are necessary to owner's business and can be removed.

trader (See *exchangor.*)

trespass To wrongfully invade the property of another.

truss A roof framework consisting of rafters and ceiling joists as well as their supports.

trust A fiduciary relationship, and instrument thereof, that places the legal title to and the control of property in the hands of a trustee for the benefit of another person. A trust may be temporary, conditional or permanent.

trust account Bank account set up by broker to deposit funds of his or her principals.

trust deed A deed that establishes a trust. It generally is an instrument that conveys legal title to property to a trustee and states the trustee's authority and the conditions binding upon him or her in dealing with the property held in trust. Frequently, trust deeds are used to secure lenders against loss. In this respect, they are similar to mortgages.

trustee One who holds title to property for the benefit of another.

trust indenture An instrument evidencing a trust arrangement.

truth-in-lending law Law requiring lender disclosure and regulating the advertising of loan terms.

turnkey project A completed construction project ready for occupancy.

under-improvement An improvement that is not the highest and best use for the site on which it is placed by reason of being smaller in size or less in cost than a building that would bring the site to its highest and best use.

unilateral contract A contract formed by performance rather than by acceptance of an offer.

unimproved As relating to land—vacant or lacking in essential appurtenant improvements required to serve a useful purpose.

unit-in-place method A method to determine replacement cost based on unit prices for various construction components.

unlawful detainer action Court eviction proceeding.

upset price Minimum acceptable bid at an auction or court-ordered sale.

urban renewal The process of rehabilitating city areas by demolishing, remodeling or repairing existing structures and buildings, public buildings, parks, roadways and individual areas on cleared sites in accordance with a more or less comprehensive plan.

use density The number of buildings in a particular use per unit of area; sometimes represented by a percentage of land coverage or density of coverage.

usury An illegal rate of interest.

vacancy factor The percentage allocated for vacancy in determining effective gross income.

value The quantity of one thing that can be exchanged for another. In real estate valuation, it is the amount of money deemed to be the equivalent in worth of the property being appraised.

variance An exception to the zoning.

void contract No contract at all.

voidable contract Contract that is valid unless voided. (May be voided by injured party.)

warranty deed Conveyance of title that contains certain assurances and guarantees by the grantor that the deed conveys a good and unencumbered title. Conveyances vary from state to state but generally assume (1) a good title to land; (2) no encumbrances except stated in deed; (3) that grantee will not be evicted or disturbed by person having a better title or lien.

water rights The rights to a water supply.

WOMEN'S COUNCIL OF REALTORS® (WCR) (See Chapter 2.)

working capital The readily convertible capital required in a business to permit the regular carrying forward of operations free from financial embarrassment. In accounting, the excess of current assets over current liabilities as of any date.

working drawing A sketch of a part or a whole structure, drawn to scale, with dimensions and instructions in such detail as is necessary to guide the worker on a construction job.

wraparound mortgage A mortgage written for the amount of the underlying debt plus the seller's equity.

writ of execution A legal order that directs a proper agent of a court (frequently a sheriff) to carry out an order of that court.

zoning Government regulation of land use; regulation by local government under police power of such matters as height, bulk, use of buildings and use of land intended to accomplish desirable social and economic ends.

zoning map A map depicting the various sections of the community and the division of the sections into zones of permitted land uses under the zoning ordinance.

zoning ordinance A law to regulate and control the use of real estate for the public health, morals, safety and general welfare.

Appendix

Exterior Structural Walls and Framing

EXTERIOR STRUCTURAL
WALLS AND FRAMING

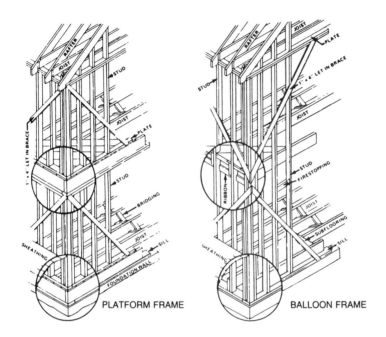

PLATFORM FRAME

BALLOON FRAME

POST AND BEAM FRAME

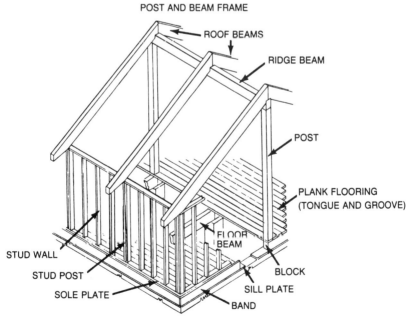

ROOF BEAMS

RIDGE BEAM

POST

PLANK FLOORING
(TONGUE AND GROOVE)

FLOOR BEAM

BLOCK

SILL PLATE

BAND

STUD WALL

STUD POST

SOLE PLATE

© Dearborn Financial Publishing, Inc. Published by Real Estate Education Company/Chicago.

EXTERIOR STRUCTURAL WALLS AND FRAMING

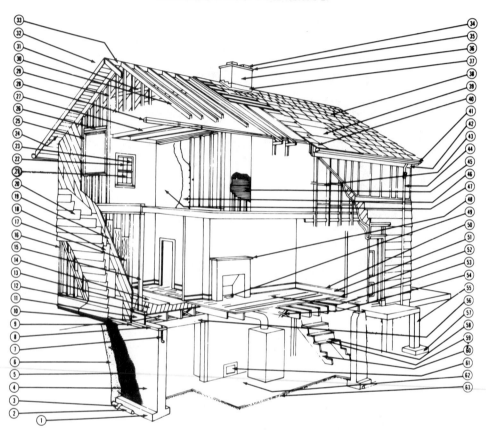

1. FOOTING
2. FOUNDATION DRAIN TILE
3. FELT JOINT COVER
4. FOUNDATION WALL
5. DAMPPROOFING OR
   WEATHERPROOFING
6. BACKFILL
7. ANCHOR BOLT
8. SILL
9. TERMITE SHIELD
10. FLOOR JOIST
11. BAND OR BOX SILL
12. PLATE
13. SUBFLOORING
14. BUILDING PAPER
15. WALL STUD
16. DOUBLE CORNER STUD
17. INSULATION
18. BUILDING PAPER
19. WALL SHEATHING
20. SIDING
21. MULLION

22. MUNTIN
23. WINDOW SASH
24. EAVE (ROOF PROJECTION)
25. WINDOW JAMB TRIM
26. DOUBLE WINDOW HEADER
27. CEILING JOIST
28. DOUBLE PLATE
29. STUD
30. RAFTERS
31. COLLAR BEAM
32. GABLE END OF ROOF
33. RIDGE BOARD
34. CHIMNEY POTS
35. CHIMNEY CAP
36. CHIMNEY
37. CHIMNEY FLASHING
38. ROOFING SHINGLES
39. ROOFING FELTS
40. ROOF SHEATHING
41. EAVE TROUGH OR GUTTER
42. FRIEZE BOARD

43. FIRESTOP
44. DOWNSPOUT
45. LATHS
46. PLASTER BOARD
47. PLASTER FINISH
48. MANTEL
49. ASH DUMP
50. BASE TOP MOULDING
51. BASEBOARD
52. SHOE MOULDING
53. FINISH MOULDING
54. BRIDGING
55. PIER
56. GIRDER
57. FOOTING
58. RISER
59. TREAD
60. STRINGER
61. CLEANOUT DOOR
62. CONCRETE BASEMENT FLOOR
63. CINDER FILL

Index

About the Residential Sales Council

The Residential Sales Council (RSC) is one of the two operating divisions of the REALTORS® National Marketing Institute, a not-for-profit corporation and an affiliate of the National Association of REALTORS® (NAR). The goal of the RSC is to provide superior member benefits that will enable residential sales specialists to maximize their professional performance. The RSC strives to meet that goal by offering the latest educational opportunities, exceptional products and publications and the Certified Residential Specialist designation (CRS).

Since 1977, the CRS has been the symbol of achievement in residential sales education and experience. The CRS means:

- *Recognition* that comes from receiving the highest professional designation in the residential real estate industry.
- *Networking* that enables you to tap into a network of top-notch professionals eager to share information and referrals.
- *Growth* that ensures that when you earn the CRS, you will have reached the pinnacle of residential sales education and will be ready to meet the challenges of your career.

To receive more information on the RSC, or to learn about becoming a real estate agent of the highest degree by earning your CRS, call 800-462-8841.

Residential Sales Council, 430 North Michigan Avenue, Chicago, Illinois 60611-4902

274